Celluloid Sisters

Women and Popular Cinema

JANET THUMIM

Consultant Editor
Jo Campling

MACMILLAN

First published 1992

Published by
MACMILLAN ACADEMIC AND PROFESSIONAL LTD
Houndmills, Basingstoke, Hampshire RG21 2XS
and London

Companies and representatives
throughout the world

Edited and typeset by Grahame & Grahame Editorial, Brighton

Printed in Hong Kong

British Library Cataloguing in Publication Data
Thumim, Janet
Celluloid sisters: Women and popular cinema.
I. Title. II. Campling, Jo.
302.23082
ISBN 0–333–48040–6
ISBN 0–333–48041–4 pbk

For my sister Sue

Susanna Lawson (1947–67)

Contents

List of Plates

PLATE CREDITS

The author and publishers acknowledge with thanks the following sources for photographs. They have made every effort to contact all the copyright holders, but in the event of any omission will be pleased to make the necessary arrangements and acknowledgements at the earliest opportunity.

Eon Productions Ltd, for numbers 20 and 21 from *Goldfinger* © 1964, Danjaq S. A. and United Artists Company. All rights reserved.

Picturegoer for numbers 1, 2, 14 and 15.

Stills from the films *The Wicked Lady* and *Madonna of the Seven Moons* (numbers 4 to 11) , from *Doctor at Sea* (numbers 12 and 13)and *Marnie* (numbers 23 and 24) by courtesy of the Rank Organisation Plc.

Women's Own, IPC Magazines, for numbers 3, 16, 17, 18 and 19.

Thanks are due, also, to the British Film Institute and the British Library at Colindale for providing prints and to Roger Jones for the frame enlargements from *The Wicked Lady* and *Madonna of the Seven Moons*.

Acknowledgements

Though I am the author of this book and the words are mine, the energy and commitment which the project required are the product of the sympathetic and imaginative support of many people. It was Jo Campling's novel proposal that I should develop my ideas into book form. I am immensely grateful to her for that and for her continuous encouragement, as well as that of Susan Sellers whose participation in some key stages of the book's conception and production was invaluable. I am indebted to my Ph.D. supervisor, Phillip Drummond, who has been consistently encouraging over what is now a considerable number of years: I have both valued and enjoyed his rigorous attention to my work as it has progressed. Many friends have taken time to read different chapters in draft form, enabling me to keep sight of the whole while entangled with the details of parts – amongst them I am particularly grateful to Gill Swanson and Liz Mason for their expertise and their useful comments.

I am also very grateful to Melinda Mash for access to her fascinating research materials; to the BFI 4th year diploma class of 1989–90 for their enthusiastic interest in my questions; to the BFI Archive viewings department, particularly Elaine Burrows and Jackie Morris, for their generous help in arranging viewings; and to my old friends Stewart and Sandra Kington for their substantial assistance with the printing of successive drafts.

Life continues around this kind of work, sometimes threatening to engulf it altogether: my close friends Wendy Pearce, Heather Lavis, Virginia Whiles, Jo Murphy and Pat Kirkham have all periodically reassured me that the work was worth completing – very warm thanks to all of them. Last, but really first, the cheerful commitment of my three children Joshua, Nancy and Ella Thumim has been crucial to the completion of the work. They have looked at films with me, discussed characterisations, checked my language on the computer screen or the discarded drafts littering the house, taken over household tasks: in short they have lived through the work with me, entering into the fun of it and making sure my feet stayed on the ground.

JANET THUMIM

Introduction:
What Does 'Popular
Cinema' Mean to Women?

During the period immediately following the Second World War cinema was the dominant form of popular culture in Britain: to say this, though, is to raise all sorts of further questions. These concern the idea of 'the popular' itself as well as questions about what 'dominant' might mean in a plural, democratically organised society with a market-based economy. For feminists it also implies recognition of the continuing struggles of gender politics.

It is a common assumption that there is some kind of causal link between people's understanding of themselves and their place in society, and the fictional representations of social life offered in the most widely consumed cultural forms. Today attention is focused mainly on broadcast television and advertising practices as the major source of such representations, the 'dominant' cultural forms, but in the days before television, cinema occupied this position. Whether or not there is, in fact, such a causal relation remains a subject for debate: certainly the advertising industry assumes there is, and current discussion of satellite and cable television and the deregulation, in the UK, of television, has provoked a renewed consideration of the idea that viewers are necessarily influenced by what they see.

The Second World War entailed enormous and rapid changes in British society: not just those consequent on the mobilisation of the country's resources for armed struggle, but also, as the war progressed, in a widespread consciousness that it was possible, indeed desirable, to 'mobilise' for the peacetime reconstruction after the war of a more 'just' and harmonious society. In popular consciousness, evidenced in the Labour electoral victory of 1945, the hardship and sufferings of the period 1939–1945 were to be justified by an improvement in post-1945 British society over that remembered from before 1939.[1]

During the war period cinema, like other forms of mass com-

1

munication, was often a vehicle for the dissemination of relatively short-term goals. The 1943 film *Millions Like Us* (Launder and Gilliat), for example, propagandized the then necessary call-up of women into the armed forces or into munitions factories: 'Mr Bevan needs another million women. I don't think we should disappoint him, do you?' asks the recruitment officer as she prepares to draft Patricia Roc to a factory far from her home on the south coast. This is not to suggest, however, that the cinema industry was directly controlled by government. At the other extreme the story of the Powell and Pressburger film *The Life and Death of Colonel Blimp*, also made in 1943, shows that there was often a considerable gap between the propaganda requirements of government and the independent activity of the film industry.[2] Cinema, as always, was shaped more by the operation of 'market forces' than by the propaganda requirements of any particular group. Yet since, by the end of the war, there was such a widespread and heightened consciousness of social change, and a general readiness to perceive a relation between this and the content of popular films, it seems more than likely that audiences in the later forties would attend with particular interest to the imagined social orders purveyed through cinematic representations: these might be contemporary stories set in familiar post-war locations (*It Always Rains on Sunday*, Hamer 1947; *Hue and Cry*, Crichton 1946; *Passport to Pimlico*, Cornelius 1949), or the highly popular costume dramas set in another time or place (*The Wicked Lady*, Arliss 1945; *Caravan*, Crabtree 1946; *Jassy*, Knowles 1947).

To my generation, born during the second half of the forties, all this was a thing of the past by the time our conscious memories begin in the early fifties. By the sixties we were, more or less, adult. Hence one of the central questions motivating this study concerns the apparent changes in the models of 'society' offered in the most widely consumed films – those that achieved the status of box office hit – during my generation's formative period. The other question entails an enquiry into the way audiences, particularly female audience members, make use of film texts: in other words how far did the girls and young women of the forties, fifties and sixties – my generation and our mothers' – develop our understandings of what it is to be a woman, from our viewings of popular cinema? That such understandings *were* routinely derived from popular cultural forms is well documented – most recently in Helen Taylor's intriguing study of the significance of the biggest box office success of them all,

Gone With the Wind (Fleming, Cukor, Wood 1939), to its successive generations of female fans.[3] For female audience members to derive use value from patriarchally ordered film texts, however, must involve a considerably more sophisticated readerly activity than is allowed for in the formulations of censorship regulations,[4] for example, or in the assumptions of such organisations as Mary Whitehouse's Listeners and Viewers Association; more recently Teresa de Lauretis, amongst other feminist theoreticians, argues persuasively that cinema is a 'technology of gender';[5] in other words that cinema is one of the means by which patriarchal order constantly renews itself.

In attempting to pursue these questions, then, this book begins with a consideration of the idea of the popular; with the general contours of the cinema industry and society in Britain during the twenty years following the Second World War; and with the particular operations of genre and the star system since these determine publicity and marketing strategies and thus partly inform the audience choices which, in the end, decide whether or not a film is a commercial success or a box office hit. But the questions I want to ask require a close reading of film texts: since it would, clearly, be impossible to examine *all* the films available to audiences during the period, or even all the box office hits, some sampling method is necessary. Taking success at the British box office as the arbiter I have selected three groups of six films from the beginning, middle and end of the period: the latter part of the book is based on detailed readings of these eighteen films and their discursive contexts.

Any sampling method, of course, is bound to be subject to major ommissions. Though Doris Day, for example, was unarguably the most popular female star of the fifties in Britain, none of her films is accorded detailed analysis here. But the general features of popular cinema's representation of women, discovered through my analyses, will apply equally to other contemporary films and stars, and the range of these is indicated in Chapter 3.

In order to make it possible to compare the representations of women in the very different types of film yielded by my correlation of various assessments of box office success, I have used an analytic method which pays particular attention to two terms in the construction of fictional female characters. These are, firstly, the narrative function of the character and, secondly, the way in which she is positioned in relation to the audience, that is to say how much access the audience is offered to the character's own point of view. Before proceeding to the discussion of the popular which properly begins this book, it will be useful to consider these analytic methods a little more closely, bearing in mind the question which follows from de Lauretis' proposition: if popular cinema is a 'technology of gender', how does it work?

The Analysis of Fictional Characters

To answer the question posed by de Lauretis' work we need to outline the terms in which screen women from such diverse films as *The Wicked Lady*, *Doctor at Sea* or *Mary Poppins* may be compared: the intention of such a comparison being to discover whether, if, and in what ways, the typical representations of women on screen changed between the forties and the sixties, and then to consider the functional meanings of such change – or lack of it – for the female audience. In short, we wish to ask what popular cinema assumed women were like. The film, however is a complex object: in order to explore its assumptions we require a method which will allow for discrimination between the various strategies used, often simultaneously, to depict characters and events. Hence the conceptual distinction, in the chapters that follow, between those strategies called on in the introduction or initial presentation of a character, those called on in the various definitions of a character which build up as the narrative unfolds, and those deployed in the narrative resolution of a character – what happens to her 'in the end'. These analytical terms will be introduced here and explored more fully in terms of the female characters in specific films, in Chapters 4 and 5, after the broader discussion of the sample films themselves which is the subject of Chapter 3.

The Introduction of Female Characters

The way in which a character is first introduced to the audience has an effect on their subsequent understanding of that character's actions, motivations and desires. It is by these means that information is offered to the audience about the relative importance of the character to the narrative, and it may also determine whether the audience feels sympathy or antipathy for the character. This understanding and estimation of the character may of course be modified by the subsequent unfolding of the narrative, but exists in a dynamic relation to this unfolding because of its centrality to the provisional meanings audiences make in their textual reading. Previous knowledge, such as that deriving from the persona of the actor performing the character, will also have important consequences for the audience's initial perceptions. When John Wayne as Ethan strides into the Edwards homestead near the beginning of *The Searchers* it is his reputation rather than the yet to be established character of Ethan, which elicits the audience's attention, suggesting to them that this character is indeed likely to be central to the narrative. At the opening of *East of Eden*, by contrast, contemporary audiences could have little idea whether the figure of James Dean, whose first starring role this was, would turn out to be more or less central than the woman he seems to be following – or indeed whether either character will be of any importance at all.

But it is not simply a question of whether or not the audience recognises a familiar face on the screen: this, indeed, can be an impediment to the internal authority of a particular text. Sean Connery's presence as James Bond signals, very precisely, the successful resolution of enigmas yet to be posed in the narrative – hence the pleasures of these texts typically derive from spectacular displays of one kind and another, rather than from the unfolding of the plot. The appearance, location, actions and speech of a character are all deployed to suggest to the audience who it is that they are watching, why this individual may be of interest and what kind of person she or he is. Our first sight of Francesca (Ann Todd) in *The Seventh Veil*, for example, is a close-up of her inanimate and impeccably composed face on a pillow: this shot is closely followed by her cunning escape from the room and the building which we understand, because of a brief glimpse of a uniformed nurse, to be some kind of medical establishment, and then by her suicide attempt. At the very least this introduction defines her for the audience as a character in crisis, a definition which is subsequently confirmed by the psychiatrist's speech comparing the human mind to Salome and her seven veils. It is a suggestion which clearly has important consequences for the audience's understanding of Francesca's story as it unfolds and of the narrative resolution in which her crisis is declared solved. She is 'cured' at the end of the film. Sometimes an initial estimation of a character is proposed to the audience by another character. Maddalena (Phyllis Calvert), for example, in *Madonna of the Seven Moons*, is suggested to be both modest and retiring in her husband Giuseppe's speech to the nuns in which he warns that she will not accept their proposal to name the children's ward after her. Maddalena's alter ego, Rosanna, is introduced by her lover Nino's mother in conversation with Victoria (Jean Kent), the kitchen girl with whom Nino (Stewart Granger) has been consoling himself during Rosanna's long absence:

> There's only one not like the others – Rosanna
> When she left they came and went, came and went,
> as you will.

Thus Maddalena the pure is introduced by a man, her husband, and Rosanna the wild by a wise old woman. In *The Wicked Lady* Caroline's implicit assertion to the audience that being nineteen she knows her own mind is modified by Ralph's previous definition of her as a child, ignorant of the world:

> *Ralph*: You're such a child, Caroline. I sometimes wonder
> if it's fair to marry you before you're old enough to know your
> own mind.
> *Caroline*: I'm nineteen.
> *Ralph*: You've seen so little of the world
> and other men.

The variety of means deployed in the initial introduction of a character to the audience varies, of course, with the relative importance of the character to the narrative. The more central the character, the more complex their introduction is likely to be. Our exploration of the typical representations of women offered in popular film will, however, require as much attention to minor characters, those whose main function is to motivate the narrative or simply to people the screen, as to the major characters whose experience we are invited to consider.

The Definition of Female Characters

By the end of the film the audience has received, in a particular sequence, a sum of information about a character. Whereas the initial presentation of a character has functional consequences for the audience's understanding of the plot structure, the overall defining strategies, those deployed throughout the film, are concerned rather with establishing the diegetic parameters within which the narrative unfolds. The functional consequences of these definitions, the audience's overall understanding of who the character is, what she is like, and so on, are implicated in the narrative resolution of the character. At the end of the film the audience is in a position to evaluate the resolutions of plot and character by referring to the definitions of character gradually established through the film. There are three qualitatively different ways of defining a character, all of which are routinely used. The social, national or racial group to which the character belongs; the gender, age and sexual status of the character; and her avowed occupations and/or aims are all drawn upon in establishing, for the audience, who and what she is. Not all these terms, of course, are always called upon for all characters, and, just as the initial presentation tends to be more complex with central characters, so the modes of definition are also more varied when the character is an important one. A character is considered to be defined in the terms suggested here either if the audience's attention is specifically drawn to this aspect in the character's construction or if, by the end of the film, the audience clearly understands that a character has a particular attribute.

It is of central importance to our understanding of Edie Doyle (Eve Marie Saint) in *On The Waterfront*, for example, that she is different from the other dockers' womenfolk by virtue of her education, though we never see her study, nor do we know anything of her life away at college: her decision to stay with Terry (Marlon Brando) is nevertheless understood to be a momentous one since it involves, it seems, abandoning her career. We first see her, a young woman with loose blonde hair, in a rear view medium long shot as she kneels by the body of her brother in the opening scene of the film. She refuses to be comforted by the priest and accuses him of 'hiding' in the church. The scene closes with a high angle close-up of her asking the question that drives her through the narrative: 'who killed my brother?' to which the audience already knows the answer. Thus we know that she is a part of the Irish-American dockers community, and that she has at least one aim in this narrative. Her angry outburst at the priest suggests that she will persevere in the search for an answer to her question. This assessment of her as a 'strong' character is reinforced in the next scene in which she appears – the brawl following the daily hiring at the docks. She attacks Terry, wins back the 'tab' and gives it to her father thus ensuring his day's work. Although the audience is privy to more information than Edie herself she also functions as an important positioning device for the audience in revealing, through her own discoveries, the extent of the dockers' code of solidarity and silence even in the face of murder threats. We are invited, through the narrative construction, to share her point of view and thus, implicitly, her incredulous frustration at the power of this code. When the mob's attack breaks up the poorly attended meeting at the church Edie is frightened and allows Terry to lead her to safety: in their ensuing conversation the audience learns, with Terry, that she is training to be a teacher at a catholic college somewhere in the country and that despite having spent her childhood in dockland she is now an outsider by virtue of both her aspirations and her domicile. By now, well into the film, we know that she is a student and aims to be a teacher; that she is unmarried and has so far led a sheltered life. On her return to her father's apartment she refuses his order to go back to the Sisters in her convent training school:

> How can I keep my mind on things that are just in books and that aren't people living?

So we learn that her choice is for the immediate, the 'real' world of 'people living', rather than for the delayed and apparently inconsequential gratifications of education, 'things that are just in books'. This concern with the here and now is translated in the narrative closure into her love for, and desire to be with Terry: but, through the multiple aspects of her character which have been offered through the film, the audience is in a position to evaluate her decision. Their ability is dependent on the various definitions of her which have been offered through the entire course of the film.

The Resolution of Female Characters

The degree of synonymity between the initial presentation of the character and the overall definitions to which, by the end of the film, they have been subject is fixed in the film's closure, in the resolution of the narrative. The closer these are, the more persuasive is the preferred reading of the narrative overall. At the end of the film the diegetic[6] world and all its inhabitants are left forever in a kind of suspended animation. They survive, if at all, in the memory of the audience: hence the consequences of the narrative resolutions for central characters are of crucial importance in the audience's summary recollections. Barbara (Margaret Lockwood) for example, in *The Wicked Lady*, may have offered an exciting example of a woman refusing to play according to the rules, but she came to a sad and bad end whereas Caroline (Patricia Roc), is brought at the end to a new beginning: fair days ahead are promised to her. The eponymous Marnie articulates, in her honeymoon rejection of Mark (Sean Connery), ideas which though they may touch directly on the day-to-day experience of women are unacceptable to patriarchal order.

> Oh men!
> You say no thanks to one of them and bingo, you're a candidate for the funny farm.
> It would be hilarious if it weren't pathetic.

In the narrative resolution Marnie must eat her words. Her final utterance of the film is 'Oh Mark, I'd rather stay with you'. The preferred reading – that understanding of the film's propositions which is inscribed in the narratives construction and its positioning of the audience – suggests that the narrative resolutions of these characters Barbara, Caroline and Marnie are earned. They are a direct consequence not only of their actions and motivations but also, by implication, of their *values* which produced these actions. The audience, from its position of superior knowledge, knows what these values are. The intersection of this paradigmatic textual structure and the operations of verisimilitude transforms these fictional causes and effects into ethical truths, for the audience. Hence the importance, for film historians and social historians alike, of an examination of the minutiae of these discourses purveyed in and through popular cultural forms. These suggested 'ethical truths' are immeasurably strengthened by their inevitable positioning within the satisfaction the audience is invited to experience at the narrative closure, as a consequence of narrative form. Questions are answered, enigmas resolved; equilibrium is re-established.

Now it is certainly true that in watching any given film individual audience members are unlikely to engage in such close readings of characters as those proposed in the analytic methods suggested here. Nevertheless particular details of various narratives may be of great significance for particular individuals in the audience. The consensus which, as we shall see in Chapter 3, exists in the preferred readings and narrative resolutions about acceptable social and behavioural values, about the issues of the day which solicit and hold the attention of cinema audiences, justifies close attention to the films which were the outstanding successes of their day. The films discussed in detail in this book have been selected according to a careful correlation of different sources which will be outlined in Chapter 1: their representations of women can, therefore, be appropriately considered as a form of evidence, in Carr's sense of the word,[7] subject to the constraints of genre and star personae noted in Chapter 2. Evidence of what? Of contemporary understandings about women's social roles; of struggles over the definition of these roles; of myths and assertions about the nature and objects of female desire; of claims about what is or is not acceptable in terms of the goals and behaviour of girls and women. These are the issues which will be explored through an examination of the introduction, definition and resolution of the female characters in selected films from the forties, fifties and sixties in Chapters 5 and 6. Firstly, however, we shall turn to a general discussion of 'the popular' in the context of British society between 1945 and 1965.

1
Popular Forms and Popularity

The Idea of the Popular

The study of popular culture in any given period offers insights into both the conditions of social formation and into the language and attitudes of the various social groups competing with each other for dominance – what we might call hegemonic struggle – at the time. This chapter is concerned with the qualifications which must be borne in mind while engaging in such an exploration of cinema popular in Britain between 1945–1965. The book as a whole is, precisely, a speculation about the available meanings of Woman in circulation at a time when cinema could be said to be the dominant form of mass culture.

The concept of popularity and the associated adjective 'popular' are freely, even glibly exchanged as if their meaning was clear. But on closer consideration a proliferation of meanings is evident, some of which are in direct contradiction. Looked at in the widest sense we might conclude with some justification that the misunderstandings generated by the idea of popularity are crucial agents of hegemonic struggle, in the cultural arena at least, since it is here that propositions are routinely made by one group about the tastes, preoccupations and desires of other groups. If we examine the consequences of such propositions, however, we invariably find that it is the interests of the articulate group that are served. It is precisely the conflicting idea of the popular which allows this sleight of hand.

Some Meanings of 'The Popular'

What, then, is understood by the phrase 'popular culture'? Most answers to this question would probably begin by referring to

11

ideas of entertainment and relaxation, as well as invoking the
post-industrial mass audience. Here already are at least two quite
distinct notions: one concerning the content of the objects of popular
culture and their functions, hence concerned with the qualities of
the object which is well-liked; the other a quantitative idea implying
that the objects in question are popular by definition because
they are accessible on a large scale – the scale of late capitalist
society. The quantitative understanding implies the ubiquity of
the objects in question, the qualitative one asserts their status as
enjoyable, providers of pleasure. Perhaps the question is a simple
one, simply answered; an object or event providing pleasure on a
large scale is popular. But this simple answer begs too many other
important questions: what kind of pleasure, for whom, and what
are its consequences? How do we know what 'large scale' means
– don't these meanings depend on other criteria, other parameters? Who provides the pleasures to be had from these popular
cultural objects and events, and why? Where does the original,
quasi anthropological definition of the term popularity fit into this
simple answer? The historian Raymond Williams provides further
definitions (Keywords, 1976), tracing the history of the term from its
latin origins in popularis = belonging to the people, through its legal
and political usages from the medieval period onwards till its widespread synonymity with 'well-liked' by the late nineteenth century.
He draws attention to the implicitly denigratory connotations of the
term in its association with culture along the high art/low art axis,
and he points out the characteristic ambiguities of the term which
have allowed its contradictory usages during the modern period.
Once we introduce the idea of the popular as emanating from the
people, as being, in a folkloric sense, the *production of* the people, the
initial simple answer is no longer satisfactory.

'The Popular' in Critical Discourse'

In quantitative terms it is true that the mass choice of the object
allows its designation as popular, but in no sense can the cultural
object in the modern period be understood to have arisen out of the
creative activity of the people. On qualitative grounds the problem
assumes almost sinister overtones since here we must have recourse
to the discursive activities of critics whose characteristic terminology is rooted in aesthetic judgements equating the popular with the
low grade and mindless, and granting approval, and the consequent

status of being worthy of critical analysis, only to objects which can be understood to conform in some way to the prevailing canons of high art. The typical critical discourse in the period with which we are concerned is additionally constrained by the class basis of the critic. An example will clarify the point. Simon Harcourt-Smith wrote in *Tribune*:

> This, on the whole, is a time when the new films can claim no privilege as works of art . . . . *The Wicked Lady* arouses in me a nausea out of all proportion to the subject . . . . Six months hence one of my friends in the industry will announce that this portentous piece of shabbiness has broken all records in, let us say, Middlesbrough. My argument will, however, remain valid.[1]

Now this film was the box office hit of 1946, thus in quantitative terms an immense popular success. This very popular object, however, gave rise to Harcourt-Smith's admittedly disproportionate nausea: it was not well-liked by him. His choice of the term 'nausea' indeed suggests such an extreme revulsion that we may well wonder what it was about the film that so disturbed him. It is hard to believe, as he claimed elsewhere in his review, that it was simply a question of his historical sensibilities being offended. Though he recognised that the film might break all records in 'let us say, Middlesbrough' he was still unable to address the question of why this should be so and, more importantly, what this implied about the appropriateness of the canon by which he judged works whose *raison d'être*, let us remember, is a commercial one. The most interesting question about the contemporary popularity of this film – what was it about 'this portentous piece of shabbiness' that was so well-liked – is one that Harcourt-Smith was incapable of asking simply because it had not occurred to him that it was worth answering.

'The Popular' and the Trade Press

Whereas for the critical press the status 'popular' thus has potentially negative connotations, for the trade press it is a positive and longed for harbinger of profit. *To-Day's Cinema*,[2] for example, announced the same film as:

Attractively full-blooded entertainment, with outstanding star
appeal.

while *Kinematograph Weekly*[3] promised their readers an

Outstanding money spinner for popular, provincial and suburban halls.

For the cultural historian it is the very success of this film which
provokes questions about its content: what pleasures did it offer,
what widespread desires did it satisfy? In other words the ascer-
tainable fact of its popularity in quantitative terms makes it an ideal
candidate for an exploration of the qualitative aspects of popularity:
despite Harcourt-Smith's nausea large numbers of people chose to
view this film – why *this* film?

Why is 'The Popular' Important?

It is becoming clear that investigation of the popular is fraught with
pitfalls: the first problem must be to discover what the popular
actually was in the period we are concerned with. We cannot rely on
the opinions of the likes of Harcourt-Smith, neither can we wholly
trust the claims of producers and distributors. We must take account
of the success of a film at the box office since this is evidence of its
choice by large numbers of people and it also assures us that the
object of our attention was familiar to large numbers of people. Since
published critical response to films emanated from a relatively small
group we must beware of accepting their assessments of quality
and content too easily, yet we are still bound to depend on their
writings as a trace of the contemporary audience now lost to us
except through this writing. At this point we might well ask why it
is necessary to pursue this elusive and slippery idea of the popular
through its various and labyrinthine operations. The urgency of the
project is clear if we accept that the concept of popularity is crucial
to hegemonic struggle in the arena of communications, particularly
those touching on, for example, class conflict or gender politics. A
notable feature of popular cinema during the period, for example,
is the striking change in the typical heroine: the transgressive adult
woman portrayed by Margaret Lockwood in *The Wicked Lady* gives
way by 1964 to the troubled child woman played by Tippi Hedren
in *Marnie*.

Those concerned with investigating the inequities of patriarchy for its female subjects may well wonder just what part the compelling models offered in popular cinema have played in the continuing subjugation of women. Similarly a concern with the practical mechanics of class conflict requires close scrutiny of the flow of the various kinds of information which circulate in mass society and, arguably, contribute to the formation and maintenance of power relations between different groupings within it.

THE TRADE

There is a bewildering plethora of quantitative assessments of popularity available for the perusal of the cultural historian: some are more accessible than others, some appeared more consistently, and, though they evaluated the same set of objects (films), they did so for a wide variety of reasons. In order for such assessments to have any meaning we must know what these reasons were. Who produced the assessments, for what purpose, to whom were they addressed? The apparently innocent, not to say naïve question 'what was the most popular film' in a particular year may be answered in a variety of ways. Broadly speaking, there are two types of periodic, quantitatively based assessments of popularity made *à-propos* the films available to the British audience during the period 1945–1965. One type concerns the operations of the industry – primarily those of distribution and exhibition – while the other purports to record and celebrate the choices made by audience members. It is hardly surprising to note the considerable degree of correlation between the results recorded by different bodies at any particular time, nevertheless if we wish to draw conclusions based on the assertion that this or that film was markedly popular we are obliged to take account of the specific source of such an assertion, and we would do well to check its correlation in other sources.

Carr's reminder,[4] that the historian is in a position to select those facts which support the case he wishes to make, is germane here in so far as it draws attention to the meaninglessness of facts separated from their context: we must have some idea of how the fact came into existence before we are in a position to use it. Thus the delicacy of the cultural historian's explorations is demonstrated: if our object of study is effects we must deal with the apparent relations between phenomena before we may approach the phenomena themselves.

One of the more intriguing features of popular cinema is the paradoxical relation between the film and the audience. Though the audience – certainly in the period with which we are concerned – is invariably composed of large numbers of individuals, yet each separate audience member engages solitarily in the act of reading the film, of making meanings from it. We shall return to the significance of this observation later; for our present purposes we note that the cinematic apparatus as a whole makes various attempts to compensate for this apparent isolation of audience members. The press and, latterly, the institutions of broadcasting, routinely comment upon the products of the film industry and in so doing celebrate the all important activity of audiences in a manner which, by virtue of its periodicity, achieves the status of ritual. A current example of this is broadcast television's coverage of the film industry's own ritual Oscar and Bafta awards; an historical example is the fan magazine *Picturegoer*'s annual poll of its readers to discover their favourite actors and actresses. These forms of activity are important in generating audiences but they also serve to give the individuals of which the audience is composed a sense, however illusory this may be, that their participation in the cinematic apparatus is substantive. The audience is presented to itself as a coherent body, thus the potentially alienating process of consumption in the darkened auditorium is counteracted.

Correlating Popularity

The periodic evaluations conducted within the industry trade papers such as *Kinematograph Weekly* and *Motion Picture Herald* are rather more straightforward: they are addressed to participants in the business of selling films to audiences and accordingly aim to inform their readers about the degree of success achieved by various products. The problem for the historian in dealing with these assessments is their inconsistency and variety and, most difficult of all, the lack of information about how given judgements have been formed. *Kinematograph Weekly*, the major British trade paper during the period with which we are concerned, used over forty different categories in its annual assessments published in December each year: only four of these, however, appeared in every year's assessments. Not only this, but also the evaluation of products implicit in these so called 'awards' appear to be the consequence of a single reviewer's professional judgement. Fortunately for the historian it was the same reviewer, Josh Billings, who was responsible for these evaluations from their inception in the 1930s until the mid-1960s. Here at least there is some consistency. Less fortunately, perhaps, Billings never gave details of his methods though he did repeatedly assert his experience, his familiarity with the market, in the chatty prose which accompanied his annual summaries.

> We've not only seen every film mentioned here but, wherever possible, traced its fate from the West End to the suburbs and sticks.[5]

There are several factors which account both for the lack of simple data about the box office receipts for particular films and for the sometimes rather desperate proliferation of categories in Kine Weekly's annual awards.

During the latter part of the 1940s cinema was undoubtedly the dominant form of popular culture and seemed, to optimists at any rate, to be an expanding industry. The economic relations between Britain and the dominant American film industry in the austere post-war years were complicated by the 1947 Marshall Plan as well as by the British government's sporadic and ill-judged attempts to protect the home industry. In this context plotting the fiscal performance of individual products must have been an accountant's nightmare; this, combined with the hope that the market would become more and more buoyant, explains the lack of reliable data. But cinema audiences peaked in Britain in the late 1940s with 1600 million admissions per year thereafter declining continuously through the 1950s, the most dramatic fall occurring between 1955 (1182 million) and 1960 (501 million). By 1965 they were down to 327 million and the relentless fall continued, reaching a mere 97 million in 1980.[6] Therefore, though the British economy as a whole appeared healthier during the consumer boom of the 1950s, the cinema industry had no respite. The major competitor in the field of entertainment was of course broadcast television, and references to this competition litter the cinema trade papers throughout the 1950s. This accounts for the proliferation of award categories which can be seen as evidence of the cinema industry's increasingly desperate attempts to offer that which was not available on the small domestic screen, as well as to predict the best financial bets for the future in the face of the relentless onslaught of television.

Bearing Carr's advice in mind then, how is the historian to select quantitative evidence of the success of films at the British box office from this confusing array of possible sources? In order that we may be able to speak with some assurance about the qualitative content of popular cinema in the period it is, clearly, important that we ascertain which films were in fact popular in advance of any detailed textual analyses. Carr suggests that the historian discovers his 'facts' through an analysis of 'documents' but he warns that in order for these 'facts' to carry any weight they must be corroborated by facts yielded from other documents of the same period.[7]

As we have seen the fan magazine *Picturegoer* carried out an annual poll of its readers and awarded, as a consequence, their 'gold medal' to the most popular actor and actress in respect of their performance in a particular film; they also published the top ten names in each category yielded in the poll. From the 1930s until 1958 when the magazine ceased publication this is a consistent and useful summary of audience preferences, albeit confined to those audience members who regularly subscribed to the magazine. On its own this would be an inadequate guarantor of the popular success of individual actors or films, but corre-lated with distributors' summaries it offers a useful corrective to their annual assessments which were more directly concerned with the profitability of films, or the market potential of stars. The most frequently quoted distributors' assessment is that published in the *Motion Picture Almanac*: this is an American publication summarising the activities of the American film industry at home and abroad in which a simple list of the ten most popular films and stars at the British box office during the preceding year is given, apparently based on returns from distributors in Britain and presumably intended for the benefit of the American industry. The entry for the British box office occupies less than a page of the thousand pages in the publication. It is a useful rough guide to the dominant trends in popular cinema, and is far more easily accessible than other sources since it was published in book form. What it offers, however, is limited by the fact of its deri-vation from the experience of those distributors routinely dealing with the American industry (if not owned by American inter-ests) and by its address which was primarily to these interests which were, we should remember, in direct and often bitter com-petition with the British home industry during the period. The major British trade paper was *Kinematograph Weekly* and here, as we have seen, Josh Billings presided over the assemblage of a wide variety of annual celebrations of success intended, it seems, both to reassure the readers and to offer them clues as to the likely directions future marketing strategies should take in order to ensure the continued profitability of cinemas. For the purposes of correlation with the assessments published in *Picturegoer* and *Motion Picture Almanac* only those categories which are both comparable and consistent are useful: these were the *Top Box Office Film*, the *Best Individual Performance*, and the *Most Popular Stars* categories, all of which appeared in every year of our period and for each of which between one and seven titles or actors' names were cited.

A correlation of the films and stars cited in all these varied categories and sources offers a more trustworthy picture of 'popularity' than dependence on any one category or source alone can do because any biases in selection are corrected in the course of references to other selections. The instrument at our disposal is still, however, a pretty rough one yielding generalised, not detailed information. We may compensate for its crudity by performing our textual analyses on a relatively large sample of the films which appear, according to this correlation, to have been most popular at the British box office during the period. The detailed discussion of film texts selected according to the method outlined here will offer interesting historical insights to set alongside those available in existing studies whose *raisons d'être* and starting points are, typically, more firmly located in questions about particular genres, directors, stars or production strategies. The problem with such studies has always been their tendency to over value film texts whose actual exposure to the mass audience was relatively marginal, because of their intrinsic interest for critics and scholars. This overvaluation becomes problematic once conclusions about the social implications are drawn because, as we have suggested, the canons by which critics and scholars have evaluated the films, finding them then to be of intrinsic interest, are not always those by which it is legitimate to understand the predilections or the reading activities of the mass audience. Once the tastes of the mass audience are invoked, as must be the case when the social implications of popular culture are under discussion, we find ourselves at the active centre of hegemonic struggle over definitions of the real. It is these definitions, particularly those concerning women and their social and cultural construction, which are the central concern of this book.

Competition from Broadcast Television

An examination of *Kinematograph Weekly* through the fifties reveals more specific attention to the universal problem for the British industry of competition from broadcast television than that available by reading between the lines of the annual review categories. Apart from routine news coverage of the various negotiations conducted between industry bodies and TV companies there are occasional feature articles which address the problem in general terms. An audience survey of 1956, for example, urged exhibitors to look to their laurels and attempted to assert that TV, while unarguably an alternative form of entertainment, was not necessarily a replacement for the cinema.

If these figures represent a majority feeling, it is clear that, although television may result in some smaller attendances at the box office, the main thing that is keeping people away is unattractive programming.[8]

A few years earlier, in 1953, Josh Billings went even further. In the chatty prose which accompanied his annual review he referred to the extremely popular Rank Organisation documentary about the coronation *A Queen is Crowned*:

Every exhibitor who played the film, and most did, makes it his top . . . Rank Organisation deserves full credit for its foresight and courage in tackling the subject . . . despite fears by many that the broadcasting and televising of the memorable ceremony would destroy the commercial potentialities of the celluloid impression. As it turned out the BBC recordings furnished the finest and most widely distributed trailer in the annals of show business . . . [9]

Despite Billings' optimism and the rather more circumspect findings of the 1956 audience survey, however, there seems little doubt in retrospect about the deleterious effect that the rise of broadcast television had on cinema audiences in Britain. The number of television licences issued rose from not quite 350,000 in 1950 to well over 13 million in 1965.[10] In the same period, as we have seen, cinema lost over three-quarters of its audience. It was a spiralling decline as admissions fell, cinemas closed and audiences dwindled; and though the drop in overall revenue was less steep than that in audience numbers because of the rise in admission prices nevertheless gross revenue declined by about half between the mid-fifties and the mid-sixties.[11] In 1952 the CEA (Cinematograph Exhibitors Association) attempted to institute a boycott against companies which sold films to television companies but were unable to prevent, in 1956, other trade associations from signing an agreement with the BBC for the sale of films. It is interesting to note that the routine screening of films on broadcast television, which began in 1956–1957 coincided with the sharpest fall in cinema attendance (from 1182 million in 1955 to 501 million in 1960). By 1958 the two television channels in Britain were broadcasting, between them, about a hundred and fifty films a year – an average of three every week.

During the sixties British film producers acquired interests in television companies thus by the end of our period it is no longer possible to make a clear separation between the economic activities of the film and broadcasting industries. Indeed, by the 1980s it was almost a truism of the trade that any indigenous production virtually depended on the financial engagement of television companies. The apparent revival of British cinema during the eighties was perceived in some quarters as intimately related to the commissioning policy of the fourth television channel.

Thus with hindsight the period 1945–1965 in the film industry in Britain was characterised by declining admissions, cinema closures, competition and then negotiation with broadcast television: it is a story of the downward spiral of film in cinema as a dominant popular form, reaching a qualitatively different level in the mid-sixties than that which had characterised it in the mid-forties.

Competition from America

A similar pattern can be traced in the increasing American involvement in British industry affairs. Partly no doubt in response to the sporadic and unpredictable interventions of the state into the workings of the industry – particularly into its dealings with American finance and its access to the competitive American product – and partly as a consequence of developments within the United States *à-propos* its own industrial organisation,[12] the American share of British distribution increased from 20 per cent to 60 per cent during our twenty-year period. The same pattern is evident on the production side of the industry where, according to NFFC (National Film Finance Corporation) by the late sixties 80 to 90 per cent of films made in Britain had American backing.[13] By the mid sixties, therefore, even films which were widely celebrated as 'British' productions such as *Goldfinger* (dir. Guy Hamilton, prod. UA/Eon UK 1964) and *Tom Jones* (dir Richardson, prod. UA/Woodfall UK 1963) had in fact entailed substantial American financial participation. Each retained a million dollars from the Eady Levy. Thus the original purpose of the levy, which was to channel revenue from the British box office into home production and stem the flow of profits overseas, was subverted.[14]

Leaving aside for the moment the issue of American 'investment' in the British industry which was, like the struggle for audiences with broadcast television, a perpetual source of insecurity in the trade, and turning our attention to the clearer issue of the straightforward competition between British and American products at the British box office, we find that here too the evident anxieties of the trade were only too well justified.

A cursory glance at the list of films popular at the British box office between 1945 and 1965, according to the correlation of sources outlined above, shows that overall the British market was dominated by the American (Hollywood) product. In the late forties the share was more even and the continuing success of American films with British audiences masked by the fact that the smaller number of top box office hits was dominated by British titles. Hence the celebration, in many histories of the cinema, of British production at this time. During the fifties, however, the American product was dominant both in numbers of popular successes and in the handful of top selling titles in each year. Towards the end of the fifties and for the first few years of the sixties British films once again figure significantly both in their share of the market overall and in the top hits listings, though bearing in mind the contribution of American finance to these productions we should perhaps be wary of the claims about the 'revival' of the British cinema which abounded in the press of the period. By the mid-sixties in any case the situation was back to what, in this post-war period at least, must be regarded as 'normal'; that is a market dominated by imported material with a nonetheless significant minority of popular box office successes emerging from the home industry.

Now the overall pattern described here was, clearly, not available in this form for the scrutiny of contemporary participants in and

observers of the industry, and its detail was the subject of speculation and argument; nevertheless a general sense that British cinema
audiences received on the whole a diet that was inappropriately
dominated by Hollywood pervades both critical writing and trade
reviews, as well as informing the various governmental interventions into the regulation of the trade. In contemporary discussion of
the industry there are two main issues at stake: these are revenue
and culture. The matter of revenue is the more straightforward:
here the domination of the Hollywood product was deplored since
its profits were accrued at the expense of the home industry thus
reducing investment which resulted in declining production with
consequent further loss of profits and of jobs. There seems to be
a general consensus that the presence of an indigenous British
production base was desirable both to generate profits and jobs
and, more importantly, to assert 'Britishness' in the international
arena. Hence the economic dominance of the American industry not
only threatened the financial security of the home industry but also,
by extension, Britain's cultural influence in the world. Not only that
but also the converse, that British audiences were being exposed to
dangerously large doses of an 'alien' culture, seems to have given
cause for concern.

Governmental Intervention

The labyrinthine detail of governmental intervention into the industry's affairs is beyond the scope of this study and is in any case
well documented by Dickinson and Street (1985). However in this
discussion of 'the popular' we must bear in mind that it is only possible to evaluate the popularity of those films over which audiences
had the opportunity to exercise their choice. While this does not
diminish the validity of the discussion it does indicate the necessity
for some attention to the politics of distribution in any consideration
of the mechanics of hegemonic struggles in the cultural arena.
The complexity of these politics is a consequence of the large
number of different interest groups and their apparent failure, in
Britain between 1945 and 1965, not only to agree a strategy for
the British industry but even to communicate adequately between
themselves.

For the government, where responsibility lay with the Treasury
and the Board of Trade, the imperatives were it seems largely fiscal
ones. The regulation of imports and exports and the generation of

revenue through taxation were often, however, in direct contradiction to the dual necessities of protecting and nurturing the domestic industry and maintaining electoral support. Within the industry the requirements of production which welcomed, for example, a high Quota percentage were frequently opposed to those of exhibitors for whom a low Quota percentage allowed more freedom to programme their cinemas. The priorities of producers and investors were, similarly, routinely opposed to those of workers represented by the unions Equity and ACT (Association of Cinematograph Technicians).[15] The interests of the actors in Equity were not always the same as the technicians in ACT, and so on. Running through the shifting alliances and discords which emerged from these disparate groupings from 1945 onwards there is a thread of agreement, an anxiety shared by all though expressed and understood, it seems, in implacably different ways, about the growing cultural dominance of Britain by America. Stafford Cripps at the Board of Trade in 1945, for example, experienced the problem in terms of imports and exports when he understood the Rank Organisation to be an effective British competitor:

> I am anxious to leave the strong Rank combine effective for meeting and possibly dealing with American competition.[16]

Whereas Ralph Bond, a member of ACT, perceived the dual imperatives of Rank's export drive in America and his investment in distribution and exhibition within Britain rather differently:

> It is a curious but evident fact that the more cinemas Mr Rank owns the more he is dependent on America to provide films to fill them.[17]

Lord Reith, appointed in April 1949 as the first chairman of NFFC (National Film Finance Corporation), the body set up to administer funds acquired through the Eady Levy to British production, certainly felt his task to be at least as much a cultural as an industrial one:

> Let us be clear as to the issues at stake . . . The most compelling are of the moral order – evidenced in the influence which the industry can exercise over so considerable a proportion of the population – interests, outlook and behaviour; in the projection

of England and the English way of life to the Dominions and foreign countries; in the enhancement of the prestige and worth of England.[18]

Harold Wilson, then President of the Board of Trade, to whom the above memorandum was addressed, took up the point in more detail during a parliamentary debate on the film industry in June 1948:

> We are getting tired of some of the gangster, sadistic and psychological films of which we seem to have so many, of diseased minds, schizophrenia, amnesia and diseases which occupy so much of our screen time. I should like to see more films which genuinely show our way of life, and I am not aware . . . that amnesia and schizophrenia are stock parts of our social life.[19]

The latent antipathy towards America which lurks beneath the surface of remarks such as these also surfaces, as we shall see in Chapter 2, as a thematic element in many British productions during the fifties. This and the implicit chauvinism of *Kinematograph Weekly*'s blithe division of the world into British, American and Continental in its annual review categories, can perhaps both be understood as examples of the same defensive attitude which characterised Britain's stumbling progress through the post-war period towards the final dissolution of the nineteenth century Empire.

The major new legislative features of the period were contained in the 1948 act which established the Eady Levy and the NFFC, both designed to protect and stimulate domestic industry. The Eady Levy, named after the Treasury official whose idea it was, required that a proportion of the box office earnings of films be paid into a fund, administered by the NFFC, for producers of British films. Henceforward argument centred on the detail of the percentages involved, not to mention the terms under which it might be tapped, while the wider issue of what constituted a British film was largely ignored – though not by American producers whose investment in 'British' productions allowed them, by the sixties, considerable access to 'Eady money' despite the intentions behind the 1948 Act. The unpopular Entertainment tax on admission tickets was substantially reduced in the late forties but not finally abolished until 1960, thus remaining a counter in the game. The Quota legislation whereby exhibitors were required to show a proportion of British productions, introduced in the 1927 Act, remained on the statute book; here again argument centred on the detail of percentages to the exclusion of any sustained consideration of what, in the light of increasing American investment at all levels of the industry did in fact constitute a 'British production'. The consequences of this fragmented and piecemeal approach were succintly summarised by the President of the Writers' Guild, Ted Willis, in a House of Lords debate in 1966:

> These three measures [Quota, NFFC, Eady Levy] . . . were all intended to help British film production, and were mainly directed to the task of preventing our own native film industry from being swallowed up and dominated by the immensely powerful American industry . . . By a strange paradox, most of our film legislation has had an effect which is the precise opposite of its intentions. Far from giving British film producers greater independence and finance, it has weakened them. And far from preventing American domination of the British film industry, American domination was never so complete and overwhelming as it is today.[20]

By the mid-sixties, as we have seen, broadcast television had supplanted the cinema as the major purveyor of popular culture and subequently anxieties about American 'influence' in Britain can be traced in the debates about the regulation and content of television programming through the seventies and eighties. These anxieties became particularly acute in the later eighties in the face of possible deregulation and an influx of satellite channels which, detractors feared, would further pollute and weaken indigenous popular cultural forms.

British Production

The domination of the industry by American interests, however, had an arguably less stultifying effect on production in Britain than the stranglehold of the two British majors, Rank and ABPC (Associated British Picture Corporation) which between them controlled the distribution circuits as well as all the major studio facilities. Both Ealing and Gainsborough, the two most celebrated production outfits of the forties, were controlled by Rank: Gainsborough as part of Gaumont British was bought outright in 1941, while Ealing survived from

1944 till 1955 only by virtue of a distribution agreement made with Rank. The third major was Korda's British Lion, though without its own circuit it was at a constant disadvantage in its competition with Rank and ABPC. There were other small production units, mostly associated with the creative talents of particular individuals such as David Lean's Cineguild, Powell and Pressburger's Archer Films, or Launder and Gilliat's Individual Pictures: the emphasis for these companies, however, was on the whole on individual productions rather than on the drive to control of large sections of the industry which motivated the majors and in any case many of these 'independent' companies relied heavily on support from Rank. The single and notable exception to this general rule is that of Hammer films. This company, formed in 1947, initially concentrated on the production of low-cost, quickly-made B-features. Following the success of *The Curse of Frankenstein* (dir Terence Fisher 1956) in the American domestic market Hammer specialised in one genre, horror. Their productions enjoyed considerable success in the late fifties and sixties, achieving an almost cult status amongst certain sections of the increasingly fragmented audience, though they never matched the box office popularity of the contemporary Carry On series of comedies, made by Rank's Anglo Amalgamated between 1958 and 1980. The two genres, or series – it is hard to know which is the more appropriate term – are comparable in their dependence on stereotypical plot and characterisations as well as in their cultivation of a 'dedicated' audience.

Consequently while it is true to say that the films made by the smaller production companies spring quickly to mind as examples of peculiarly British film making – films such as David Lean's *Brief Encounter* (prod. Cineguild UK 1945), Powell and Pressburger's *Black Narcissus* (prod. The Archers UK 1947) or Launder and Gilliat's *The Happiest Days of Your Life* (prod. Individual Pictures UK 1950) it is nevertheless also the case that such films represent a relatively small proportion of British production as a whole. In addition to this it is also important to note that during the course of the fifties these companies relied increasingly on the co-operation of the majors to continue in production.

Towards the end of the fifties new groupings of writers and directors emerged and were responsible for the appearance of the films celebrated as the 'New Wave' of British cinema: they fared no better than their predecessors however in maintaining anything more than temporary independence from either British or

American majors despite support from NFFC and finance from outside the industry. By 1965 three companies formed in 1959, Allied Film Makers (Attenborough, Forbes, Dearden, Relph, Hawkins and Green), Bryanston (Michael Balcon) and Woodfall (John Osborne and Tony Richardson) were either out of business altogether or heavily dependent on American finance: *Tom Jones*, produced by Woodfall in 1963 was financed entirely by United Artists. Even Hammer films were in trouble, finally vacating the studios at Bray, in which all their successful horror cycles had been produced, in 1968.

THE AUDIENCE

The vicissitudes of the various branches of the film industry are germane to our discussion of popularity because they have an effect on both the number and type of films offered to audiences. As far as audiences themselves are concerned we might speculate that though the number of cinemas had substantially diminished by the mid-sixties, and the typical admission price had risen appreciably, yet the overall range of choices open to audience members had not actually changed as much as these facts might imply. Going to the cinema, in the 1960s, was just one amongst a range of entertainment options. What this qualitative social change does suggest, however, is that the concept of popularity as applied to the cinema has a different meaning in the sixties than that which we can understand from it in the forties. This will have further implications for our understanding of the social consequences of cinematic representations towards the end of our period. Popular cinematic imagery, we can say, was far less widely consumed in the sixties than it was in the forties: we must note that our correlations of the various assessments of popularity in any particular year are conducted against the background of an overall and absolute decline in the popularity of the institution of cinema. The demise of the fan magazine in the late fifties is a reminder of this.

British Society

It is in the later fifties, in fact, that many changes in British society of which the overall decline in cinema as the dominant popular form is symptomatic rather than causal, are most sharply apparent. By this time a post-war generation was reaching maturity, a generation born during the period of austerity and reconstruction following the Second World War, educated according to the 1944 Education Act and accustomed to the joint provisions of the National Health Service set up in 1948 and the National Insurance Act of 1946. The 'consumer boom' of the 1950s, accompanied by virtually full employment and a low inflation rate (3.7 per cent average 1945–1964)[21] allowed increasing material affluence to the people in general. Although some food rationing lingered on until 1954 the days of post-war austerity were largely over by the early fifties and the 1951 Festival of Britain heralded a style of living qualitatively different from that which characterised the pre-war years. During the decade of the 1950s per capita consumption rose by 25 per cent, and on the surface at least, measured in such things as ownership of cars, television sets and domestic appliances, it did indeed seem as though, to quote the conservative Prime Minister Macmillan yet again, the people of Britain had 'never had it so good'.

Yet beneath this increasingly glossy surface there were complex struggles taking place. The 1944 Act ensured free education for all, but the grammar or secondary modern structure of secondary education perpetuated class divisions which were masked by the general increase in affluence. The expansion of university provision resulted in more places being available but failed to keep pace with the rising birth-rate so that by 1961 only 4.6 per cent of eighteen year olds obtained a university place, and almost half of these came from professional, middle-class families. Full employment and the expansion of manufacturing to fuel the consumer boom resulted in the large-scale immigration of black colonial subjects, invited to the UK to carry out the less popular tasks in service industries. The scale of this influx and the almost total absence of any provision for its social consequences produced a new and difficult dimension to the indigenous system of class and privilege, and these difficulties began to surface in the Notting Hill race riots of 1958.

The dissatisfaction of newly articulate groupings such as youth, blacks and homosexuals with the status quo was noted and understood in different ways by academics and intellectuals as well as by government agencies and public bodies. While the catch-all term 'permissive society' satisfied some as sufficient explanation, others looked for reasons. Many regarded the pervasiveness of American cultural influence as the root of the problem, and turned to explorations of British culture and society in an attempt to find solutions. With the benefit of hindsight, the historian Richard Hoggart and the psychiatrist R. D. Laing appear to exemplify best the extremes in the range of positions taken by British intellectuals in their analyses of contemporary social ills. Richard Hoggart's influential book, *The Uses of Literacy* (1957), attempted rather nostalgically to locate 'Britishness' in his study of working class culture which, while celebrating the consequences of the post-war meritocratic ideal, also looked back to the pre-war 1930s as the repository of indigenous popular cultural values. In a sense we can understand Hoggart's work, as well as that of Raymond Williams (*Culture and Society* 1961) and E. P. Thompson (*The Making of the English Working Class* 1968), as an attempt to come to terms with the changing experience of the contemporary individual through an exploration of social structures amongst which class was understood to be predominant. R. D. Laing (*The Divided Self* 1965; *The Bird of Paradise and the Politics of Experience* 1967; Laing and Esterson: *Sanity, Madness and the Family* 1964) approached the problem the other way round, as it were, studying the details of individual consciousness in order to arrive at a functional understanding of more general social structures, and cited the family as the major agent of repression.

Over all, of course, hung the threat of nuclear catastrophe kept to the fore of public consciousness both by the continuing 'cold war' between NATO and the Warsaw Alliance and by the activities of CND, formed in 1958 following the explosion of the British H-bomb in 1957.

Women in Britain

For women in Britain the situation was ambivalent, as the war time exhortations about female equality and independence and the propagandist attention to the 'noble housewife' gave way to a new form of the old double standard. Education for girls was, in legislative terms, the same as that provided for boys yet in practice debates about curriculum content gave increasing precedence to those who saw the purpose of girls' education as primarily a preparation for wife and motherhood. Newsom, for example, in *The Education of Girls* (1948) wrote:

> The future of women's education lies not in attempting to iron out their differences from men, to reduce them to neuters, but to teach girls how to grow into women and to relearn the graces which so many have forgotten in the last thirty years.[22]

Apart from implicitly deploring the introduction of female suffrage thirty years earlier, he clearly conceived the purposes of
education for women differently from those of education in general
(for men). Not only must girls 'relearn the graces' but they should
also be properly equipped to fulfil their role as safeguarders of
'national standards':

> Woman as purchaser holds the future standard of living in this
> country in her hands . . . If she buys in ignorance then our
> national standards will degenerate.[23]

His reactionary views, though by no means the only ones, dominated curriculum development in secondary schools through the
fifties and he was still an influential figure in 1964 when he suggested, in an *Observer* article, that girls should concentrate on
'feminine' skills such as flower arranging. Though it is true that
this proposition caused a furore in the columns of the quality press
yet, as Elizabeth Wilson notes:

> liberal indignation was largely focused on the effect such propo-
> sals would have on middle class women – or grammar-school
> girls might be a more accurate way of putting it – and Newsom's
> views on 'vocational' – by which he meant domestic – education
> for the average girl (or rather the working class girl), whose
> vocation was still seen as marriage and family, were not only
> still widely accepted, but even became more popular as sex
> education was introduced into schools after 1956 under the
> rubric of 'preparation for parenthood' – in theory for boys as
> well as girls, but in practice aimed primarily at the female half
> of the school population.[24]

But despite the baby boom of the late forties and the flurry of
home making, both of which dominate the pages of womens'
magazines at the start of the fifties, women were needed to contribute their labour to the expanding factory production of goods of
which they were also expected to be the major consumers. Women
were thus crucial to the economic expansion of the UK during the
fifties – just as crucial as they had been to the maintenance of the
'home front' during the forties. But whereas in the forties their
dual role had been both recognised and celebrated, in the fifties the
problems they experienced as a consequence of the fragmentation

of their daily lives into mother, wife, worker and so on came increasingly to be regarded as the result of their own inadequacies and incompetence. By the sixties the 'bad mother' was being held responsible for all manner of social ills.

One of the intentions of this book is to examine what images of women were offered to audiences in Britain during these years. How did the narrated experiences of fictional women on the screen compare with the day to day realities of the women in the audience? During the twenty-year period issues of specific concern to women appeared on the agendas of various public bodies – the medical profession, the politicians, sociologists and so on. In the forties the degree of state intervention into the detail of family life was an important issue. Beveridge noted, in 1948, that:

> The housewife's job with a large family is frankly impossible, and will remain so, unless some of what has now to be done separately in every home – washing all clothes, cooking every meal, being in charge of every child for every moment when it is not in school – can be done communally outside the home.[25]

However just as the provisions of the post-war legislation, the 'Welfare State', were only a faint echo of the far more radical propositions contained in the 1943 Beveridge report, so the discussion of women's 'frankly impossible' domestic role boiled down in practice to the question of pre-school provision such as creches and nurseries on the one hand and on the other hand to consideration of the 'family allowance' and the concept of the family wage. During the fifties attention was focused on fertility control and sexuality – encouraged by the publication of the two Kinsey reports[26] – and as fears about the falling population were allayed by the marked rise in the birth rate the notion of 'family planning' became not only a respectable one but the subject of discussion and surveys. Despite the apparent liberalism of such debate, however, it had the effect of reinforcing the family as the only acceptable site for the expression of sexuality. As Elizabeth Wilson puts it:

> Sexuality was both to expand and flower in liberated fashion *and* to be organised within marriage.[27]

Liberal attitudes were thus concerned with the terms of marriage contracts and the accessibility of birth control, never with an interrogation of the inevitable contradictions generated within the family unit as a consequence of its multiple functions. Hence divorce became easier to obtain and increasingly widespread, but marriage and domestic management were generally regarded as the major goal in life for women. Debates among educationalists about the school curriculum acknowledged this in their different provision for and expectations of boys and girls at secondary level, and these differences became more marked as the decade progressed. By the sixties the appearance of the contraceptive pill, the Wolfenden report (1957) heralding changes in the laws relating to male homosexuality and the increasingly articulate exasperation of the young with regard to the mores and conventions of their parents' generation all contributed to the myth of 'the permissive society' and the widespread fears about promiscuity and immorality in circulation at the time.

The Historical Audience

Whereas the distinguishing feature of British society in the forties was a stoical collectivism, by the sixties there was instead an impatient fragmentation. Is there any evidence of these concerns in the content of films achieving large-scale box office success? It is certainly true to say that the characteristic themes treated in popular film underwent marked changes through the period, and that at any given moment all the most popular films tended to share some common concerns, as we shall see in Chapter 2. However, unless we are to subscribe to the simple idea that films in some way reflect the society in which they circulate, it is a more complex matter to understand the significance of such changes. Given that the meanings of a film are the product of an active negotiation between the reader and the film text, how did female audience members 'read' the images they were offered of their celluloid counterparts?

Here we are immediately plunged into the realm of speculation. We can never know the answer to this question, but we can consider some of its determinants. We can take a sample of box office successes yielded through a correlation of different sources as outlined above. We can engage in detailed analysis of these films, considering not only the narratives' overall themes, structures and resolutions but also details of the representations of female characters and the nuances of their relation to overall narrative development. So far, so good: but all this only attends to the film object itself. What of the audience, particularly the female audience? What forms of evidence are available to us here? It is possible to envisage an oral history enquiry which would attempt to reconstruct through interviews and questionnaires some traces of the audience.[28] However, apart from the logistic difficulties of such an undertaking, any conclusions it came to would be subject to all the limitations inherent in such methods. Reconstruction through hindsight, faulty memory and unrepresentative samples of respondents would all contribute to the unreliability of any conclusions drawn, though such conclusions would, admittedly, offer fascinating correlative material along the lines of the Mass Observation survey of cinema audiences in Bolton in 1938.[29] More satisfactory would be an examination of contemporary published material: though the audiences themselves cannot be resurrected yet we can have access to the discursive materials routinely circulating among them. We have available to us in this form empirical evidence of the terms in which various films, characters, plots and stars were discussed. We can discover which representations were acceptable, which were the subject of controversy. In short, while we cannot meet with the audience, we can know something of the context in which their viewings took place and in which their meanings were formed.

Such material is available from a variety of sources: the national press in which films were routinely reviewed; the trade press in which, as we have seen, the likely response of audiences was the subject of sometimes quite detailed speculation – the idea of the differentiated audience was certainly an important one for this readership. Fan magazines, in addition to reviews and features aimed to assist the readership in its choice of viewing, also published readers' letters and articles taking issue with themes regarded as controversial. A substantial overlap may be assumed between female audience members and the readership of magazines addressed specifically to women; here is empirical evidence about issues which concerned female readers of both the magazines and the films. All this empirical data will be useful in moderating the preferred reading suggested through the narrative construction of any particular film text. So here we have two distinct sources of data – the films themselves, and contemporary publications – upon which to draw. The particular uses we make of this data will be ordered according to our theoretical understanding of the processes of reading. Here there are differing models concerned with the mechanics of spectatorial pleasure, the range of possible operations between the text and the reader, the epistemological status of language and experience, and so on. These matters will be taken up in Chapter 6. For the present it will be sufficient to note, referring once again to Carr's dictum about the correlation from multiple documents to specific facts, that in considering the relation between a film and the female members of its audience we are not dealing with facts but rather with the interpretation of attitudes, the discovery of constraints, the status of particular ethical positions. All these are part of the wider field of determinants affecting female behaviour and expectations, part of the socialisation, the acculturation of girls and women. We might also note here Simone de Beauvoir's simple reminder (*The Second Sex*, 1948) that those maintained by a dominant group in a position of inferiority are, of course, inferior. The point is that they are not inevitably so but are so as a consequence of their oppression. Hence the primary question informing the contents of this study: how far can popular cinema be understood to have contributed to the continuing subjugation of women in the post-war period?

2
Popular Cinema in Britain, 1945–1965

THE FILMS

Having considered the concept of popularity as it is applied to the cinema, and having sketched the broad outlines of social history in the UK during our period it is now time to turn our attention to the films themselves.[1] In this chapter we shall attend to the general thematic features typical of the majority of films popular in the mid-forties, mid-fifties and mid-sixties, and to the two aspects of the cinema which particularly inflected marketing strategies, audience choices and, most important, audience readings of film – which are genre and stars.

The Forties

A cursory glance at the titles popular at the beginning, middle and end of our period allows some very general observations about the kinds of films which the mass audience chose to see. During the forties melodrama was by far the most popular genre; various interpretations of the overall generic type from the (recently) celebrated Gainsborough melodramas such as *Madonna of the Seven Moons* (dir Arthur Cratree, UK 1944), *They Were Sisters* (dir Arthur Crabtree, UK 1945), *A Place of One's Own* (dir Bernard Knowles UK 1944), *The Wicked Lady* (dir Leslie Arliss UK 1945), *Caravan* (dir Arthur Crabtree UK 1946), to the no more lavish but far more glossy Warner productions such as *Mr Skeffington* (dir Vincent Sherman, US 1944), *Old Acquaintance* (dir Vincent Sherman US 1943), *The Corn is Green* (dir Irving Rapper US 1945) and *Mildred Pierce* (dir Michael Curtiz US 1945). The Ealing film *The Captive Heart* (dir Basil Dearden UK 1946) interpreted the genre with a story about the British inmates of a German prisoner of war camp, and Two Cities' *The Way to the Stars* (dir Anthony Asquith UK 1945) also dealt with subject matter drawn from the experience of war, but these two films were unusual. On the whole the war is more significant by its absence in films of the later forties. Where it is present it is usually as a background to stories whose substance concerns the emotional and familial ties of the protagonists, such as in *Piccadilly Incident* (dir Wilcox, ABP, UK 1946). Two epic historical/literary dramas, Rank's expensive and prestigious *Henry V* (dir Laurence Olivier UK 1944) and *Caesar and Cleopatra* (dir Gabriel Pascal UK 1945) were successful at this time, and there were several fairly light hearted musical comedies – *I Live in Grosvenor Square* (dir Herbert Wilcox, ABP, UK 1945), *Here Come the Waves* (dir Mark Sandrich, Paramount, US 1944), *The Road to Utopia* (dir Hal Walker, Paramount, US 1945) – and one or two thrillers *Conflict* (dir Curtis Bernhardt, Warner, US 1945) and *Spellbound* (dir Alfred Hitchcock, David Selznick, US 1945). In general however the melodrama was the dominant form, from studies of contemporary life in *Brief Encounter* (dir David Lean, Cineguild, UK 1945) and *Mildred Pierce* to historical extravaganzas such as *A Song to Remember* (dir Charles Vidor, Columbia, US 1944) or *Caravan*. The most striking feature of films popular at this time is the emphasis on the individual, as we shall see frequently a woman, in the narratives. Even where wider social or historical issues appear to be the primary subject matter it is the fine detail of individual emotion on which the audience is invited to dwell. A typical example is the narrative resolution of *The Bells of St Mary's* (dir Leo McCarey US 1946). This is essentially a fairy tale dealing with the opposing methods employed by 'reason' and 'emotion' in the context of education. Both methods are validated at the end of the film when the spiritual man, Father O'Malley, and the medical man, Dr Mackay, agree that the object of their endeavours, the 'good heart', is the same. Yet despite their agreement the 'happy ending' of the film is a consequence, finally, not of the school being saved but of the trust between the central characters Sister Mary Benedict (Ingrid Bergman) and Father O'Malley (Bing Crosby) being renewed at the last minute. Hence the audience satisfaction at the narrative's close is constructed around the relationship between the central female and male protagonists rather than around the ostensibly central plot element which concerns the institution, the school itself.

The Fifties

By the mid-fifties this emphasis on the personal appears to have shifted and the detailed delineation of individuals serves a more generalised purpose: now the audience is not invited to empathise with the special and unique joys and sorrows of a particular character so much as to understand the character's apparent uniqueness as exemplary of one or other position in a wider debate about social values. Marlon Brando as Terry Mulloy in *On the Waterfront* (dir Elia Kazan, Columbia, US 1954) moves, during the course of the narrative, from the position of 'side-kick' to his brother in the group of union officials terrorising the 'ordinary' dockers, to being the champion of the oppressed dockers in their challenge of corrupt hiring practices. The last scene of the film shows a bloodied but not bowed Brando staggering in to work followed by the dockers and watched approvingly by his two mentors, the Padre (Karl Malden) and the 'educated' heroine Edie played by Eve Marie Saint. Though Brando's method style of acting and the numerous intimate scenes where he wrestles with his emergent conscience combine to allow insight into the special difficulties his character experiences, yet the final scene generalises from this experience, pointing out its wider social significance. The 'message' of this film is precisely about the functioning of the individual *within* the collective. The individual is valued in so far as she or he contributes to the well-being of the group. Another example is the biopic *Reach For The Sky* (dir Lewis Gilbert, Rank, UK 1956) in which Kenneth More plays Douglas Bader: here the entire film is a study of the career of this celebrated hero of the Battle of Britain and the appalling physical handicaps he overcame in pursuit of his goal. Yet the character, as played by More, is carefully constructed to exemplify the Churchillian requirements of the British people in their historic struggle. The climactic action sequences of the Battle of Britain follow a series of slow pans around close-ups of pilot's faces as they listen to Churchill's exhortatory radio speech announcing the forthcoming battle and ending on the stirring 'finest hour' phrase. The positioning of this famous speech in the narrative invites an understanding of Bader's career and his personality as exemplary of all the qualities Churchill called for in the patriot of the war period. The events of Bader's career thus become symbolic of the national struggle and eventual victory: Germany, as Churchill's stentorian tones announce, threatens the 'abyss of a new dark age' and this, through the film's construction, is made equivalent to the catastrophic accident through which Bader himself had been threatened, and which in previous scenes we have witnessed him slowly, painfully and with difficulty surviving, against all the odds.

Though in the fifties the melodrama remained a popular genre, as evidenced by the success of such films as *Hobson's Choice* (dir David Lean, British Lion, UK 1954), *Marty* (dir Delbert Mann, UA, US 1955), *All that Heaven Allows* (dir Douglas Sirk, U-I, US 1955) and *East of Eden* (dir Elia Kazan, Warner, US 1955), there is a greater variety of distinct generic types represented amongst the major box office hits of the period. Unlike the forties the war film is a popular genre – not only *Reach For The Sky* but also *From Here to Eternity* (dir Fred Zinneman, Columbia, US 1953), *The Dam Busters* (dir Michael Anderson, ABPC, UK 1955) and *A Town Like Alice* (dir Jack Lee, Rank, UK 1956). Comedy emerges as a distinct genre, in marketing terms, with the earliest titles of the long running series of Doctor films, *Doctor in the House* (dir Ralph Thomas, Rank, UK 1954) and *Doctor at Sea* (dir Ralph Thomas, Rank, UK 1955), the first of the St Trinians cycle, *The Belles of St Trinians* (dir Frank Launder, British Lion, UK 1954) and the first of the Boulting brothers' comedies, *Private's Progress* (dir John Boulting, British Lion, UK 1956). Thrillers figure less frequently than comedies but nevertheless *Rear Window* (dir Alfred Hitcock, Hitchcock, US 1954) and *The Man Who Knew Too Much* (dir Alfred Hitchcock, Paramount, US 1956) were both extremely popular. However the genre that, with hindsight, seems to characterise the mid fifties best of all – to be equivalent in popularity to the melodrama in the forties – is the musical. *The Glenn Miller Story* (dir Anthony Mann, U-I, US 1954), *Calamity Jane* (dir David Butler, Warner, US 1954), *The King and I* (dir Walter Lang, TCF, US 1956), *Guys and Dolls* (dir Joseph Mankiewicz, Samuel Goldwyn, US 1955), *Oklahoma* (dir Fred Zinneman, Magna US 1955) and *High Society* (dir Charles Walters, MGM, US 1956) are amongst the best remembered of these successes. The thing that characterises these films and other examples of the genre such as *Seven Brides for Seven Brothers* (dir Stanley Donen, MGM, US 1954) and *South Pacific* (dir Joshua Logan, Magna, US 1958), apart from the music itself, is their appropriations from the real world in the service of fantasy. History, biography, popular myth, contemporary society are all plundered for plots, locations, and characters whose most striking feature is their un-likeness to their referents. The success of this production strategy – this focus on pleasurable fantasy delivered by means of colourful visual spectacle and catchy tunes – we find developed further in the box office successes of the sixties.

The Sixties

There is in the majority of sixties films a kind of narrative self-consciousness about the artifices involved in film making which is on the whole lacking in the fifties musicals and which as we shall see forms a substantial common link between the films which achieved the greatest box office success during the decade.

The public enjoyment, implicit in the success of these films, of their recognition of the complexity of the film object is in part a consequence of the increasing access to broadcast television. Once it is no longer the only available source of mass entertainment an expedition to the cinema involves a conscious choice between various options. It seems likely that it is also a consequence of the public's increasing perception of the star persona as an element separable from the 'vehicle' through which it is marketed. Through the fifties as we have seen distributors and exhibitors became, with good reason, more and more concerned about the profitability of their endeavours and consequently contributed, in their marketing strategies, to the emphasis on star performers in the discourses surrounding the exchange of popular film. This phenomena is of course nothing new in the history of cinema. The earliest and most celebrated example was the innovatory naming of stars in the struggle between the MPPC (Motion Picture Patents Company) cartel and the 'independents' in the USA before the First World War in which the 'Biograph girl' became the star Florence Lawrence. It does seem, however, to be particularly marked in the fifties and early sixties – a time, like the teens of the century, of major structural changes in the organisation of the film industry.

This attention to stars, this perception of film as a vehicle for its performers, is most clearly evident in the overlap between the film industry and the rapidly expanding popular music business, an overlap which is often conveniently explained as either the evidence or the consequence of the increased affluence of youth. The film and music industries thus collaborated in the production of film vehicles for popular music stars in order to tap the surplus income of this sector of the population. Hence for example the Cliff Richard films *The Young Ones* (dir Sidney Furie, ABP, UK 1961) and *Summer Holiday* (dir Peter Yates, ABP, UK 1963) and the Beatles' films *A Hard*

Day's Night (dir Richard Lester, UA, UK 1964) and *Help* (dir Richard Lester, UA UK 1965) which appear amongst the top box office hits of the early sixties. The corollary to this apparent development in audiences' recognition of the discrete elements operative in film is their recognition of and pleasure in the practices of film making which, it seems, were now enjoyed in their own right. Pleasure in the artifice itself is clearly an important element in the success of *Mary Poppins* (dir Robert Sephenson, Disney, US 1965) in which the clever juxtaposition of animation and live action was a central and much celebrated device. The spectacular thrills of near science fiction gadgetry was a crucial factor in the success of the James Bond pictures *Dr No* (dir Terence Young, UA/Eon, UK 1962) *From Russia With Love* (dir Terence Young, UA/Eon, UK 1963) and *Goldfinger* (dir Guy Hamilton, UA/Eon, UK 1964). The inventive cinematography of the contemporary Hammer horror cycle was clearly enjoyed for its own sake though these films, while moderately successful, never achieved sufficiently widespread popularity to appear amongst the titles yielded by the correlation employed here. Most striking of all perhaps is the number of films in which the comedy depends on the audience's recognition of specifically cinematic 'games': the eponymous Tom Jones hangs his hat on the camera, thus obscuring the audience's vision and turning the screen black; the Beatles perform a concert in the guard's van of their train from Liverpool to London in *A Hard Day's Night* ; Norman Wisdom depends heavily on a peculiarly cinematic form of slapstick in *A Stitch in Time* (dir Robert Asher, Rank, UK 1963). The point is not that these devices in film are new, rather that, as with the increasing reliance on the persona of particular stars from the late fifties onwards, that they appear consistently in the films that enjoyed the biggest success at the contemporary box office.

In addition to what we might characterise as a fragmentation of the pleasures of cinema, evident in popular sixties films, there is also a thematic emphasis on the 'liberation' of the individual from the constraints of the past; from their upbringing, from existing conventions and so on, with a parallel emphasis on the validity of the individual's pursuit of pleasure. Here there is another about turn from the location of the individual within the collective which we have suggested was characteristic of the mid-fifties films. In the sixties the weight of the collective is more likely to be represented as an unnecessary constraint on the all important freedom of the (usually youthful) individual. But the dominant feature evident in consideration of all aspects of the cinema in the sixties seems to be fragmentation.

Cinematic pleasure is fragmented – the star is a box office draw, the cinematic artifice is enjoyed for its own sake, gadgetry and locations are frequently applauded for their simple presence. The audience too is fragmented – there is an appeal in both marketing and production strategies to distinct audience groupings. Films purveying currently popular music stars aimed for the youth audience; Hammer horror movies developed a specialised following as did the endlessly repeated formulaic films such as the Doctor series, the Carry On films, and the James Bond movies. The widely acclaimed 'kitchen sink' dramas, celebrated for their revival of 'British' cinema are in fact most notable for their insistent fragmentation of the idea of Britishness. Class and regional differences were typically emphasised in these films though their frequent juxtapositions of tradition and innovation, conformity and independence, allowed for considerable ambiguity about the meanings of Britishness which they offered.

The movement towards plurality in the genres popular at the box office which we noted *à-propos* mid-fifties films continued in the sixties, most likely as the dual consequences of the fragmentation of the audience and of its overall decline. Cinema-going in the sixties became, as we have noted, a specialist leisure pursuit: it is not surprising therefore to find the institution of cinema adapting itself to cater for a series of specialist audience groupings. Thus comedy, music (though not the musical itself), science fiction, horror and realist drama were the dominant forms amongst box office hits. The war film was still a popular genre: *The Great Escape* (dir John Sturges, UA, US 1963), *Zulu* (dir Cy Endfield, Paramount/Diamond, UK 1964) and *Von Ryan's Express* (dir Mark Robson, TCF, US 1965) were all among the handful of top box office hits in their year of release.[2]

There is considerable overlapping of genres, no doubt evidence of the attempt on the part of the industry to ensure maximum exposure for their product by appealing to more than one audience grouping as well as of what Cawelti (1979) terms 'generic transformation' – that is the tendency within any particular genre to maintain audience interest both by reproducing the expected contours of the genre and by 'breaking' generic rules.[3] The dissolution of generic boundaries implied in the notion of 'transformation', which conforms to the widespread technical self-consciousness typical of this period, is certainly a striking feature of popular cinema in the sixties. The comedy *Carry On Spying* (dir Gerald Thomas, Anglo-Amalgamated UK 1963), for example, derives much of its comedy through its references to the contours of the spy thriller. The James Bond movies – primarily thrillers though also celebrated for their science fiction spectacle and lavish representations of consumer durables – construct both suspense and comedy on the assumption of audience familiarity with the thriller form. The suspense in such movies is never about *whether* our hero will survive, but rather about *how* he will escape from the desperate straits in which, time and again, he finds himself. The comedy derives from the knowledge, shared between Bond and the audience, that he *will* survive since the formula requires it.

The broad outline of the characterics of films popular at the box office given above is necessarily schematic; there are of course important exceptions to most of the generalisations offered. It should be noted at this point,however, that the films so characterised are precisely those which achieved box office success as defined by the careful and systematic correlation outlined in Chapter 1. Any homogeneity evident in the form and content of films achieving the status of box office hit at any one moment is a consequence of audience choice, not of production strategy.

Audience choice is inevitably constrained by a plurality of factors: we have already considered the social context of viewing, and production and marketing strategies within the industry. As we have seen in the summary of the period given here there are other issues more specific to the discourse surrounding film itself which need to be taken into account. Principal among these are genre and star personae.

GENRE

The organisation of textual forms and narrative content within an overall system of generic modes is crucial to the functioning of the institution of cinema. It is the means whereby the industry defines its products in order to sell them and it is also the means by which audiences order their choice of particular films from among the multiplicity on offer. Within each particular text and through generic types as a whole there is a simultaneous articulation of repetition and difference: repetition – of narrative strategies, stylistic devices, certain themes and character types – is concerned with the expectation of the audience while difference – the continuous presentation of the new, the *un*-expected and *un*-familiar – ensures the novelty of each text and is thus concerned with its desirability at the box office, hence its profitability.

The generic classification of film texts is fundamental to the activity of disparate groupings within the institution of cinema. It is evident in the exhibition and distribution branches of the industry as an attempt to distinguish and define products in order to mount more effective sales campaigns and thus maximise profits. It is evident in the production branch of the industry since generic specialisation tends to be encouraged, as in the case of Gainsborough's melodramas of the late forties and Hammer's horror films of the late fifties and sixties, by the success of a particular product and the ensuing capitalisation on already existing resources. It is also evident in theoretical studies of film where attention to genre has been developed as an alternative to the auteurist approach to film criticism: here the generic attributes of the text are privileged and various examples of the genre, albeit from different directors, studios and so on, are considered as a group and the 'metadiscourse' of the genre itself is revealed and analysed to display the underlying cultural celebrations and/or anxieties implicit in it.

But there are problems implicit in these different motivations behind generic classification. The industry, though it experimented with the generic descriptions of products during a period when the popularity of cinema as a whole was declining rapidly, used a relatively small number of generic 'labels' (Cartoon, Musical, Documentary, Comedy, Western, Horror) during the period under discussion, of which only the categories Musical, Western and Horror appeared in the trade papers consistently. Film historians and theoreticians, on the other hand, applying the concept of genre for quite different reasons, have tended to cite a far greater variety. Thus Pam Cook's invaluable summary of film studies[4] cites six categories (Western, Gangster/Crime, Film Noir, Musical, Melodrama, Horror) while Steve Neale,[5] compiling a list of genres as a teaching aid, cites eleven (Western, Gangster, Detective, Thriller, Horror, Sci-Fi, Musical, Melodrama, Comedy, Phantasy/Adventure, Epic). Genre theory was in fact first elaborated on the basis of film noir and the western; the former primarily noted for its stylistic features, the latter for its thematics. Subsequently work focusing on genre has attended to the musical, the horror film, the melodrama and so on. The consequence of such a proliferation of categories is not only the tendency on the part of film scholars to lose sight of the industry in their concentration on individual texts but also to risk losing sight of the text itself since discussion centres on generic specification and critical attention is in danger of being limited to the business of classifying the text forgetting, or at least marginalising, the primary task of analysing the activity of the text in respect of its readers, the audience. A consideration of meaning gives way to a preoccupation with ordering.

Nevertheless the formulation with which Neale closes his exposition is a useful one:

> genres also provide a means of regulating memory and expectation, a means of containing the possibilities of reading.[6]

Its references to the audience's experience, 'memory', its desires, 'expectation' and, most importantly, its suggestion of the way readings may be constrained by generic conventions are all productive ones. This 'containing' of the 'possibilities' may operate to privilege one reading to the extent that alternative readings implicit in ambiguities of the text become impossible – an example is the thriller construction of Hitchcock's film *Marnie* (Universal, US 1964) in which the female reader, despite textual invitations to the contrary implicit in many of Marnie's own utterances, is obliged in the narrative closure to subscribe to the male hero's formulation of Marnie's 'problem'.

Mildred Pierce (dir Michael Curtiz, Warner, US 1946) draws on the codes of both film noir and the melodrama, calling on audience recognition of these conventions for their understanding of the logic of plot development. But the dark and troubled world of film noir is evoked primarily for the scenes detailing Mildred's 'independent' life as a successful entrepreneur, her relationship with Monty and her difficulties with her daughter, Veda. The sunny, by comparison almost pastoral world of the family melodrama is reserved for the flashback segments chronicling the domestic life of Mildred's past. It is this latter, of course, which is validated as the solution to the intractable problems posed to Mildred through the generic codes of film noir, in the emblematic final shot of the film in which Mildred and her previously estranged husband step out of the night time world of the film noir police station into the dawn of a new, melodramatic, day. Thus the audience's understanding of

Mildred's dilemma is organised according to generic conventions.
So seamlessly organised, in fact, that many contemporary reviewers
referred to the film as a 'realist tract'; *Newsweek*, for example,
characterised it as 'a bitter commentary on suburbia' (15 October
1945). Public discussion centred on Mildred's qualities as a mother
rather than on the contexts in which she exercised this function:

> Parents' and women's clubs throughout USA discussed the prob-
> lem 'was Mildred Pierce a good mother?' Some argue that
> Mildred was weak to give in to her daughter. Others that she set
> no example that she could happily expect her daughter to follow.
> Still others that she was a misunderstood wife and mother whose
> love proved too indulgent . . . [7]

In the process the rather more interesting question, about the
social dimensions of Mildred's attempt to lead a professional as
well as a domestic life, was missed.

However the co-existence of different generic modes within a
single text does not always guarantee such clarity. The 1956 film,
The Searchers (dir John Ford, Warner), drew on the codes of two
quite different genres, the family melodrama and the western, in its
complex tale of quest and vengeance set in America's mythic past.
The interaction between these two well established genres tends
to reveal the essential differences between them and, implicitly,
between the models they offer of contemporary American society.
These are differences which cannot, in the end, be successfully
resolved within the terms of the diegesis, hence the almost epistemological fracture at the point where Ethan (John Wayne) rescues
rather than shoots Debbie (Natalie Wood), near the end of the film.
The locations, period and overall structure of the film proclaim it a
western – an understanding strengthened by the central presence
of John Wayne – but the excruciatingly protracted western quest
is punctuated by temporally parallel domestic episodes with all
the hallmarks of family melodrama. The assertive young woman,
Laurie Jorgensen (Vera Miles), the ineffectual and near comic male
characters of her father (John Qualen) and her would-be husband
Charlie (Ken Curtis) – both feminised by their exclusion from the
western segments of the film – and the details of domestic ritual all
require that the audience call on the codes of melodrama in their
understanding of these scenes. It is these familial, melodramatic
codes again that dominate in the narrative closure as the door

of the Jorgensen home is closed and the western hero, his quest completed, rides away into the desert. But the western convention of 'feminising' the non-white, savage, childlike – the un-cultured, in short – in order to delineate the more clearly the culture of the male, white hero standing as he does for America and the future, works against the conventions of the melodrama in which women are typically offered as the central stabilising force with the prerogative – albeit often expressed in servile terms – of maintaining the fabric of civilisation. This accounts for the inconsistencies of the central characters Ethan and Debbie, though their inconsistencies cannot, of course, ever be resolved within the terms offered in this film. It also accounts for the confusing mixed address of the film most evident in the exchange between Laurie and Marty (Jeffrey Hunter) just before Marty leaves, once again, to attempt Debbie's rescue:

> *Laurie*: Martin, you're not going, not this time.
> *Marty*: You crazy?
> *Laurie*: But it's too late, she's a grown woman now.
> *Marty*: But I gotta go, Laurie. I gotta fetch her home.
> *Laurie*: Fetch what home? The leavin's of Comanche bucks sold time and again to the highest bidder, with savage brats of her own now.
> *Marty*: Laurie shut your mouth.
> *Laurie*: Do you know what Ethan'll do if he has the chance? He'll put a bullet in her brain. I tell you Martha would want him to.

Here the typical position of each genre, *vis-à-vis* the position of women, is given from the wrong place, so to speak: Laurie, the heroine of the family melodrama, about to be united, finally, with the object of her affections, repudiates her 'sister' Debbie as dehumanised because of miscegenation. Marty, the hero of the western odyssey about to reach his 'grail', defends the centrality of the family in the home. The interweaving of these two generic modes in this film thus produces serious epistemological problems for the reader since it is the logic of the melodrama that emasculates the resolution of the western: the scene in which Ethan Edwards (John Wayne) at the last minute saves Debbie (Natalie Wood) rather than killing her being virtually inexplicable through the western codes by which Wayne's character has been constructed.

Reviewers understood the film as a western but found it deeply flawed, perhaps because of its 'contamination' by the codes of melodrama:

> When his story reaches a point where only dishonesty can conceal an essential falsity – he simply throws it in our faces . . . all the climax of The Searchers with its preposterous rescue and Edward's unbelievable change of heart, is like this.[8]

> The Searchers had the makings of a classic if only the master had kept his eye on the ball.[9]

> The picture rides steadily away from the opening climax into anti climax and dullness . . . dramatically the Master is at a low ebb this time. All is far too quiet on the western front.[10]

The insistence on the film as a potentially 'classic' western, despite its apparent inadequacies, is striking in these and other reviews; speculation on the reasons for this, though intriguing, would be out of place here. It is sufficient simply to observe that an acknowledgement of the generic codes upon which any particular film text draws is central to understanding the film's contemporary meanings. The generic reflexivity which we have already noted as a common feature amongst films popular at the box office in the sixties is evidence not only of audience recognition of such codes but also of their pleasure in the play on codes typical of these films.

STAR PERSONAE

But why was *The Searchers* understood as an inadequate western rather than as an inadequate melodrama since, as we have seen, it drew on the codes of both genres? Apart from the fact that the film was dircted by John Ford, acknowledged as the 'master' of the western, there is also the central presence of the actor John Wayne whose star persona was closely identified with this genre.

When audiences make their choice of films to see, when fan magazines synopsise and comment on the latest new releases and when reviewers in the press offer their opinions about currently available titles they all depend heavily on existing, and shared, knowledge about the typical attributes of individual performers. The marketing of films recognises and capitalises on this fact, invariably including actors' names prominently in their publicity materials. Thus when the audience pays at the box office to view the film they are also, perhaps even primarily, paying for the sight of a favourite performer in action. In making this payment they are anticipating the pleasure not only of the unexpected contours of the particular, as yet unknown film but also of the familiar and well liked aspects of particular performers. Thus they come to the viewing with certain expectations. The term 'persona' summarises these expectations: it derives from the previous performances and public utterances of the actor and is constructed over time in specific ways.[11] In terms of the audience's reading of a new film, however, their familiarity with the personae of performers is likely to inflect their understanding of the narrative as it unfolds. Sean Connery's first appearance on screen is likely to command attention of a different order from that accorded to an 'unknown' actor in the James Bond films of the early sixties. The centrality of his performances as James Bond to his persona is also likely to have consequences for the audience's understanding of his character Mark Rutland in Hitchcock's film *Marnie*, which was released in the same year as *Goldfinger*, 1964. This public conception of the characteristics of certain performers, the star persona, is in many ways more durable than their memory of the details of particular films: certainly star's names are frequently used to recall past films. When *The Slipper and the Rose* (dir Brian Forbes, Paradine, UK 1976) was reviewed, Margaret Lockwood as the stepmother was characterised as 'surely the best known and most elegant Wicked Lady of them all':[12] after thirty years her performance in the 1946 film *The Wicked Lady* was still an enduring element of her persona.

Many of the periodic assessments of popularity conducted by various parts of the industry focussed particularly on the names of stars; in trying to trace the changing attributes of popular film it is of interest to note who were, in fact, the most popular stars in each of our three decades. Our primary questions about the models of female behaviour offered to audiences also require attention to changes in the typical features of the personae of the top female box office stars. Referring again to the correlation outlined in Chapter 1 one striking feature is immediately apparent: whereas in the mid forties the numbers of male and female stars that can be regarded as, in the terms of the trade, box office winners, are roughly equal there is a steady decline in the relative popularity of male and female stars through the fifties and into the sixties. In the early sixties nearly all the most popular box office stars were men.

Box Office Winners

In the forties Stewart Granger, James Mason, Bing Crosby, Bob Hope, Alan Ladd, Humphrey Bogart and Lawrence Olivier were the most popular male stars: Bette Davis, Greer Garson, Margaret Lockwood, Joan Fontaine, Ann Todd, Phyllis Calvert, Ingrid Bergman, Anna Neagle and Celia Johnson the most popular female stars. In the fifties amongst the men there were James Stewart, Richard Todd, Dirk Bogarde and Kenneth More at the top of the list – the only female star matching their box office popularity was Doris Day: Gregory Peck and Frank Sinatra were next most popular, and so was Julie Harris. Finally there were Marlon Brando, John Mills, Rock Hudson, Norman Wisdom, Audie Murphy, Danny Kaye, Ernest Borgnine, Yul Brynner and James Dean and, still as popular as they had been in the forties Alan Ladd, Humphrey Bogart, and Bing Crosby. The women were Audrey Hepburn, Grace Kelly, Judy Garland, Deborah Kerr, Anna Magnani and Kim Novak. The top female stars at the box office in the early sixties were Elizabeth Taylor, Hayley Mills, Sophia Loren and Julie Andrews, with Audrey Hepburn still a major attraction at the very beginning of the decade. Just five names, yet the list of male stars with equivalent popularity at the box office is long (thirteen if the Beatles are counted as one): they were Peter Sellers, Sean Connery, Cliff Richard, Albert Finney, Elvis Presley, Stanley Baker, Rex Harrison and the (four) Beatles, with Kenneth More, Dirk Bogarde, John Mills and Norman Wisdom still retaining the popularity they had enjoyed during the fifties. This remarkable imbalance between the genders, in terms of box office popularity, mirrors the relative presence of central male and female characters in the most popular films of the period, as we shall see. What we have here is, in effect, a most striking decline in the overall visibility of women in popular film which raises important questions both about the audience and about the social positioning of women during our period. Of one thing we can be sure, and that is that the absence of women on the screen did not reflect a similar absence of women amongst the population. We must ask, then, why it was that in the forties there were numerous highly popular female stars whereas during the fifties and sixties there were, relatively, so few? More importantly, perhaps, we may wonder what effect this dearth of women amongst the top box office stars of the day had on audience understanding of womanhood – particularly for the meanings that might have been construed by female audience members.

In one sense this is yet another impossible question: in the chapters that follow we shall look closely at the details of screen representations of women and at their narrative experience – what happened to them 'in the end' – but we should also attend to the discourses surrounding the personae of the female stars that *were* highly popular. We can now say that on the whole male stars were far more popular at the box office than female stars for the major part of our period: how then did reviewers deal with the female stars that did achieve 'top ten' status, and what were the characteristic features of the most popular female star personae in each of the three decades?

From the 'Artful Female' to the 'Grown Up Doll': the Personae of Top Female Stars

The commentaries on the top female stars of the forties typically emphasise their professionalism, their resilience and their competence in researching and representing complex characters on screen. Bette Davis, arguably the most popular of all, was celebrated for her portayals of powerful though often tragic female characters and in these celebratory reviews her own forceful professionalism was also acknowledged. A *New Statesman* review of her performance in the 1950 Mankiewicz film *All About Eve* refers – as is often the case in the construction of star personae – to the reputation of earlier stars, in this case Tallulah Bankhead and Greta Garbo:

> Bette Davis' bewitching portrayal of a middleaged star: flamboyant, maudlin, kind-hearted, irritating, pathetic, her great lady of the theatre a la Talullah is one of the three finest things in a screen career surpassed only by Garbo's.[13]

But though the screen career is Davis' own, and the 'great lady of the theatre' is, strictly speaking, the character Margot Channing which she plays in the film, there is an elision between the great theatre star and the great screen star: the consequence is that the string of adjectives also apply to Bette Davis. Margaret Lockwood's

performance in *The Wicked Lady* was admired for its ebullience: she
was seen to be 'romping through the man crazy, trigger happy title
role'[14] but also to be displaying a 'mastery of all the emotions
known to the artful female'.[15] The validation of female independence implicit in the popularity of stars such as these two was,
however, accompanied by the substantial popular success of stars
whose personae emphasised quite different aspects of woman. Celia
Johnson, for example, in *Brief Encounter* (David Lean, Cineguild, UK
1945) was:

> delightfully naive and feminine as a happily married woman
> who drifts into romance and discovers before it is too late that
> her domestic happiness really comes first.[16]

In a feature article later in the year her own domesticity was
heavily emphasised:

> Celia Johnson is something quite unique in film stars. She is
> an extremely personable young woman who has never found
> the time nor the zeal to settle down in front of a mirror and
> deliberately acquire glamour. 'Perhaps I ought to try to be
> glamorous, in the evenings anyhow,' she says, spreading out her
> practical hands with the short, unvarnished nails, and looking
> ruefully at the marks left by potato peelings.[17]

And so was her class position:

> When Nicholas is older he will go to Eton, where his father
> went. His mother, born in Richmond, went to St Paul's Girls'
> School.[18]

Ingrid Bergman too was celebrated in the forties for her modesty,
dignity and gentility:

> It is something of a paradox that this natural gentility which now
> brings her to the foremost position among the great actresses of
> the screen was at first, the most potent threat to her professional
> success in Hollywood. There is no use denying it. When she first
> came here her qualities were too rare to be fully appreciated

and her approach was such that she could not hope for quick recognition as a great dramatic actress.[19]

She wore a plain, ordinary looking rain coat, a pair of black and beige rubber over-boots and on her head, tied peasant fashion, a coloured scarf. She might have stepped clear off the Yorkshire moors. Her face, practically untouched by any make-up, glowed with health. Her lips were of the shape and colour decided by nature.[20]

Like Bergman, Joan Fontaine and Greer Garson were also regarded as 'classy' stars. It was the 'type' of woman occupying the proverbial pedestal, rather than her abilities as a performer, that was implicitly celebrated in fifties reviewers' contributions to star personae. Hence an emphasis on the simple physical presence, rather than on the complexities of character associated with Bette Davis or the ebullient sexuality of Margaret Lockwood's performances, dominated in the formation of the personae of popular female stars in the fifties.

Grace Kelly's or Deborah Kerr's distinguished and somewhat restrained elegance exemplify the 'classy' type; at the other extreme a childish, naive and vulnerable sexuality was celebrated in the popularity of Julie Harris. *Today's Cinema*, reviewing her performance in *East of Eden* (dir Kazan, Warner, US 1955) wrote:

Julie Harris as Abra exudes the unworldly but passionate charm which typifies all her work.[21]

Other reviewers compared her to the 'wispy but 'pure' rebel tamer' played by Eve Marie Saint in *On The Waterfront*[22] and likened her, evocatively, to the 'Wendy figure' of J. M. Barrie's Peter Pan.[23] Most explicit of all was the *Hollywood Reporter* review:

Julie Harris, as Abra, combines a young girl's silliness with a mystic, almost breathless, virginal delicacy.[24]

'Unworldliness', 'purity', 'a young girl's silliness': these terms, used in connection with a top box office star, indicate a significant qualitative difference in the apparent taste of audiences between the forties and fifties. There is an opposition here between the self-contained adult appreciated in Grace Kelly's performances and the impetuous child which Julie Harris presented. In between the two is the archetypically wholesome Doris Day, by far the most popular female star of the fifties, as *Woman*'s gossip column 'Show People' noted:

> Her frank and friendly manner, a combination of high-powered glamour and simplicity, certainly captivated everyone who met her. Doris, I would say, comes as near having universal appeal as anybody in films. One curious fact is that her admirers can't agree on the secret of Doris's appeal. Some say it's her voice, some go for her wholesome personality, others love her vitality.[25]

It is interesting to note that although the stereotypical sex symbol, best exemplified in Marilyn Monroe's persona, has been taken to represent the fifties' ideal star most closely, the fact is that at the time, in the middle of the decade, such stars as Monroe, Bardot or Kim Novak (more popular than either at the British box office) were noted, like Julie Harris, more for their qualities of naïveté than for any independent assertion of their sexuality. The paradoxical coexistence of a desirable and glamorous physical appearance with vulnerable innocence, developed, during the decade, into almost a paradigm for female sexuality: and we should note the striking difference between this and the assertive sexuality represented in the performances of Bette Davis, Margaret Lockwood or Joan Crawford in the forties.

Diana Dors is a rather interesting exception: hailed as the 'British answer' to Marilyn Monroe, she was certainly discussed in terms of her physique. She was also, however, both an assertive woman and a competent actress as her performance in *Yield to the Night* (dir J. Lee-Thompson, ABP UK 1956) showed. With hindsight it is possible to perceive Dors' own manipulation of the extreme objectification of female stars which typifies the fifties: her celebrated (or notorious) publicity stunt with the mink bikini being one example. But Dors was not among the most popular actresses at the British box office according to the correlation employed here: the fact that retrospectively she has come to 'signify' the British fifties, as Monroe signifies the fifties in the USA, is a testament to the strength of her persona rather than to her contemporary popularity.

By the sixties not only were there far fewer top female stars, but also this fragmentation of the typically complex personae of forties stars had gone even further. The most popular female stars by then were, on the one hand, the childlike Audrey Hepburn and the child Hayley Mills, and on the other hand the sensual, adult figures of

Elizabeth Taylor and Sophia Loren with the asexual figure of Julie Andrews bridging the gap and inheriting, perhaps, the mantle of Doris Day. Andrews, already celebrated for her success in the stage production of *My Fair Lady*, made her screen debut in *Mary Poppins* (dir Robert Stevenson, Disney, US 1964). Reviewers drew on her existing reputation, but went further in their typecasting:

> Disney's fair lady has a pure sincerity that no amount of sweetness can cloy.[26]

> Her well scrubbed, plain Jane beauty has never looked more transparently radiant.[27]

> She is a very dream of a nanny, a pretty grown-up doll in Edwardian dress and sensible shoes.[28]

It was Julie Andrews, 'well scrubbed' with 'sensible shoes', recalling Celia Johnson's 'short, unvarnished nails' and 'practical hands', or Ingrid Bergman's 'glowing healthy' face 'practically untouched by any make-up' who was unconditionally admired for her professional skills whereas Taylor and Loren, both highly accomplished actresses, are frequently demeaned by the lascivious attention to their private lives or their physical characteristics or both – often at the expense of their performances. Thus the *Daily Express*'s grudging report of Elizabeth Taylor's Oscar award for her performance in *Butterfield 8*:

> No-one should play down her award, but this looks like a 'sympathy Oscar'. A gesture, in her convalescence, to the woman who is a symbol of the 100% glamour brigade.[29]

The *Evening Standard* announced Sophia Loren's forthcoming projects in a similarly demeaning fashion:

> I think I can promise you a torrid summer. Sophia Loren is returning to Britain to make two more films. Both give wide scope for Miss Loren to exhibit the tropical side of her personality. Both will follow the principle established by *The Millionairess* that the combination of highbrows and ample bosoms are the greatest insurance for success at the box office. In these ventures Miss Loren will have the literary backing of John Mortimer and John Osborne.[30]

Their antipathetic reporting of Taylor continued, this time in connection with her reputed earnings in the film of Cleopatra, which,
in the early sixties, seemed rarely to be out of the headlines:

> The million dollar fee is real enough in hard cash, but it is more
> important as the appropriately fabulous market price of a myth
> surrounding a woman who has achieved success on the most
> preposterous scale. How has she done it? Frankly, she has not
> got there by her acting, which is professional enough, but unless
> she has a notable director, is nothing more.[31]

The simple reference to the name of a popular star can summon up,
evoke, a particular historical period: thus through their personae,
stars come to stand as signifiers of the time in which they achieved
their greatest popularity. Anna Neagle, for example, continued her
career until the seventies but is forever associated with the late
thirties and forties, the time in which, as a *Picturegoer* reviewer
wrote in 1951, 'she (was) as much a part of Britain as Dover's white
cliffs'. But do the personae of popular stars reflect, or mirror the
generally held assumptions of a period, or should we understand
them rather as evidence of contemporary aspirations? Do they
exemplify and affirm existing social practices or are they role
models for each new generation of moviegoers? Relevant to these
questions is a consideration of the narrative experience of such
stars in the popular films of the day; in other words we need to
examine the intersection of the film text and the star text.[32] More
crucially still we must attempt to understand the activity of female
audience members in their readings of fictional female characters –
their sisters in celulloid. We shall return to this question in Chapters
6 and 7.

3

The Films: Narrative Themes

At each of the three 'moments' – the mid-forties, mid-fifties and mid-sixties – there are marked thematic unities between films which, at first glance, seem to be quite disparate. We should of course bear in mind the overriding common factor that all the films achieved enormous success at the box office when they were first released. In general terms we can perhaps deduce from their popularity evidence that their thematic concerns bore some relation to the wider social experience of the audiences who, through their choice, made them so popular. This is not to suggest that the themes of these films simply mirror or reflect the concerns of the times, but rather that there are likely to be points of intersection between the fictional and the real, exemplified in the films and the audiences respectively, evident in the themes which appear concurrently in different films. This proposition is endorsed by the marked differences evident in themes current at each of the three 'moments'.

THE FORTIES: WOMEN AND SACRIFICE

The Bells of St. Mary's (dir Leo McCarey, RKO, US 1946); *Brief Encounter* (dir David Lean, Cineguild, UK 1946); *Madonna of the Seven Moons* (dir Arthur Crabtree, Gainsborough, UK 1945); *Piccadilly Incident* (dir Herbert Wilcox, ABP, UK 1946); *The Seventh Veil* (dir Compton Bennett, Theatrecraft, UK 1945); *The Wicked Lady* (dir Leslie Arliss, Gainsborough, UK 1946).

The most striking attribute of these films, considered as a group, is their concentration on the activities and motivations of women. This theme is offered by means of overt reference to mental ill-health such as the 'split mind' of Maddalena/Rosanna (Phyllis Calvert) in *Madonna of the Seven Moons*, or the traumatic 'paralysis' of her hands

suffered by Francesca (Ann Todd) in *The Seventh Veil*, and through
close attention to the mental processes of central female characters
such as Laura (Celia Johnson) in *Brief Encounter*, and Diana (Anna
Neagle) in *Piccadilly Incident*: in all these cases audience access
to and sympathy for the central female character whose mental
processes are under such scrutiny is carefully constructed early
in the narrative and emphasised throughout the film. The other
recurring thematic device with a similar intention is the opposition
within a narrative of two clearly defined characters who symbolise
different aspects of femininity such as Caroline (Patricia Roc) and
Barbara (Margaret Lockwood) in *The Wicked Lady*, or Maddalena
and Rosanna in *Madonna of the Seven Moons*, or two aspects of a
single character which are developed through their interaction with
an opposing pair of less central characters. Laura expresses different
aspects of herself with her lover Alec (Trevor Howard) than with her
husband Fred (Cyril Raymond), in *Brief Encounter*, and in *Madonna
of the Seven Moons* Maddalena is the devout and retiring wife of
Giuseppe (Peter Glenville) while her alter ego, Rosanna, is the
stormy and passionate mistress to the gang leader Nino (Stewart
Granger). This theme can be understood as a representation of
choice – often associated in these films with loss, alienation or
loneliness. The individual either *feels* isolated in her predicament,
as Laura does in *Brief Encounter*, or is indeed physically isolated like
Diana in *Piccadilly Incident*, shipwrecked on an island in the middle
of the ocean. The dilemmas confronting this group of characters are
the consequence of either the intervention of fate, such as Laura's
chance meeting with Alec in *Brief Encounter* or Diana's shipwreck in
Piccadilly Incident, or of childhood trauma such as that experienced
by Francesca in *The Seventh Veil*, or by Maddalena in *Madonna of the
Seven Moons*. The substance of the narrative is their negotiation of
the choice which will, in the end, define them.

But the audience has more to do: in one group we participate in
the suffering of the heroine – often through the device of the voice
over (*Brief Encounter, The Seventh Veil*) – in another we ourselves are
engaged, because of the suspense construction of the narrative, in
weighing the relative merits of conflicting value systems – thus
in moral and ethical considerations. In *The Bells of St. Mary's* the
audience is invited to evaluate the pedagogic methods favoured
by Sister Mary Benedict (Ingrid Bergman) and Father O'Malley
(Bing Crosby); in *The Wicked Lady*, Barbara's and Caroline's differing understandings of love, desire and marriage are constantly

juxtaposed and implicated in their narrative experiences; and in *Madonna of the Seven Moons* the confusing and apparently contradictory attributes of conventional femininity are, quite literally, split into the figures of the cherished, fragile wife and mother and the assertive, sensual mistress. An associated theme which overlays all the rest is an exploration of love – romance, sexuality, commitment – between men and women.

To be more explicit, to use today's terminology, we can say that these films deal with sexual politics using an exploration of the female psyche as the key to the mystery. It could and should be argued that this exploration of the politics of gender is overdetermined by the consensus evident in these films that it is the mysterious female who can, if examined sufficiently, offer solutions to the problems perceived in relations between the genders. Indeed in those films which dealt specifically with mental ill-health such as *The Seventh Veil* and *Madonna of the Seven Moons* the (male) medical figure pronounced authoritatively on 'the human mind'.

> The human mind is like Salome hidden by her seven veils. With a lover she will take off four or five or even six, never the seventh. Under hypnosis, down comes the seventh veil.
>
> Dr Larsen (Herbert Lom) in *The Seventh Veil*.

> We know very little of the workings of the human mind. You see, something happened to split her mind in two. It may have been a shock in childhood. When things became too much for her she broke away from all ties, all mental torments, and took refuge in her other self. A door in her mind closed and another opened.
>
> Dr Ackroyd (John Stuart) in *Madonna of the Seven Moons*

Yet we must note that it is the female 'human mind' that is under analysis. This feature of the films allows considerable activity to the female audience member, and considerable scope for readings at variance with those indicated in both the address and the narrative closures of the films – the 'preferred reading'. For a modern female reader then, not only are gender politics and personal choices depicted but also, and more importantly, the tension between these and patriarchal social structures is revealed. Whether we can assume that such meanings were as clear for contemporary readers of the films is more problematic; consideration of this question will require our attention to the processes of reading, and this will be the substance of Chapter 6. For the present we shall simply note that in these films the dilemma of women, in a society whose language and institutions are predicated on a patriarchal order, appears to be clearly acknowledged.

All the films are melodramas: they chronicle domestic and emotional struggles within a small group of people, typically offered as a 'family'. Whether the struggle takes place within an individual, such as Laura's tussle with her conscience in *Brief Encounter*, or between individuals, such as the fight for power between Francesca and Nicholas (James Mason) in *The Seventh Veil*, it invariably deals with efforts to establish, maintain or defend the family. This social unit is, admittedly, interpreted in several ways within these films: *Brief Encounter* deals with the discrete bourgeois unit of parents and children; *Piccadilly Incident* and *The Wicked Lady* work within the slightly broader constraints of the extended family, the 'line' designated jointly by a family name and an ancestral home; *The Bells of St. Mary's* substitutes the catholic sister- (and brother-) hood for the family based on ties of blood or legal contract. Nevertheless the common feature is that the self-definition of the individuals concerned is inextricably linked to their position within this matrix, and the preservation of the family, however it is understood, invariably transcends the importance of the individual.

Techniques of story telling special, though not unique, to film making such as flashbacks, cross-cutting on parallel action and the insertion of subjective fantasy sequences, are deployed to assert the interdependence of the internal world of the family with various other experiential domains. Thus Laura's fantasy in *Brief Enounter* of a possible future with Alec, pictured in her daydreams, is juxtaposed with the prosaic mundanity of the suburban train, and sandwiched between domestic scenes of her 'real' life. Diana's long ordeal in *Piccadilly Incident* as a member of the shipwrecked group – itself constituted as a kind of family, albeit an unsatisfactory one – is cross-cut with the simultaneous experience of her supposedly bereaved husband as he mourns her loss, remarries and celebrates his son's christening. The opening scene of *Madonna of the Seven Moons*, a kind of preamble to the film, details Maddalena's traumatic experience while at her convent school: this is subsequently revealed to be a flashback since the main action of the film takes place twenty years later and tells the story of the tragic consequences of her experience and their effects on her family. Francesca's unhappy childhood and repressed adolescence is offered in the series of flashbacks which punctuate *The Seventh Veil*'s narrative of her psychiatric treatment. In all these cases the present consequences for the family unit are offered as the arbiter by which past events, future fantasies and so on must be judged. The flashback, particularly, insists on the importance of past events in their consequences for the present and, by implication, for the future. This attitude persists in the group of films popular in the mid fifties though, as we shall see, the past by then is understood as inherently problematic. By the sixties the past is regarded exclusively as an impediment, and the only film in that group to employ the flashback is *Marnie*, in which it is used in the narrative closure to resolve the enigma posed by Marnie's 'deviant' behaviour.

The films are, on the whole, set in the present or very recent past: only one, *The Wicked Lady*, is unequivocally a 'period' film. Although this allows considerable scope for the set and costume designers and the consequent pleasures of spectacle for the audience, an important consideration in post-war Britain as the Gainsborough studios discovered to their advantage, both the central concerns of the film and the manner in which they are exemplified in particular characters conforms to the rest of the group. Though the setting may be restoration England, the issues and problems are clearly those of post-war Britain. Several films entail a more or less detailed consideration of a series of past events and their contribution to present problems – in *Brief Encounter* for example there is an almost Proustian attention to the minutiae of a short period of time. Although there is substantial attention to the passage of time in all the films, it is a fairly short and clearly defined time span which is reviewed. The narratives of *The Wicked Lady*, *The Bells of St Mary's* and *Madonna of the Seven Moons* all move forward in time consistently, covering a few months. In contrast to the sixties films, audience attention, in the unfolding of the narrative, is continuously drawn to the passage of time. Caroline, for example, in *The Wicked Lady*, refers to the six months she has been housekeeping for Barbara; the narrative of *The Bells of St Mary's* is punctuated by various incidents whose temporal relation is frequently remarked upon, such as the arrival of Father O'Malley, the passage of the school year, and so on; *Madonna of the Seven Moons* opens with Angela's journey home which is closely followed by Maddalenas's disappearance. The other three films – *The Seventh Veil*, *Brief Encounter* and *Piccadilly Incident* – employ flashbacks to unfold the narrative, to reveal the history of the present dilemma, and the segments of time offered are both short and well defined.

All the films make consistent reference to social structure – to manners, mores, value systems – but these are on the whole marginal to the drama of the character whose relation to the structure is the central concern of all the films. There is a curious and distinctive distance established between the protagonist and the social context, even when the latter is an important element in the problems faced by the protagonist. In _Piccadilly Incident_, for example, even though it is crucial to the narrative that we are clearly in the London of the Blitz, or marooned off Singapore after the Allied evacuation, it is always the fine detail of Alan's (Michael Wilding) or Diana's emotional state that really concerns us. The clearest example of this distancing from society as a whole is in _Brief Encounter_ where Laura in her voice over constantly refers to her ordinariness and to the kind of life she leads, to her companions and so on and yet the very fact of her account of changing her library book or buying a new toothbrush for her son draws our attention not to the book or the toothbrush or the son – but to Laura herself and the paradoxical extraordinariness she is experiencing. In the _Bells of St Mary's_, though the central enigma concerns the fate of the school, it is the nuances of the tension between the characters Sister Benedict (Ingrid Bergman) and Father O'Malley (Bing Crosby) constructed as they appear to be to exemplify conflicting male and female attitudes to the education of children, to which our attention is continuously drawn.

This group of forties films, then, typically deals with the moral problems experienced by female protagonists in their relation to contemporary social structures. The primacy of the family as the fundamental social structure is asserted, thus by implication the woman is deemed to be responsible for the maintenance of the family. Inadequacy, incompetence or immorality in the female, the narratives of these films suggest, will have serious consequences for the integrity of the family and thus for the social fabric as a whole. The audience is invited, by means of the filmic construction of the characters, both to empathise with their dilemmas and to concur with value judgement inscribed in the preferred reading of the film. The relation between the characters' desires and the social conventions which order their proper actions is presented as problematic and, through the depiction of the characters, the audience is required to participate in an evaluation of these conventions. Finally it is most striking that the different and often contradictory models of behaviour are invariably personified, such personifications typically taking female form.

THE FIFTIES: MEN AND NATIONAL UNITY

The Dam Busters (dir Michael Anderson, ABPC, UK 1955); *Doctor at Sea* (dir Ralph Thomas, Rank, UK 1955); *East of Eden* (dir Elia Kazan, Warner, US 1955); *Reach For the Sky* (dir Lewis Gilbert, Rank, UK 1956); *Rebel Without a Cause* (dir Nicholas Ray, Warner, US 1956); *The Searchers* (dir John Ford, Warner, US 1956).

Whereas the forties films invited their audiences to participate in an exploration of the female psyche, these films, on the contrary, typically offer a variety of models of masculinity. Central characters are invariably male – the films are *about* men. But not only are we offered men rather than women, we are also invited to consider the consequences for the nation of the different value systems exemplified in the various heroes, rather than for the individual: the dominant theme is the relation between masculinity and the nation.

There are basically two strategies through which masculinity is explored. Some films entail close study of an exceptional individual such as the pilot Douglas Bader (Kenneth More) in *Reach for the Sky*, the inventor Barnes Wallace (Michael Redgrave) in *The Dam Busters*, or the western hero Ethan Edwards (John Wayne) in *The Searchers*. Others deal with the passage from adolescence to manhood of a central character such as Cal Trask (James Dean) in *East of Eden*, Jim Stark (James Dean again) in *Rebel Without a Cause*, and Martin Pawley in *The Searchers*. *Reach for the Sky* and *The Dam Busters*, based as they are on true stories of the celebrated individuals Douglas Bader and Barnes Wallace, are essentially 'biopics'. This emphasis on the attributes and experience of a single individual is of course strengthened by the centrality of star personae to readings of the roles. Indeed in the comedy *Doctor at Sea* the central figure of the enormously popular Dirk Bogarde seems to be the main, if not the only justification for the film's existence. His is the only character to whom the audience has any direct access: in the context of the other films in this group it is tempting to regard Dr Simon Sparrow as a parody of the 'exceptional individual' around which many of the other narratives revolve. Dr Sparrow is exceptionally ordinary in contrast to the farcical stereotypes represented by other characters such as Captain Hogg (James Robertson Justice), Miss Mallet (Brenda da Banzie) and the various officers and seamen constituting the crew of the SS *Lotus*. The central figures of Ethan Edwards and Reverend Samuel Clayton (Ward Bond) in *The Searchers* represent, within the generic terms of the film, an exploration of the qualities of the stereotypical heroes of the mythic west. Posed between the terms of these two figures, so to speak, is the adolescent Martin Pawley (Jeffrey Hunter) who becomes a man during the course of the protracted search: through its empathy with this young man the audience is invited to evaluate the consequences for the future of America of the ethical positions taken by the older men. As we have seen this evaluation is complicated considerably by the uneasy coexistence, within the film, of two distinct and often mutually hostile generic modes. The narratives of both *East of Eden* and *Rebel Without a Cause* are concerned with precisely the same point. In these two films, however, we are invited to participate in the adolescent struggles of the central characters Cal Trask and Jim Stark, both played by James Dean, to 'find' themselves in opposition to the models offered by their fathers and, as we shall see, despite the counterproductive activities of their mothers. Both characters must discover how to act rightly, in Jim Stark's phrase 'for once to do something right'. The centrality of their dilemma to the future health of the nation is underlined, for the audience, in the exchange between Jim and the agent of the state, Ray Arthur (Ed Platt).

> *Jim*: How can a man grow up in a circus like that?
> *Ray*: Beats me, son, but they do.

Parental responsibility is clearly invoked; the nation needs *men*. For Cal, in *East of Eden*, it is his father's approbation which is crucial:

> Talk to me father
> I gotta know who I am
> I gotta know what I'm like.

His girlfriend Abra recognises that

> you have to give him some sign that you love him

or else he'll never be a man.

It is interesting to note, *à-propos* this group of films, that though the preferred reading generally entails a suggestion to the audience about which of the various models of masculinity depicted is the more acceptable or appropriate in its diegetic context, there is far more ambiguity about the qualities of the 'discredited' models than in typical forties films' summaries of the morality of their heroines. In the narrative closure of *East of Eden*, for example, we are invited to subscribe to Cal's pragmatic approach in preference to the inappropriately straitlaced attitudes of his father, Adam (Raymond Massey), and his brother, Aron (Richard Davalos) but we are also offered sufficient information about Adam both to understand and to respect his intransigeance. In the penultimate scene of *Rebel Without a Cause* Jim has finally acted on his proposition that 'we are all involved' and, despite Plato's tragic death, is able to take his place in the adult world as he introduces Judy to his parents:

> Mother, Dad, this is Judy.
> She's my friend.

But his father's reasoning, his abhorrence and fear of 'getting involved' are seen to be justified: we never doubt his care for Jim, though we are invited to consider it misdirected. The transition from confused and chaotic adolescence to ordered and controlled manhood which the film delineates through Jim's experience is summarised in the visual contrast between the opening and closing shots. In the opening shot an extreme low angle close up shows us the adolescent Jim sprawled drunk on a city street at night, cuddling with one hand a child's toy found among the litter while, like an infant in a crib, he sucks the thumb of his other hand. The final image of the film is an extreme high angle long shot, symmetrically composed and showing the facade and forecourt of the observatory in daylight. An adult male carrying a briefcase walks towards the central door, reaching it as the end title comes up. Though the narrative closures of *Rebel Without a Cause*, *East of Eden* and *The Searchers* have implicitly discredited the morality and ethics of Frank Stark (Jim Backus), Adam Trask and Ethan Edwards, yet the history and logic of their positions has been sufficiently well established through the course of the narratives to allow the audience to perceive their 'discrediting' as tragic rather than as the well deserved consequence of their immoral or unethical actions.

This is in striking contrast to the narrative closure of *The Wicked Lady*, for example where the death of Barbara (Margaret Lockwood) can only be understood, in the film's preferred reading, as the direct and well deserved consequence of her amorality. The opening and closing shots of this film are virtually identical – Ralph and Caroline riding through a pastoral landscape: in retrospect Barbara's story is an obstacle to be overcome by the couple before they can 'really' know love and, through their marriage, maintain the Skelton family. There is an emphasis on pragmatism in the definitions of individual behaviour proffered in these fifties films – the audience is invited to consider not so much the absolute propriety of individual's actions, as in the forties group, as their effectivity in the wider project of building and maintaining the social cohesion necessary to the health of the nation. In *The Searchers* though Ethan's racist repudiation of Debbie (Natalie Wood) after she became the wife, the 'squaw', of the Indian chief Scar must be itself repudiated yet we are still invited, by our witnessing of the Indians' savage brutality, to empathise with both his reasoning and the emotional scars which have produced his own savagery.

A preoccupation with the cohesion of society, symbolised and summarised in the concept of the nation, manifests itself in all these films. In some a simple recognition that society is indeed composed of disparate groupings is a sufficient basis for the hermeneutics.[1] In *Reach For the Sky* for example, the world is roughly composed of two groups, the civilian and the military, and it is self-evident that Bader's exclusion from the airforce gives rise to questions about how and when he will be readmitted. In *Doctor at Sea* British society is organised according to rigid groupings of class and occupation, and much of the film's comedy depends on a gradual democratisation in which humour is to be had as much from debunking the social elite of the medical profession as from debunking the hidebound solidarity of the working class, represented by the seamen whose delegation finally accepts Simon Sparrow after he has successfully performed an appendectomy on one of their number. In *Rebel Without a Cause* the central enigma of the plot, which concerns the socialisation of Jim Stark, rests on the apparently uncontentious observation that there is an almost unbridgeable gap between the young and old generations represented by the teenagers and their parents, but the film is addressed as much to the parental generation as to their children, despite the presence of James Dean in the starring role.

In the western/melodrama *The Searchers* the major dilemma concerns the coexistence of white America with the indigenous Indians, stereotypically characterised as barbaric and uncivilised. It also touches on problems consequent upon the co-existence of the civilian and the military – one of the many complex and ambiguous representations in this film is that of the U.S. Cavalry. Whereas the classic western offers the military as an heroic group, in *The Searchers* their heroism is in question, their abilities compared unfavorably with those of the Texas Rangers and their barbarism equated with that of the 'uncivilised' Indians. The ubiquitous and relatively straightforward groupings based in age, class and ethnicity are similarly problematised in many of the films.

Though the plot events of *East of Eden* centre around the efforts of the confused and disturbed adolescent Cal to discover himself and to win his father's love, his story also stands as a metaphor for the process of self-discovery of the nation as a whole – that is America in the early twentieth century. This is the time, historically, when the economic bases for American dominance over the 'free' world were being laid, when British hegemony in world trade was successfully challenged by the United States. The relevance of this self assessment to post World War Two, post-McCarthy America is clear: an exploration of the question 'what is America' being discreetly positioned in the distant past of nearly half a century ago. Hence the constant preoccupation, in the film, with definitions of 'good' and 'evil', with law and convention, and hence also the dominant preoccupation of the film – the morality of money and profit – since US hegemony in the 1950s was based, precisely, on the concept of the free market. The moral rectitude and idealistic intransigeance exemplified in both Cal's father Adam and his 'good' twin brother Aron is revealed to be inadequate to contemporary needs: it is the 'bad' Cal's point of view that is privileged in both the plot's unfolding and in the narrative closure. Thus the old American way, the simple and old fashioned understanding of good and bad (right and wrong) is put into question and the audience invited to a more pragmatic consideration of the opposition good:bad.

The theme of this opposition, developed principally through the device of the twin boys, is announced in an opening credit which locates the action in the twin towns of Monterey and Salinas, separated by the 'dark and brooding Santa Lucia mountains' which 'stand like a wall' between them. Monterey, where the film opens, is a 'rough and tumble fishing port' and an urban centre, albeit a small one, with a main street, a bank, a jail and a brothel. Salinas, in contrast, is a 'peaceful agricultural town' whose ordered fields offer a striking visual contrast to the rocky coastline and untidy fishing nets of Monterey. Salinas stands for settled, rural America where biblical values are upheld and life is quiet and ordered. Monterey offers a microcosm of urban America and significantly, by virtue of its being a seaport, of the interface between America and the rest of the world. It is Cal who bridges the gap between Monterey and Salinas. His curiosity leads him to Monterey where he discovers his mother, now the owner of a thriving bar/brothel 'on the outskirts of town'. His desire to please his father is demonstrated in his efforts with refrigeration and the lettuce harvest and his investment, just before America's entry into the First World War, in bean futures. Thus he constructs a connection between his mother's world of business and knowing 'what people are really like, what they want' and his father's idealism, wanting to do 'some little thing for humanity'.

The opposition outlined here between the different values of the urban and rural communities, between the farmers and the traders, is also apparent in *The Searchers'* juxtaposition of the settlers and fighters from an earlier period in the history of the United States, just after the civil war of the 1860s. The relevance to concerns of the fifties is, however, similar in its insistence on the question 'what is America' and the recognition implicit in the narrative closure that the success of the future may depend on relinquishing some of the tenets of the past. The articulation of these issues in *The Searchers* is complicated, as we have seen, by the coexistence of two generic modes. In the end it is the settled, domestic values of the melodrama which prevail over those of the western. Ethan Edwards rides away from the Jorgensen ranch as the door is closed: the audience is inside with the family, with Debbie, Martin Pawley and, significantly, with the Reverend Samuel Clayton. His is a key character in which the the contradictions between the old and the new, the military and the religious, the masculine and the ridiculous, are presented in uneasy and often comic coexistence. He possesses a double authority in the community in that he is both the preacher, performer of baptism, wedding and funeral rites, and the Captain of the Texas Rangers. He fought in the civil war for the confederates, but unlike Ethan accepted defeat and found a place in the new order of things.

Ethan has been 'wandering' during the three years since the end of the war:

> Don't believe in surrender
> No – I still got my sabre, Reverend.
> Didn't turn it into no ploughshare, neither.

The Rev. Clayton, on the other hand, is firmly established as one operating 'within' society and the law – in the family melodrama segments of the film – yet he is also offered, particularly in the closing scenes dealing with the final, successful assault on Scar's village, as an experienced and convincing inhabitant of the western generic mode. The distance between Clayton and Ethan, often a diametric opposition, is in these scenes so narrowed that we are invited to view them, as they stand in close up on the bluff overlooking the Indian village they are about to attack, which is visible in the far distance of the desert landscape, as equivalent if not equal. This harmony, however, is violently disrupted, in generic terms, in the resolution of the attack. Here we have the sombre suggestion of Ethan's barbaric scalping of the dead Scar juxtaposed with the comic scene of Clayton squatting with his trousers down while his men perform a minor operation on his backside. Throughout the film Clayton has been offered as a comic opposite to the exceptionally independent and self sufficient Ethan, yet in the denouement he and Ethan act together, and he mediates between Ethan and Marty over the crucial question of Debbie's worth. Thus Reverend Clayton, despite often being a comic figure, is also shown to be pragmatic in his ability to re-evaluate his experience in the light of new situations.

The concern over the defining values of the nation apparent in *East of Eden* and *The Searchers* is evident in most films in this group. In *Doctor at Sea* the general democratisation of the nation underlying much of the comedy is accompanied by chauvinism verging on the xenophobic. Stereotypical British chauvinism is developed in this film in the large central segment chronicling the period when S.S. *Lotus* is in port at Bellos. Not only are the 'foreigners' themselves an embarassing representation of stupidity, cupidity and general unseemliness but also the town of Bellos itself is a curious amalgam of signs of foreignness rather than being any recognisable global location. Thus we have heat, references to the tropics, to the local British colony; we have various shades of skin colour from the latin to the negroid; we have oriental music, spanish shawls, and mediterranean/arab building styles. In the end the reader is forced to conclude that it doesn't really matter where this place is – the point is simply that it is abroad, it is *other* than Britain. And yet there is a kind of critical selfconsciousness at work, fuelling the comedy. The British are so inappropriately themselves in this exotic location – summarised in the shot of Second Officer Archer going ashore in his suit, bowler hat and rolled umbrella – that the laughs are based on the interface between 'Britishness' and the 'other', rather than simply on the manifest absurdities of the 'other'. British rigidity of mind is constantly highlighted – for example in the exchange between Simon Sparrow and the US ship's captain, unrecognisable as such to Simon since he is informally dressed in a brightly coloured shirt.

Reach for the Sky and *The Dam Busters* both purvey chauvinism through their study of aspects of the British experience of the Second World War, yet it is an uneasy matter in these films too, and underlying queries about the constitution of the nation which is the subject of such chauvinism continually break through to the surface. This is a feature of *East of Eden*, as we have seen, and a constituent of the wry humour in *Doctor at Sea*. It is less evident in the heavy handed assertion of British superiority given in *Reach for the Sky*, but particularly clear in the subtlety of the opposition posed in *The Dam Busters* between the scientist inventor Barnes Wallace and the heroic pilot, Squadron Leader Gibson (Richard Todd).

The film is paradoxical in its attitude to Barnes Wallace, a most complex and interesting character whose unworldliness and naïveté is repeatedly emphasised, indeed it is almost suggested to be a consequence of his exceptional brilliance and perseverance. The audience is invited, in various key scenes, to be alternately sympathetic to and dismissive of Barnes Wallace's apparently simplistic approach to the problems inherent in translating pure research into practical advantage. But the meritocratic ideal of the fifties is assumed in the mutual understanding and respect suggested between Barnes Wallace and Squadron Leader Gibson. These men are both exceptional in their chosen fields and recognise each other as such. Thus they exemplify the premise of meritocracy, that innate ability will eventually overcome any odds. Barnes Wallace's obstacle is the stifling inertia of bureaucracy represented by a rather cliched view of Whitehall administration. Gibson's are the limits of skill and the properties of matter: the bomb designed by

Barnes Wallace will only work if dropped from exactly the right height at the right speed and distance from the objective. Thus we can understand Gibson's struggle as being with the physical environment and Wallace's with the social one. Their co-operation produces the desired end, in the interests of the nation's survival. The narrative is rather more subtle than this schematic summary would suggest, since Wallace also deals with the physical world in the sense that his mathematical researches produce the initial idea, and Gibson deals with the social world in his selection and training of the squadron and his nurture and care of the crews. Yet neither mathematics, for Wallace, nor command, for Gibson, are constructed in the film as problematic. The nation depends on a combination of their qualities of imagination and faith (Wallace) and courage and skill (Gibson) and the film details their differences, thus revealing the tenuous balancing of unlike elements assumed in the concept of national unity.

All the films except *Doctor at Sea* and *Rebel Without a Cause* are set in the past. *Reach for the Sky* and *The Dam Busters* both deal with the Second World War, *East of Eden* and *The Searchers* locate their action in specific periods of American history – the First World War and the aftermath of the civil war respectively. All the films chronicle rather longer passages of time than is typically the case with either the forties or the sixties films. The unfolding of the relation between exemplary masculine figures and crucial problems of national definition requires, it seems, more temporal space than the close attention to the female psyche characteristic of the forties group or the sixties fables of pleasure. The only exception is *Rebel Without a Cause* which chronicles twenty four hours in the 'growing up' of its hero: here it is the psyche of the adolescent Jim Stark which we are invited to examine, in his negotiation of the contemporary values represented by the different social groups with which he has to deal – his parents, his peer group, and the benevolent state in the person of the Police Juvenile officer, Ray Arthur.

The most striking difference, however, between this group of films and those popular in the mid forties is the almost total absence of central female characters. There are women in these films but – with some important exceptions which we will consider in later chapters – they are at best passive, and frequently constructed to be understood as irredeemably negative within the terms of their diegeses. Insofar as women are active at all in these films, it is invariably in relation to the more central development of male characters. The height of female activity is to motivate narrative events. Thelma (Muriel Pavlow), for example, in *Reach for the Sky*, provides through her presence the spur which enables Douglas Bader's will to overcome his physical disability. In its construction of these scenes the film summarises this point by suggesting that it is because he wants to take her dancing that he learns to use his artificial limbs. Judy (Natalie Wood), in *Rebel Without a Cause*, through her taunts provokes Jim into the confrontation with Buzz that culminates in the fatal 'chicken run': Jim's opportunity to 'for once do something right' arises directly out of the consequences of this incident. The paradigm for the female characters in this group of films is Debbie in *The Searchers*. Though we see little of her on screen and though her character is barely developed, yet she is the pretext for the search which the film chronicles: it is because of her that all of the film's action takes place – not because of her own desires, of which we know practically nothing, but because of what she represents. Women in this film are, to use Mulvey's phrase, 'bearers not makers of meaning'.[2] The problem of savagery versus civility, inhumanity versus humanity, is articulated around the possession of a woman. Valuing a woman, the film suggests, is a 'civilised' trait, and it is Debbie's restoration to the settlers group which marks the end of the film. In the cases where female characters exceed the boundaries of such passivity, however, they are unequivocally negative. Miss Mallet's inappropriate girlishness and her unwelcome pursuit of the misogynist Captain Hogg is an example from the comedy *Doctor at Sea*: Jim Stark's mother (Ann Doran) in *Rebel Without a Cause* is another. In Jim's view which, as we have seen, is the one to which the audience is invited to subscribe, his mother is the chief cause of his problems:

> Every time you can't face yourself
> You blame it on me.

His father's spineless inability to 'stand up' to her renders him invalid as a role model, and Jim's solution to this problem, given early in the film in his initial interview at the police station, is validated in the narrative closure when Jim and his father both 'stand up':

> I mean if he had the guts to knock Mum cold once
> then maybe she'd be happy.

And then she'd stop picking.

Cal's mother Kate (Jo Van Fleet) in *East of Eden* has a more ambiguous role in the development of the plot since she is allowed to articulate the film's criticism of Adam's excessive and outdated puritanism, as well as to offer a model of pragmatism essential to Cal's development. But her positive contribution to her son's education is compromised in the film by her position as the owner of a brothel 'on the outskirts of town': thus she remains an outsider, a negative character.

Central to these fifties films is an exploration of the various groupings within society, often perceived as existing in uneasy alliance, but nevertheless constituting the nation through their necessary unity. Unlike the forties films individuals, invariably male, serve primarily to exemplify discrete social groups or ethical positions, and are of interest in those terms rather than as a consequence of their individual dilemmas. Ethan Edwards represents the old: despite his inexplicable change of heart he must ride away from the united group at the end of the film. So too, the intransigeant Adam Trask suffers a heart attack at the end of *East of Eden*. The individuals whose motives and emotions are most closely examined in these films are Jim in *Rebel Without a Cause* and Barnes Wallace in *The Dam Busters*, but Jim represents adolescence in general, and Barnes Wallace stands for the contemplative, for creative science in his juxtaposition with the man of action, Gibson. Even the subject of the biopic *Reach for the Sky*, Douglas Bader, is made to 'stand for' ideal Britishness through his juxtaposition with Churchill's famous speech. So problems in national coherence are explored through the depiction of paradigmatic masculine figures, and women, where they appear, do so in order to motivate or impede the narrative progress of central male characters.

THE SIXTIES: YOUTH, PLEASURE AND AUTHENTICITY

Goldfinger (dir Guy Hamilton, UA/Eon, UK 1964); *A Hard Day's Night* (dir Richard Lester, UA/Proscenium, UK 1964); *Marnie* (dir Hitchcock, Universal, US 1964); *Mary Poppins* (dir Robert Stevenson, Disney, US 1965); *Summer Holiday* (dir Peter Yates, ABP, UK 1963); *Tom Jones* (dir Tony Richardson, UA/Woodfall, UK 1963).

In this group of films there is an emphasis on personal liberation and freedom, accompanied by an insistent privileging of the young and the new. At the surface level this is expressed in the pleasures of spectacle, purveyed and understood in a variety of ways, but underlying many of the films is a deeper concern with authenticity: structures of class, nationality and power being interrogated to reveal their justifications in terms of the individual. All the films make reference to, or depend for their meanings on an acknowledgement of the practices of film making, thus they assume a familiarity on the part of their audiences with such practices. A feature typical of all these texts, then, is an overt celebration of the pleasures of the text itself. The play of techniques, from the 'magical' juxtaposition of animation and live action in *Mary Poppins*, to the elaborate optical punctuations of the episodes in *Tom Jones* and the direct address to camera in both these films, are in themselves pleasurable. All the films except for *Marnie* are comic fantasies of one kind or another; but even in *Marnie* the codes of realism are suspended periodically in service of the hermeneutics. Soft focus and a flood of red light across the screen each indicate stages in Marnie's control over herself and/or events. The former indicates to the audience her vulnerability, her own sense of unease, while the latter signifies her regression into clinical trauma.

Generic reflexivity is, as we have seen, characteristic of popular films of the sixties, and in terms of genre these are all hybrid texts. *Goldfinger* draws on the spy thriller mode but is also, by virtue of its near parodic excesses, in many ways a comedy as well as a fantasy. *Mary Poppins* mixes its fantasy with the musical and the melodrama, *Summer Holiday* combines the musical and the travelogue, *A Hard Day's Night* is at the same time a documentary and a near farcical fantasy for which the justification is the spectacle of the Beatles and their music. *Tom Jones* is a kind of episodic melodrama, but it depends on the suspense construction of the thriller to sustain its narrative flow and includes many comic set pieces. Where the conventions of the thriller are in use – in *Marnie, Goldfinger, Tom Jones* – it is interesting to note that the questions posed invariably concern *how* events will unfold rather than *what* the resolution of the enigma will be. *Marnie* opens with the discovered crime, but there is no mystery for the audience about the identity of its perpetrator. We are never in any doubt, in *Tom Jones*, as to whether he and the heroine will eventually be united; and neither do the pleasures of *Goldfinger* derive from the shock of the new, but rather from the unfolding of the expected against a background of the spectacular.

The films are, in this respect, like fairy stories or mythic tales where the format is well known to the audience, whose pleasure is thus primarily derived from the novel articulation of familiar forms. *Tom Jones*, with its extra-diegetic narrator and *Mary Poppins* both refer overtly to the story telling form. Bert (Dick Van Dyke) tells us, early in the film:

> Can't put my finger on what lies in store
> But I feel what's to happen all happened before

Thus generic reflexivity, the fairy story form and the central importance of musical performance and spectacular locations, gadgetry and so forth all contribute to the sense of the world as playground. Even the much more sober film, *Marnie*, refers to the experiences of childhood, validating their importance through the assertion that her deviance stems precisely from traumatic events which are inappropriate to childhood experience.

Not only is the world offered in the majority of these films a playground, but its inhabitants have a right, if not a positive duty to participate in or consume the pleasures to be had there. In *Tom Jones* there is a consistent and engaging attention to pleasure: pleasure in the simple appearance of things such as sunlit landscapes, rich interiors, the human body both adorned and unadorned by clothes and jewels. Particular pleasure is to be had from the contemplation of surface appearances: polished wood, glowing embers, fine lace, worn leather, healthy animals, weathered brick and stone, and so on. There are sensual pleasures in abundance such as eating, drinking and lovemaking. Not least, as we have seen, there is pleasure in the text itself, thus the film is not only pleasurable in the spectacles it offers, but it also offers pleasure in its own frequent acknowledgement of its artifices: the audience is invited to enjoy not only the thrills and spills of the heroes and villains but also the skill and wit of the film maker. Since we are encouraged through the film's construction never to forget that it is 'only a story' we are also given licence, so to speak, to empathise with the virtuousness, lasciviousness, villainy and so on of the characters in their picturesque settings.

In *Goldfinger*, similarly, the fantasy operates much like the classic fairy tale in which the essential nature of the characters is known in advance of their engagement with any specific plot events. This information, the signifiers of the particular stereotype to be called on, is communicated to the audience through the dress, deportment and/or location of the characters. The spectacles offered are those of luxury living: the best hotel in Miami, the private Lockheed jet plane, the interior of the gold bullion vaults, and so on; of cars, planes and the latest applications of science and technology to gadgetry of various kinds from the industrial laser to the tranquilliser gun, from the sinister car crushing machine to the remote controlled death dealing gas canisters; not to mention Bond's Aston Martin with its plethora of hidden secrets diligently described to the audience before being shown, one by one, in use. The representation of various sports is an important ingredient – here we have horses, golf, and various martial arts. Not least of all these, of course, is the spectacle of James Bond (Sean Connery) himself: a vital constituent of the playground world of sixties films would seem to be the male star. Sean Connery is on screen for a substantial part of the time in both *Goldfinger* and *Marnie*; The Beatles and Cliff Richard are clearly the prime *raisons d'être* for *A Hard Day's Night* and *Summer Holiday* respectively, and Albert Finney, having established his popularity in *Saturday Night and Sunday Morning* (dir Karel Reisz, Bryanston/Woodfall, UK 1960), is continually offered as a pleasurable spectacle to audiences of *Tom Jones*. It is interesting to note, *à-propos* this film, that though the narrator defines Tom as a man with a considerable sexual appetite:

> To those who find our hero's behaviour startling
> the answer is simple
> Tom had always thought that any woman was better than none.

Tom is, in fact, always passive in the initiation of his sexual encounters as he disarmingly admits to Lady Belleston (Joan Greenwood)

> *Lady B*:   Tell me, Mr Jones, are you used to making these sudden conquests?
> *Tom*:   I'm used to submitting.

James Bond too, though he engages, like Tom Jones, in plenty of swashbuckling action, is frequently offered as a passive, immobile object for our gaze in ways reminiscent of the conventional objectification of women on the screen. In both these films and, to a lesser extent, in *A Hard Day's Night* and *Summer Holiday* oppositions between activity and passivity, dominance and subjection, masculinity and femininity, are deployed with intriguing complexity to problematise conventional attributes of gender. It is a deployment, however, which is invariably concerned with representations of the male: women in these sixties films, with the important exceptions of Marnie (Tipi Hedren) and Mary Poppins (Julie Andrews) are most notable for their absence. Where they do appear on screen, in *Tom Jones, Goldfinger* and *Summer Holiday*, for example, it is always and only to partner the primary, male, characters or to motivate narrative events which centre on male characters.

A preoccupation with personal liberation, with the freedom of the unique individual, accompanies this emphasis on pleasure. The forms which this liberation takes vary according to the logical requirements of specific texts but the underlying thematic assertion is common to all films in this group. Thus in the psychoanalytical thriller *Marnie* the eponymous heroine must be liberated from the repression of her childhood trauma before she can atone for her transgressions. In the fantasy musical *Mary Poppins* it is the paterfamilias, George Banks (David Tomlinson), who must learn to recognise the value of childhood innocence and curiosity as a model for adult behaviour. In this film too there are numerous unmistakeable references to youth culture of the sixties with its emphases not only on personal liberation but also on instant fulfilment as a kind of hedonistic birthright of all who cared to claim it. The song 'Spoonful of Sugar' and the emphasis on gravity and logic defying adventures such as flying through the air or 'popping through pavement pictures' inescapably suggest the hallucinogenic 'trips' provided by LSD.[3] The more general association of laughing and getting 'high' such as at Uncle Albert's tea party where uncontrollable laughter propels the assembled company to float near the ceiling in helpless giggles, only to be 'brought down' by the thought of something sad, refers just as compellingly to the use of other drugs such as marijuana which was widely enjoyed amongst sections of the affluent youth of the sixties. The twenty-four hours in the life of the Beatles, chronicled in *A Hard Day's Night* is an almost paradigmatic study of the anarchic fun associated with the concept of liberation in the hedonistic, apolitical sense in which it is offered in these films. The slapstick, zany humour of this film also recalls many quintessentially British precedents from the Goon shows of the 1950s and the contemporary Carry On films, to the nonsense poetry of Edward Lear or the crude wit of the Edwardian music halls. It is a humour premised on the illogical or absurd conjunction of individual desire acted out without reference to the constraints of convention – precisely the scenario enacted in many of this group of films.

The anarchic defiance of convention, characteristic of these films, is accompanied by a privileging of the young and the new: liberation implies not just untrammeled self-expression but also the refusal or abandoning of previously respected constraints. Constraints of class and age (but interestingly not those deriving from gender) are variously explored and found to be inappropriate. The problem which fuels the narrative of *Tom Jones*, for example, relates to class and social conventions. Tom and Sophie (Susannah York) cannot marry because they are of a different class by virtue of their birth. The propriety of this obstacle is never questioned by any of the characters nor by the narrator, yet the film constantly offers examples of the abuse of class privilege, and by this means implicitly holds class divisions up to ridicule.

Similarly money, which though by no means synonymous with class is often used as an indicator of it, is shown to be an inappropriate motive for action. Money is the main reason for Blifil's dastardly campaign against Tom; the presence or absence of money causes minor characters, such as the innkeeper at the first inn, to behave quite differently whereas it is unimportant to 'good' characters like the retired housekeeper Mrs Miller, Tom's supposed father Partridge, or Tom himself. Through its elaborate and heavily emphasised pretence the film invites condemnation of pretentiousness in class, money or religion. In this respect it is directly comparable to *Mary Poppins*, *Summer Holiday* and *A Hard Day's Night*, and in all of these films such pretentiousness is typically located amongst the older generation. It is from the stultifying influence of the aged bankers that George, in *Mary Poppins*, must be liberated; from the grasping machinations of her mother that Barbara Winters (Lauri Peters) in *Summer Holiday* must free herself. In *A Hard Day's Night* the Beatles confront a whole series of stock authority figures – the police, the groundsman outside the television centre, Lionel, producer of the teenage TV show – asserting, in their confrontations, the absurdity of an authority which is unable to greet and evaluate each new situation with fresh eyes. The single exception to this general rule is the engaging figure of Paul's grandfather, played by Wilfrid Brambell. His exquisite performance of the anarchic, eccentric and altogether impossible old man allows the Beatles themselves to occupy the position of reasonableness and, by implication, to put the 'adults' of the film such as the businessman on the train, the TV producers, the police and so on, even further beyond the pale.

Underlying this logic of pleasure, liberation and the superiority of the young and the new is the notion of authenticity. In *Marnie* we are required, through the tight logic of the narrative's construction, to subscribe to Mark's assessment of both Marnie's criminality and her rejection of his sexual advances as deviant and *therefore* inauthentic. Marnie is sick and must be cured in order that she may become her 'real' self. Tom and Sophie are celebrated, in *Tom Jones*, for the honesty and *therefore* the authenticity of their love for each other which is contrasted with the deviousness of the other characters who, through their advances, impede the fulfillment of this love. The decadent Lady Belleston and Sophie's duplicitous cousin Harriet Fitzpatrick both make a play for Tom; Sophie is subject to the unwelcome advances of the foppish Lord Fellmer as well as those of the greedy and beastly Blifil. The implicit concern with authenticity noted here suggests an exploratory approach to the nature of truth, thus of knowledge, underlying the apparently frivolous surface of many of these texts. The epistemological paradigm is to be found in the major theme of *Mary Poppins* which, as we have suggested, concerns the transformation of the central character George Banks. The agents of his transformation are the magical outsiders Mary and Bert. Their primary assertion is of a child centred view of education in which the humanitarian displaces the materialist as the determining factor in the socialisation of the young. George tells us, early in the film, that:

> A British nanny must be a general
> The future empire lies within her hands
> And so the person who we need
> To mould the breed
> is a person who can give commands.
> Tradition discipline and rules must be the tools
> without them, disorder, catastrophe, anarchy
> In short you have a ghastly mess.

But Mary's arrival throws him into a confusion from which he attempts to extricate himself by dismissing her – as he tells his wife 'I don't propose standing idly by and letting that woman Mary Poppins undermine discipline'. Mary skilfully subverts his intention by re-presenting his song:

> *George*:   If they must go on outings
> These outings must be
> Fraught with purpose, yes, and practicality.
> These silly words like supercalli –
> and popping through pictures
> fulfill no basic need.
> They've got to learn the honest truth
> despite their youth they must learn
>   *Mary*:   About the life you lead.
> They must feel the thrill of totting up
> a balanced book
> a thousand ciphers neatly in a row.
> When gazing at a graph that shows the profits up
> their little cup of joy should overflow.
> It's time they learned to walk in your footsteps
> To tread your straight and narrow path with pride.
> Tomorrow just as you suggest, pressed and dressed
> Jane and Michael will be at your side.

In her re-presentation, in the subtle difference between the two parts of the song, lies a deeper difference. This is the difference between their respective philosophies of education. George wants to train the children, to 'mould the breed' in his own image, as Mary's song points out, whereas she wishes to open their eyes, to facilitate their exploration of the world – in short to educate them. This subtle difference between two points of view, in this case about education, recurs in the juxtaposition of the two songs about money: about the twopence Michael brings on the outing with their father, which has been engineered by Mary Poppins. Mary's song 'Feed the Birds' urges that the children give the twopence to the 'little old bird woman', whereas George with 'If you invest your twopence wisely in the Bank' requires that they invest it. In both cases, education and money, it is Mary's position with which the audience is invited to empathise. Thus education is preferable to training, and humanitarianism is preferable to capitalism. The implication is that there is a substantive link between these two oppositions. The education Mary urges leads to humanitarianism, to a more careful and caring society. The training preferred by George leads to the inhuman excesses of capitalism – it dehumanises. These inferences are borne out both by the melodies and by the visual presentation of the two songs. Finally as George leaves his disciplinary interview at the bank we understand that he has been saved from dehumanisation by his recognition of the worth of Mary's approach. The ancient patriarch asks him where he is going and George replies:

> I don't know.
> I might pop through a chalk pavement picture
> and go for an outing in the country
> seize a horse off a merry go round
> and win the Derby.
> I might just fly a kite.
> Only Poppins would know.
> She's the one that sings that ridiculous song
> A spoonful of sugar.

Behind these problematic notions of authenticity and truth lies the question of power: its morality and its meanings. This is closest to the surface of *Marnie* which details the struggle of the two central characters Mark and Marnie. In crude terms this is, precisely, a struggle for power. Yet it is also a struggle over the meanings of power in its multiple and varied guises. Sexual power, economic power; power based in social class; knowledge as power: all these are explored and the balance of power shifts between the two protagonists as the narrative unfolds. Related concepts such as the nature of love, a central concern of *Tom Jones* as we have seen; of transgression, also treated, albeit differently, in both *Goldfinger* and *A Hard Day's Night*; and of knowledge itself, so closely examined in *Mary Poppins*, are inevitably subject to audience scrutiny as a consequence of *Marnie's* focus on this struggle. The audience is skilfully led, by means of a series of epistemologically sound moves, to the position where, at the narrative's close, it is Mark's meanings that are validated, Marnie's that are shown to be unsound. Her resistance, however, has allowed considerable scope to questions concerning the validity of Mark's meanings – in particular to the question of whose interests, in social terms, they serve. Thus the relationship between epistemology and truth is revealed, the relativity of truth acknowledged despite the seamless resolution of the mystery.

Only two of the films are set in the past, and it is these two which offer the most specific critiques of Britishness, though, as we have seen, most query established conventions in one way or another. *Tom Jones*, set in eighteenth century England, implicitly ridicules the rigid social hierarchies of that period, asserting in their place the primacy of 'authentic' interpersonal love and affection. *Mary Poppins* is far more extreme in its condemnation of British tradition. An exaggeratedly stereotypical 'Britishness' is offered in a series of symbolic representations, and it is of particular interest to note the preferred readings invited *à-propos* the selected institutions. They are either the subject of ridicule or located at the negative pole of oppositions suggested in the diegetic value structure. Thus the British navy is represented by the absurd Admiral Boom marooned in his rooftop ship's deck, introduced to the audience by Bert:

> Now this imposing edifice what first greets the eye
> is the'ome of Admiral Boom, late of His Majesty's navy.
> Likes his house ship shape at all times, he does.
> Ship shape and Bristol fashion.

The British banking system is proudly announced by George:

> Money's sound.
> credit rates are moving up up up
> and the British pound is the admiration of the world.

But it is revealed, later in the film, to be hopelessly weighed down by senile and blinkered men dominated by laughable visions of the British imperial past. George, persuading his son to invest his twopence, tells him:

> You'll be part of railways through Africa
> Dams across the Nile
> Fleets of ocean greyhounds
> Majestic self advertising canals
> Plantations of ripening tea . . .

The British public school system is referred to rather more obliquely in both George's requirements of a nanny, 'a British nanny must be a general', and his ritual punishment at the bank. Here the emblems of George's position in the world of (British) men – his red carnation, his umbrella and his bowler hat – are ceremonially destroyed by the banker Dawes following his ancient father's instructions: the scene recalls the various ritual initiations and chastisements said to take place within the hallowed confines of some celebrated British public (private) schools. In the animated section of the film fox hunting and horse racing are depicted (these 'sports' also appear in *Marnie* and *Tom Jones*); the fox-hunting scene is particularly interesting for its implicit anti-Britishness. Bert, riding a merry-go-round horse, rescues the fox as it is about to be caught by the savage hounds. In a broad Irish accent the fox, now in safety on the back of Bert's horse, says:

> Faith and begorrah
> 'tis them redcoats again!

The fox is referring not only to the red hunting jackets to be seen on the screen but also to both the American war of independence and the long standing conflict between Britain and Ireland. The implication is that the British (the hunters) are the agressors, the enemy, and the fox (the Americans, the Irish) the valiant quarry who will eventually succeed/survive, having right on his side. There is another reference to the American war of independence in the final interview between George and the bankers. Here the bankers recall the only previous occasion when there had been a run on the bank (such as the one provoked by the 'bad behaviour' of George's son, Michael). It had happened when they 'unwisely' invested in the cargo dumped in Boston harbour by the 'party of colonists'. George is allowed a rather weak joke:

> As the ship lay in Boston harbour a party of colonists dressed as Red Indians boarded the vessel, behaved very rudely and threw all the tea overboard. This made it unsuitable for drinking. Even for Americans.

But far from generating laughter at the expense of the Americans the joke actually operates to draw attention to the inappropriately superior attitude adopted by the British towards their erstwhile colonists, and thus to justify the anti-Britishness which pervades the film – despite the impeccable accent of Julie Andrews.

All the films cover periods of a few months, the only exception being *A Hard Day's Night* which supposedly takes place during a fairly elastic twenty-four hours. But the diegetic construction of time is tenuous: it seems unimportant to the plots of the films how many weeks or months have actually elapsed, and, like the myths and fairy tales on whose structure these films depend, we are offered a succession of present moments whose temporal relation is remarkably vague. In these films it is always *now*. This diegetic ambiguity extends to the locations, too, which tend to function symbolically rather than according to the codes of realism. Despite the apparent documentary veracity of the hand held camera shooting in *A Hard Day's Night*, for example, what we are actually offered is a series of vignettes of typical London locations – the towpath by the river, the pub interior, the street market – which signify London rather than delineate it. In *Tom Jones* the countryside which is always sunny, where roses always bloom profusely, is separated from London, where streets are always crowded and salons elegant, by the grassy uplands and village inns through which the various flights, chases, and adventures move. There is never any sense of geographic coherence, nor is it necessary since the tale itself is, simply, a tale.

Summer Holiday, Marnie and Goldfinger all depend on clear differences being established between their various locations in Europe and the United State, but in these texts too the primary importance of the location is to signify the different value structures with which protagonists must contend. Thus in *Summer Holiday* we have France signified by the Arc de Triomphe and men in berets on bicycles; Switzerland by the Alps and a St Bernard; Austria by a waltz and some dancers in lederhosen; Yugoslavia by excitable border guards and barbaric peasants, and Greece by the Parthenon. In *Marnie* the stables where she keeps her horse, the interior of her mother's house and the mean street in the Baltimore docks where it is situated, and the lavish residence of the Rutland family are all important for developing the audience's understanding of nuances of her character which are revealed to the audience by her presence in the locations. It is in *Mary Poppins* that these geographic and temporal inconsequentialities are at their most extreme. Neither geography, weather, nor time of day are logically coherent. The cherry trees are always in bloom; the city is always damp and foggy; it is almost always evening in the park; pavements are frequently wet and there are a remarkable number of sunsets. None of this impedes the flow of the narrative, however, since what we are being offered is an idea of London, not a portrait of it. The proximity of the park, the zoo, and St Paul's Cathedral defies any interpretation based on experience of these places but nevertheless allows the various adventures of the central family to unfold as if in a series of story book illustrations.

In this group of films, then, there is a general emphasis on playfulness and innocent pleasure of various kinds in which the established structures of society are represented as repressive constraints on the all important freedom of the individual. The acceptability of such constraints is measured by their authenticity – the degree to which they can be understood to be 'real' in terms of the emotions and desires of the (invariably young) individual. The personal is opposed to the collective, and tradition usually impedes the proper expression of the new: in general this confrontation is expressed as a conflict of generations. Finally all the films invite their audiences to dwell with pleasure on the surface appearance of things, not least among which is the artifice of the film text itself.

There is some compelling material for students of both film history and social history here: our concerns, however, are specifically with the representations of female characters within the films summarised in this chapter. As these outlines suggest, there are some striking changes in the typical fictional experiences of women in each of the three periods. We will need to look more closely at the details of these representations and the fictional experience they construct, as well as considering their reception in contemporary reviews, before we can arrive at any understanding of the meanings they may have suggested to contemporary female audience members.

4

The Construction
and Definition
of Female Characters

MALE AND FEMALE CHARACTERS – NUMBERS

It is an undoubtedly tedious and rather unlikely procedure for an audience to engage in, but a count of all characters, male and female, appearing on the screen in the eighteen films under detailed consideration here shows an imbalance in the representation of gender that is nothing short of spectacular. In any one film, it may be argued, there is no logical reason why the numerical relation between the genders should in any way reflect the balance in the population outside the cinema. Particular genres, *mises-en-scène* and locations are, it is true, quite likely to require more male or more female figures on screen in the interests of verisimilitude. But we are dealing here with a relatively large sample of films selected on the basis of their contemporary success at the box office: we can perhaps assume that the audiences whose choices ensured this success were themselves a representative sample of the population in general – at least in terms of gender balance. We might expect that a count of male and female characters across an appreciable number of films would compensate for the imbalances necessary to the narratives of individual films – but this is not the case.

In Chapter 3 we noted the typical themes of films in each of the three historical moments, the mid-forties, mid-fifties and mid-sixties and observed that in general the forties films were about women, the fifties films about men and the sixties films about youth. In the forties though, despite the films' concentration on female experience, female characters account for less than half of all the figures seen on screen; by the mid-fifties male characters outnumber females by more than 2:1, and the picture in the mid-sixties is similar, the ratio being slightly less than 2:1 males:females. These ratios are to be found equally amongst the named characters, the protagonists of the films, as amongst the greater numbers of figures whose function is to people the screen rather than to participate actively in particular narrative events. Not only are there far more heroes than heroines, there are also routinely more men than women amongst the 'people in the street', the audiences, crowds, customers, patients, passengers and so on who constitute the bulk of the images of humanity in general offered in such fictional accounts. The routine epithets 'man in the street', 'mankind' and so on would appear to offer a more accurate summary, certainly of popular fictional representations addressed to the widest possible audiences, than those concerned with the politics of gender in language might care to allow.

In this chapter we shall look more closely at the ways in which such female characters as do appear on the screen are introduced to the audience; how their characters are constructed in the form of the film and the means by which the audience is invited to recognise, empathise with or criticise the details of their engagement with the narrative events unfolding in the fictional world which the film constructs, the diegesis. Our exploration of the typical representations of women offered in popular film will require as much attention to minor characters and indeed to those figures, so consistently and surprisingly outnumbered by males, whose function is simply to people the screen in the interests of verisimilitude, as to those major characters whose experiences we are invited to consider.

In order to engage in such an exploration we require a means of discriminating between characters in any one film which can be applied to all films – we need a nomenclature which will allow reference to Marnie (Tipi Hedren in *Marnie*, Hitchcock 1964) and Barbara (Margaret Lockwood in *The Wicked Lady*, Arliss 1946) on the one hand, distinguishing them from such figures as the diners in the Kardomah restaurant (*Brief Encounter*, Lean 1946) or the teenage fans pursuing their idols through London (*A Hard Day's Night*, Lester 1964). In arriving at a means of discriminating between the women (and men) we see on the screen we must bear in mind two factors: the first is the *narrative function* of the character. What is their fictional role, what part do they play in the narrative construction, the giving and withholding of information that drives the narrative forwards? The second is the degree to which the audience is specifically offered *access to the character's own point of view* of narrative events. How much can we know, or guess, about the character's private response to the events of the narrative, how far does the narrative structure encourage us to speculate about the motives, desires and fears of the character? It is precisely the delicate combination of these two factors that allows differences in the meanings to be made by different audience members from an identical film text. In Chapter 7 we shall pursue this proposition further in respect of the particular meanings female audience members might have made. In the meantime, in this chapter, we want to look closely at exactly what was there on the screen in our different films: who were the fictional women, how were they offered to the audience and, in Chapter 5, what happened to them in the end?

Central, Major and Minor Characters and Figures

We shall use the terms Central, Major and Minor characters, and Figures, to distinguish between the women on the screen in the terms outlined above. Central characters, the ones the film is 'about', are the fewest: there is generally no more than one or two in each film and, except in the forties, they are invariably male characters – the eponymous Marnie being the only exception to this rule in the group of films from the mid-fifties and mid-sixties under consideration here. Not only are these characters central to the narrative but also there is considerable audience access to their point of view and, the factor which distinguishes them from the important Major characters, they develop and change in some fundamental way during the course of the film as a consequence of narrative events.

Major characters are, typically, more numerous, nevertheless there are rarely more than two or three of each gender in any one film. These characters are crucial to the narrative and the audience is usually offered some, typically more limited, access to their point of view of narrative events. They are developed considerably during the course of the narrative – by the end of the film we may know quite a lot about them but they don't radically change as a consequence of narrative events: their major function is to enable the narrative development of the central character.

Minor characters are more numerous still, typically about nine or ten altogether, men and women, in each film. These characters are named individuals but unlike central and major characters the audience is offered minimal insight into their points of view. Their major function is to motivate narrative events and to this end they are as a rule *presented* rather than *developed* and, crucially, are not affected by the resolution of the narrative in which, generally, they do not effectively participate.

Finally there are the 'Figures', the peoplers of the diegetic world. These are sometimes individual figures but more often groups such as diners, dancers, soldiers, nurses and so on. Allowing for the fact that a group (counted as one, or as two if it is a mixed gender group) may comprise an uncountable number of individuals – such as the crowds of teenage fans pursuing the Beatles in *A Hard Day's Night* – the average number of such 'figures' varies between about forty and sixty in each film, there being rather more in mid-fifties and mid-sixties films than in those of the mid-forties. These 'figures' are rarely named, though they may be, there is never any audience access to their point of view and they do not participate in narrative events beyond their simple presence. They are of interest to us however, partly because of the extraordinary imbalance, noted above, between the genders in this group and partly because, as we shall see, these 'figures' are more likely than any of the more important female characters to be seen on screen engaged in some occupation, to work in some way. Study of the figures, then, allows access to the routine representations of female activity on the margins, as it were, of the narrative.

THE INTRODUCTION OF FEMALE CHARACTERS

The ways in which characters are first introduced to the audience, and the means by which the audience is alerted to the significance or otherwise of particular characters, are a function of film form. Here the fictional world proposed in the narrative – the diegesis – is laid out, the propositions and operations of the hermeneutics which bind the audience into the film are set into play. We may not be surprised to discover, therefore, that there is little change in the relative use of various methods of introducing characters to the audience between the central, major and minor characters and the figures peopling the screen. But though there is consistency across the whole twenty year period, there is considerable variation between the four types in any film. What we are considering here is the ways in which the special forms of cinema are deployed to delineate the characters in a story: we must bear in mind that, as we have seen in Chapter 2, factors external to any particular film text may also have a bearing on the way in which a character is initially understood by the audience. The persona of stars appearing in the film, the particular aspects of the story and characters to which audience attention has been drawn in advance of their taking their places before the screen in the darkened auditorium, in the publicity, the posters and the film reviews in various branches of the popular press: all these will nuance the meanings to be made by individual audience members of the film itself.

Central Characters

Central characters are typically offered, in their first introduction to the audience, through more complex visual unfoldings than is the case with other characters. Often a part of the body seen in close-up elicits audience questions about the identity of the whole figure, thus ensuring close attention when the figure is eventually revealed. This teasing of the audience by proposing the part as the representative, or harbinger, of the whole has a long history in the entertainment industry, recalling devices of performance routinely used in cabaret and on stage, as well as drawing on the early development of film language in which close-up shots of significant objects were inserted into the narrative flow in order to direct audience attention.

With central characters the details of the body itself and their gradual unfolding usually take precedence over the setting in which the character is first located, though it is also true that both the geographic location, the *mise-en-scène* itself and the filmic location (the juxtaposition of shots within which the image is situated) combine to form a proposition, as it were, about the narrative path about to be followed by the character; frequently this is a proposition which narrative events will, eventually, overturn or reverse. Thus the first image of Francesca at the start of *The Seventh Veil* (Compton Bennett 1945) is an extreme close-up of her face as she lies in her hospital bed, closely followed by her flight, a combination of images suggesting a character in crisis. The final image of the film is the deep focus long-shot of Francesca and Nicholas' embrace: through the course of the narrative her desire to flee is explained and resolved.

Similarly in *Marnie* (Hitchcock 1964) the initial and partial images of Marnie herself are all situated in locations suggesting transit – the railway platform, the hotel room, the railway station and so

on, whereas in the last shot of the film, though she is still in
transit, she is with her husband in his car having just told him
(and the audience) that she'd 'rather stay' with him. Sometimes
the proposition entailed in the first glimpse of a central character
prefigures or announces the general contours of the ensuing narrative such as the first shot of Barbara (Margaret Lockwood) in
The Wicked Lady (Arliss 1946). A reverse angle cut from the full
figure medium close-up of the couple Ralph (Griffith Jones) and
Caroline (Patricia Roc) is slowly faded in so that Barbara appears
in a superimposition, framed in the doorway of Ralph's house and
positioned exactly between the couple, announcing to the attentive
spectator precisely the role she will play in the forthcoming tale. Her
appearance and dress confirm Caroline's earlier enthusings about
her beauty, but her flirtatious and worldly demeanour, added to this
significant first view of her positioned between the couple, suggests
the major narrative enigma which will concern the negotiations
between the two women. Maddalena's alter ego Rosanna (Phyllis
Calvert), in *Madonna of the Seven Moons* (Crabtree 1945) is first
offered in fragmented form in an emblematic close-up view of her
face in the dressing table mirror as she loosens her hair, signalling
her passage from 'Maddalena' to 'Rosanna', a passage which is
completed on her arrival in Nino's (Stewart Granger) room at the
Venucci inn where, once again in a mirror, we see her putting on
the seven moons earrings.

But the paradigm for the way in which central characters are
introduced is that of Marnie. Our first sight of her is a rear-view
close-up of her suited elbow hugging her bulging yellow handbag.
The camera stays still as she walks away into frame, still in a rear-
view, until she's a small figure in long-shot, then cuts directly to the
angry face of her previous employer, Strutt (Martin Gabel), as he
mouths the word 'Robbed!'. After a short sequence in Strutt's office,
in which the central male character Mark Rutland (Sean Connery) is
also introduced, the film returns to Marnie. She is still seen in a rear
view, but this time disappearing down a hotel corridor preceded
by a porter laden with boxes. The film cuts fairly rapidly through a
series of shots all of which show part of Marnie's body – her hands
as she changes her ID card, the back of her half dressed figure as
she leans over the hotel basin to wash the black dye out of her hair.
Finally the audience is allowed a close-up shot of her face as she
throws back her wet blonde hair. We don't actually see Marnie in a
full figure shot until she gets out of the taxi and enters the Red Fox

Tavern where, we learn from the familiar greetings she exchanges with the receptionist, she is a regular and valued guest. By this time we have learned to pay very close attention to every small change in Marnie's appearance and demeanour, and the subsequent unfolding of the plot depends heavily on this attention for its meaning.

The fragmentation of the body of the central character is thus an important means, though not the only one, by which audience attention to the character is solicited and maintained. The location in which we first see the character is of more importance in enlightening us about the psychic make up of the character herself than in offering information about the diegetic world, though of course both functions are fulfilled. Our first view of Marnie dressed as herself, for example, is of her upper torso framed by the locked safe deposit boxes in the station. The actions and speech of the central character on the whole also serve to reinforce her enigmatic qualities, in the process reinforcing also the bonds between the audience and the character.

Major Characters

The audience's first view of major characters is more likely to be in full figure than in the fragmented state routinely employed for central characters. The relation between them and their location is privileged, suggesting to the audience what kind of person this is and prefiguring, through their 'setting', their role in the narrative to come without emphasising them as problematic characters containing some mystery or enigma to which we learn to want the answer, as is typically the case with central characters. It is often a subtle distinction, but in general the speech and actions of major characters is also perceived and understood in relation to their context rather than to some inner driving force of their personality. Major characters are more likely to be offered as a whole, existing in some kind of harmonic relation with their surroundings, whereas central characters are, as we have seen, frequently offered as a series of parts which often add up to a puzzling whole – the business of the narrative and the audience together being to 'solve' the puzzle.

Our first views of Kate (Jo Van Fleet) and Abra (Julie Harris) in *East of Eden* (Kazan 1955), for example, are in medium long-shot as they walk through surroundings which, as the plot unfolds, we learn to be analagous to their characters. Kate is walking alone between the Monterey Bank and the rough and run-down outskirts of town where her establishment is situated; she is formally dressed, wearing gloves, a hat and a veil and she ignores Cal's (James Dean) attempts to get into conversation with her as he follows her. Abra, on the other hand, bareheaded and wearing a summer dress, is strolling arm in arm with Aron (Richard Davalos) through the sunny pastoral landscape of Salinas. As the narrative unfolds we learn that the opposition town:country is indeed an important one and the initial identification of these two major female characters with a particular geographic location enables our subsequent understandings of their crucial narrative consequences for the central figure of the film, Cal, who must resolve the opposition.

In *Madonna of the Seven Moons* (Crabtree 1945) it is important that Maddalena's daughter Angela (Patricia Roc) be understood as a 'modern' girl, in order that her mother's inappropriate attachment to outmoded conventions can be better appreciated. Accordingly our first view of Angela is in a medium long-shot as, wearing slacks and with her hair loose, she runs down the steps of a Cannes hotel and jumps into the passenger seat of an open-topped sports car. Joan Draper (Frances Mercer) the second wife of the central character Alan Pearson played by Michael Wilding in *Piccadilly Incident* (Wilcox 1946) is the woman who unwittingly and tragically supplants the central character Diana (Anna Neagle) when the latter is missing, presumed dead, after the Allied evacuation of Singapore. Prefiguring this role in the narrative, we first see Joan in medium long-shot picnicing with her US service colleagues outside the gates of the Pearson country mansion where Alan is recuperating from wounds received on active service, and mourning his supposedly dead wife. The scene ends, after their first meeting, with a medium close-up of Joan's face as she leans on the No Trespass sign outside the mansion gates; a cut takes us directly to a similarly framed shot of Diana leaning against a tree on the island where she is marooned.

The introduction of Winifred Banks (Glynis Johns) in *Mary Poppins* (Robert Stevenson 1965) has her, in elegant Edwardian dress, dancing and singing her way down Cherry tree Lane to her house, which she finds in a state of chaos; undeterred she continues with her suffragette song, attempting to include the cook and maid. The juxtaposition of her suffragette gaiety with her disordered household proposes the problem to be resolved, by the end of the film, through the intervention of Mary Poppins (Julie Andrews) herself. The audience's first view of her, also in full figure, shows her seated on a cloud floating over an idealised view of the London skyline emphasising at once her distance from the day-to-day world and the magical powers which she will bring to bear on the household of Cherry Tree Lane. Mary Poppins, despite her eponymous role, cannot be regarded as a central character in the terms outlined above because she doesn't change during the course of the narrative and the audience is accorded very little opportunity to empathise with her own desires – she doesn't have any. The central character in this film is the patriarch George Banks. In order for the family's problems to be resolved it is he who must change, and this is precisely what Mary accomplishes by the end of the film.

Minor Characters

Central and Major characters are the ones the audience is required to 'know' during the course of the narrative. The more minor a character the more likely it is that the location in which we first see them, or the actions which they are performing at the time will have greater narrative importance than their personalities. Hence Mrs M. (Joyce Carey), the manageress of the station cafeteria in *Brief Encounter* (Lean 1945) is first seen in her characteristic position behind the counter: we never see her anywhere else. Her function is to motivate the narrative by providing, through her on-going and mildly comic flirtation with the station porter Mr Godbey (Stanley Holloway), a foil for the desperate and tragic affair between Laura (Celia Johnson) and Alec (Trevor Howard) which is at the centre of the film. Cousin Agatha (Martita Hunt) in *The Wicked Lady* (Arliss 1946) descends the staircase in Maryiot Cells, the Skelton Manor, accompanied by the exasperating and absurd middle-aged and identically dressed twins (Amy Dalby and Beatrice Varley) to greet Caroline as she comes in from her ride with Ralph and to give her the letter announcing Barbara's imminent arrival. We know little more of Cousin Agatha than that she is initially sceptical about Barbara:

> *Caroline*: Oh, pretty's too tame a word for her. She has beautiful green eyes, like emeralds.
> *Cousin Agatha*: Cats have green eyes, I don't like cats.

Her role in the narrative is to be the locus of recognition of Barbara's diabolical amorality. Only she shares the recognition the audience is invited to make of Caroline's suffering through the film, and this is her importance. Thus she enables and motivates narrative development, offering, within the diegetic structure, a more complex view of the play between the two central women.

Similarly Helene Colbert (Brigitte Bardot) in *Doctor at Sea* (Ralph Thomas 1955) enables, to the limited extent that any character development could be said to take place in this limp and chauvinist comedy, the humanisation of the central figure Simon Sparrow (Dirk Bogarde) by providing him with a suitable 'love interest'. This narrative function is implicit in her first scene where she is singing in cabaret in the foreign port where the SS *Lotus* has docked. She attracts the attention of the group of ship's officers with whom Dr Sparrow is drinking and from whose masculine badinage he has, so far, resolutely kept himself aloof. The scene makes it clear, however, that he is not impervious to Helene herself, and their romance subsequently develops.

In the Douglas Bader biopic *Reach For the Sky* (Lewis Gilbert 1956) Nurse Brace (Dorothy Alison) is first seen in medium close-up as she comes, smiling, through the door onto the terrace of the nursing home where Bader (Kenneth More) is convalescing, in answer to his shouted summons. As she busies herself with his welfare she also questions his interest in his girlfriend, Sally (Beverly Brooks), thus prefiguring her main narrative function which is to provoke Bader out of the state of self-pity into which he sinks during his convalescence. This provocation is crucial to the narrative since Bader has all his famous Second World War braveries ahead of him. Once he leaves the nursing home we don't see Nurse Brace again, yet her role has been an important one in motivating Bader's recovery in this section of the narrative.

Jessie Cotton in *Marnie* (Hitchcock 1964) opens the door of Bernice's house to Marnie's knock, provoking a display of jealousy from Marnie which offers further insights to the audience about her complex character, as well as ensuring close attention to the ensuing scene between Marnie and her mother, Bernice (Louise Latham), in our first view of her. The framing of the child Jessie, full figure in the doorway in a slightly high angle shot as if from the adult Marnie's point of view also announces, albeit in cryptic form, the final solution to the enigma of Marnie herself which, as we discover in the flashback sequence near the end of the film, is located in Marnie's childhood – the time when she herself would have answered the door of her mother's house.

All these minor characters are first seen by the audience in full figure, in locations which have a particular significance for narrative events concerning central and major characters rather than for the minor character who is the subject of the image. Though their actions and/or speech anounce or nuance narrative events the audience is never invited, nor given the opportunity subsequently, to consider further what the character's own subjectivity might entail.

Figures

The men, women and children – often the 'extras' or bit part players – whose roles are defined here by the term 'figure' can hardly be said to be 'characters' at all. Like buildings, props and costumes they are accoutrements of the diegetic world whose principal function is to enable the verisimilitude of location. They are primarily offered in a representation which privileges their location or their action, which typically has a reciprocal relation with the location: hence the dancers in the London restaurant where Alan (Michael Wilding) and Diana (Anna Neagle) dine in *Piccadilly Incident* (Wilcox 1946), the mourners at the Edwards' funeral in *The Searchers* (Ford 1956), the teenage fans in *A Hard Day's Night* (Lester 1964), the riders in the hunt in *Marnie* (Hitchcock 1964), the customers in the bank in *Mary Poppins* (Robert Stevenson 1965). But figures are not always, nor necessarily, plural in this way. Laura's maid Ethel in *Brief Encounter* (Lean 1946), for example, should also be classified as such since her narrative function is simply to establish the comfort of Laura's middle class home. We see Ethel once when she brings a tray of food to Laura's son as he recovers from his accident – we see considerably less of Ethel, in fact, than we do of the comfortable chintz covered armchair in which Laura sits by the fire opposite her husband. In *Reach for the Sky* (Lewis Gilbert 1956) the waitress in the mess dining hall is of no importance in herself; like the tables, chairs, trays and cutlery she is an accoutrement of the location 'officers dining hall' whose presence confirms our reading of the scene.

The key determinants, in the initial introduction of characters to the audience, are thus their appearance, their actions and/or speech, and their location: by the way in which these variables are organised the audience is offered, through film form itself, 'clues' as to the relative narrative importance of the figures on the screen.

Introduction by Another Character

In the case of central and major characters the routine methods outlined above are sometimes modified by the addition, often in advance of the character's first appearance on screen, of an introduction by another character already known, or at least already introduced, to the audience. This narrative device either serves to problematise the character so introduced or to confirm, to reinforce the reading suggested to the audience through the character's location, appearance and so on. Thus we are offered two assessments of Marnie (*Marnie*, Hitchcock 1964) before our first glimpse of her: Strutt (Martin Gabel), as we have seen, declares she is a thief and Mark Rutland (Sean Connery) affirms her good looks. Similarly before Barbara (Margaret Lockwood in *The Wicked Lady*, Arliss 1946) first appears in the superimposed fade-in discussed above the audience has already heard Caroline's enthusiastic speech about her beauty and goodness, with the acid qualification from Cousin Agatha about the green eyes of cats. Before we first see Angela Labardi (Patricia Roc in *Madonna of the Seven Moons*, Crabtree 1945) running down the steps of the Cannes hotel we have already been privy to a discussion between her parents Giuseppe (John Stuart) and Maddalena (Phyllis Calvert) about what kind of girl she is. We are alerted to the social class of Sophie Western (Susanna York in *Tom Jones*, Richardson, 1963) before we first see her in her fairytale heroine's introduction standing on the bridge over the lake dressed all in white, by the earlier exchange between Tom (Albert Finney) and his mistress Molly (Diane Cilento) daughter of the poacher Black George (Wilfred Lawson), in which Molly tells Tom:

> Miss Western's come back from Paris and'll be
> wanting a maid.

The most elaborate and intriguing use of this device occurs in *Madonna of the Seven Moons*, and it is one which considerably reinforces the opportunity for oppositional readings – readings made against the grain of that urged in the textual construction. Both Maddalena and her alter ego Rosanna are introduced, or rather their visual introduction is modified, through the speech of another character shortly after their first appearance on screen. Maddalena's husband Giuseppe joins her with the nuns in the garden of the convent hospital where she has just refused to allow them to name the new children's ward after her, and reminds the nuns of his earlier warning that Maddalena's modesty wouldn't permit their request. Thus the audience's understanding (armed with their sole possession of knowledge of her traumatic childhood experience) of Maddalena's desire for seclusion is modified by the other protagonists' reading of this desire as pious modesty. When Rosanna first appears we see her, clearly a stranger in Maddalena's bedroom where she finds herself, reflected in the mirror as she loosens her hair and puts on her gipsy shawl, and we follow her as she buys a one way ticket to Florence at the railway station. The full importance of her role as consort to the leader of the petty criminal ganger, Nino (Stewart Granger), is made clear in Mother Venucci's (Nancy Price) speech to the kitchen maid Victoria (Jean Kent) which occurs after Rosanna has left Rome but before she arrives at the thieves' kitchen in Florence. Mother Venucci says:

> There's only one not like the others – Rosanna.
> When she left they came and went,
> came and went, as you will.

These additional sources of information about the dual central character of this film concern two opposing aspects of womanhood which Maddalena/Rosanna is clearly meant to embody – two aspects which in this character are fatally irreconcilable. These are the pious, retiring but loved and respected mother and wife, Maddalena, and the impetuous, passionate and mysterious mistress, Rosanna. Some of the popular press greeted Phyllis Calvert's performance of this dual role with scepticism:

> Phyllis Calvert gives a pretty but hardly convincing demonstration of a 'split' personality . . . [1]

> . . . while Phyllis Calvert is charming as the mother she fails entirely to put the required fire and passion into the wanton she occasionally becomes.[2]

Nevertheless it is certainly true that this particular division of patriarchal definitions of femininity evident in the 'two' characters is likely to have been just as familiar to contemporary female audiences as to more recent ones. It is therefore of interest to emphasise that the wife, the pillar of the bourgeois nuclear family, is defined for the audience by a man, her husband, while the (arguably) more appealing character Rosanna is the subject of a definition given by a knowing, we might say wise, old woman. An oppositional reading of the film informed by a concern with gender politics will make more of this feature of the film than of the preferred reading which attempts to offer the 'modern' girl , Angela (Patricia Roc) as the solution to a 'problem' firmly located, as the preferred reading would have it, in the past.

THE DEFINITION OF FEMALE CHARACTERS

By the end of the film the audience's initial understandings of characters and their ability to evaluate the actions and choices they make as they confront the problems posed by the narrative has been developed. The initial perceptions of audience members may have been modified by subsequent narrative events. In any case there is more to be said by the end of the film about the female characters seen on the screen. By this time the audience is likely to have some idea of the class, race or nationality of the character; to have some notion, more or less precise, about her age and an idea about her sexual status – that is to say whether she is a young virgin, a celibate, a bride, wife or mother, or indeed whether her narrative path has led her from one such state to another; in addition to these kinds of information the audience might also know what occupation – work or profession – the character routinely engages in, whether or not such activity is foregrounded in the narrative itself; and what aims, if any, the character has for her (albeit fictional) life. In such ways the female characters are defined through their diegetic experiences offered to the audience; it is these definitions to which we shall now turn our attention.

Class, Race and Nationality

Throughout the twenty year period under consideration class is a far more important definer of fictional individuals than either race or nationality – both the latter being called on only when the designation 'other' is important to the hermeneutics. Thus in *Piccadilly Incident* (Wilcox 1946) Joan Draper (Frances Mercer) is American in distinction to the English Diana (Anna Neagle) whom she supplants; Sally, in *East of Eden* (Kazan 1955) is a negress confirming, through her proximity with Kate, the latter's position as an outsider to polite society in so far as this exists in Monterey; Plato's nanny (Marietta Canty) in *Rebel Without a Cause* (Ray 1956) is also a negress, functioning in the narrative to emphasise Plato's (Sal Mineo) 'motherless' predicament. In both these films addressed to mid-fifties America it is also apparently axiomatic that the negress is the social inferior of her white sister, so that the distinction between Sally and Kate, or between Plato's nanny and his mother could be understood as equivalent to a class distinction. The only woman of any significance in all of the films to be defined by her racial origins is the minor character Look (Beulah Archuletta) in *The Searchers* (Ford, 1956), and she is treated as a comic figure, her primary narrative function being to demonstrate Martin Pawley's (Jeff Hunter) inadequate understanding of the 'uncivilised' customs of the Indians.

Thus in the mid-forties class was the exclusive indicator of social position; in the mid-fifties the designation 'other' was of occasional importance – either race, usually expressed through colour, or nationality. In the mid-sixties, on the other hand, we are just as likely to have a clear understanding of a character's nationality as of her class background.

It would perhaps require close examination of a much larger body of films than are dealt with here to speak with any certainty on this point, but it does seem as though a preoccupation with class position in the mid-forties has, by the mid-sixties, given way to an attention to national origins as a more reliable indicator of the 'given' attributes of an individual. Certainly by the mid-sixties there is more variety in the apparent class positions of both major and minor characters – the vast majority of characters in both the mid-forties and the mid-fifties being defined as middle class.

Age and Sexual Status

All the central female characters – those characters which we can understand their respective films to be 'about' – are young. The oldest are Maddalena in *Maddona of the Seven Moons* (Crabtree 1945) and Laura in *Brief Encounter* (Lean 1946) who are both somewhere in their thirties. The rest – Francesca in *The Seventh Veil* (Compton Bennett 1945), Diana in *Piccadilly Incident* (Wilcox 1946), Barbara and Caroline in *The Wicked Lady* (Arliss 1946) and Marnie in *Marnie* (Hitchcock 1964) – are all in their early twenties at most. In the publicity photographs for *Madonna of the Seven Moons,* indeed, there is little difference in the apparent age of the two main female leads, Phyllis Calvert and Patricia Roc, and much was made, in contemporary fanzine gossip,[3] of reports that Garbo had turned down the part of Maddalena some years earlier on the grounds that she was too young to play the mother of an adult daughter whereas Phyllis Calvert, young though she also was, relished the opportunity the role offered. In other words the age of the fictional character Maddalena is effectively reduced in the fanzine gossip surrounding the part.

Amongst the major characters the picture is a similar one: the oldest women here are the problematic characters of Kate in *East of Eden* (Kazan 1955) and Bernice Edgar in *Marnie* (Hitchcock 1964), both of whom play the mothers of young adult children – Cal Trask and Marnie respectively – who are in crisis as a consequence of their mothers' past actions. Two characters are of indeterminate age as far as the narratives they inhabit are concerned – Sister Mary Benedict in *The Bells of St Mary's* (Leo McCarey 1946) and Mary Poppins in *Mary Poppins* (Robert Stevenson 1964) – but since they were played by Ingrid Bergman in 1946 and Julie Andrews in 1964 they were likely to be read by contemporary audiences as belonging to the group of younger women. The rest, like the central characters, are in their early twenties or younger: Angela (Patricia Roc) in *Madonna of the Seven Moons,* Sally Benton (Brenda Bruce) and Joan Draper (Frances Mercer) in *Piccadilly Incident,* Abra (Julie Harris) in *East of Eden,* Judy (Natalie Wood) in *Rebel Without a Cause,* Thelma (Muriel Pavlow) in *Reach for the Sky,* Debbie Edwards (Natalie Wood) and Laurie Jorgensen (Vera Miles) in *The Searchers,* the child Jane Banks (Karen Dotrice) in *Mary Poppins,* Barbara Winters (Lauri Peters) in *Summer Holiday* and Sophie Western (Susanna York) in *Tom Jones.*

Among the minor characters – those whose primary function is to motivate narrative events – there is slightly more variety in the age groups represented on screen, particularly in the group of films from the mid-forties. Looking at the spread of minor characters through the mid-forties, mid-fifties and mid-sixties though is to come to the inescapable conclusion that by the mid-sixties there are far fewer middleaged and old women seen on the screen than before. There are some exceptions: these are, on the whole, very minor characters such as the Bird woman of St Paul's (Jane Darwell), Katie-Nana (Elsa Lanchester), the Banks' cook and maid, the 'ghastly crew'

of would-be nannies blown away by the magical gust of wind
and the various oldish women in the sample crowd around Bert
(Dick Van Dyke) as he goes through his routines outside the park
gates in *Mary Poppins*. These are caricatures of 'old women' rather
than believable people like the rather more substantial Mrs Miller
(Rosalind Atkinson) and Aunt Western (Edith Evans) in *Tom Jones*.
In the other sixties hits, on the rare ocasions when there are older
women to be seen on the screen they tend to be cruelly exaggerated
stereotypes like Stella Winters (Madge Ryan), the Yugoslavian
'bride's' mother, or the old Frenchwomen magically transformed
by Don's (Cliff Richard) song into young and nubile beauties, in
Summer Holiday. In the sixties it might be comic or tragic to be
old, but never interesting. In the mid-fifties by contrast, though
the major characters are, except for Kate in *East of Eden*, all young
women, there are several older women among the minor characters.
These include Miss Mallet (Brenda da Banzie) in *Doctor at Sea*, Jim
Stark's mother (Ann Doran) and grandmother (Virginia Brissac)
in *Rebel Without a Cause*, Martha Edwards (Dorothy Jordan) and
Mrs Jorgensen (Olive Carey) in *The Searchers*. The same is true in
the mid-forties: Tessa (Amy Veness) and Mother Venucci (Nancy
Price) in *Madonna of the Seven Moons* are amongst several older
female characters in small parts; Mrs Breen (Una O'Connor), Mrs
Gallagher (Martha Sleeper) and several of the nuns in *The Bells of
St Mary's*, and the twins (Amy Dalby and Beatrice Varley), Cousin
Agatha (Martita Hunt) and Henrietta (Enid Stamp-Taylor) are by
no means the only older women to appear on the screen during *The
Wicked Lady*.

In general then we might say that in this twenty year period
only young women were of sufficient interest to justify their representation in the foreground of popular film texts, and that the
effective participation in the narrative on the part of older women
had diminished noticeably by the mid-sixties. Although this might
conceivably be explained by the concentration on youth and the
youth audience which we have noted *à-propos* successful films of
the sixties, still the comparative absence of older female characters
in the mid-forties and mid-fifties, and the routine presence of older
male characters in all periods does seem to suggest that, in popular
cinema at least, by the mid-sixties women over the age of 25–30 are
most conspicuous by their absence. Anna Neagle, for example, in an
interview for *Films and Filming* (Nov 1973) commented on the dearth
of parts for 'older women':

They are writing very few subjects now for the older woman except on the theme of a mature woman who has an affair with a young man. This has been a favorite since long before Gloria Swanson and William Holden did Sunset Boulevard, and when well done can be very successful, as *The Graduate* has proved. But it's not for me – I've been offered those kind of parts and I don't think I could play them well, because I don't want to play them.

Amongst the declining references of any kind to the cinema in the women's magazines of the sixties, the emphasis is invariably on the ages and domestic lives of the stars. *Woman's Own* wrote in May 1963:

It isn't – it can't be – but it IS Bette Davis, now well into her 50s but looking as smooth and swinging as 16 year old daughter Barbara . . . [4]

and in September of the same year

No wonder modern mothers and daughters are taken for sisters – look at Ingrid Bergman and daughter Jenny . . . [5]

Features on Sophia Loren, Elizabeth Taylor and other stars evidently regarded in the sixties as 'older' women, concentrated on their histories of marriage, divorce and custody battles – as for example a piece about Ingrid Bergman in *Woman and Beauty* (February 1964) which applauded the strength with which she had handled these difficult life situations but, in three pages, never mentioned a single film or part she had played.

The marked decline in references to either the cinema or to popular film stars in women's magazines in the late fifties and early sixties can presumably be accounted for by the decline in cinema audiences during that period. When female stars *are* featured the emphasis is almost exclusively on their management, in their 'private' lives, of what seems increasingly to have been perceived as the dominant female roles – wife and mother.

Within the film texts too there is an overwhelming preponderance of these roles: female characters are either young and (therefore) virgins and/or brides or, if they are (slightly) older they are (therefore) wives and/or mothers. The few exceptions, women (usually young) whose expression of an active and independent female sexuality is evident in the narrative's unfolding, are invariably compromised for their articulation of female desire. Examples are Rosanna in *Madonna of the Seven Moons*, Laura in *Brief Encounter* and Barbara in *The Wicked Lady* – and these are all characters in films of the mid-forties. There aren't any comparable characters in the films achieving such large-scale popularity in the mid-fifties.[6]

An interesting group of characters comprises young women whose awakening recognition of their own sexual desire is experienced by themselves (and thus, in the films' preferred readings, by the audience too) as problematic. Their 'problem' is invariably solved when their desire is reciprocated, usually in the narrative's closure. Thus Laurie spends the entire course of *The Searchers* waiting for Marty to return from his quest, which he does in the closing sequence of the film; Abra in *East of Eden* continually and uneasily examines the quality of her feelings about Aron and Cal, apparently finding peacefulness and the promise, at least, of fulfillment with Cal when he is finally reconciled with his father Adam in the last shot; Judy's malaise in *Rebel Without a Cause* is resolved by Jim's arm around her shoulders as he introduces her to his parents and the young couple, implicitly, take their place in the new light of their adult day after the horrifying events of the previous night, symbolic of their adolescent confusions; Francesca is 'cured' at the end of *The Seventh Veil* and is thus able to recognise that Nicholas is the one she has always wanted and Caroline, at the end of *The Wicked Lady*, finally gets Ralph and, so he tells her, future happiness.

But if the desires of the female character are not reciprocated they are invariably offered, in the diegetic construction, as predatory or ridiculous or both. Wendy Thomas (Joan Sims) in *Doctor at Sea* is delineated as a comic example of the appalling fate in store for a man who is the object of an unattractive woman's desire, and in the same film Miss Mallet (Brenda da Banzie) is similarly a comic figure on account of her age: in her case, though, she gets her man but this resolution is offered as a hideous punishment for the man in question, Captain Hogg (James Robertson Justice).

In the mid-sixties film *Tom Jones* the eponymous hero meets, as fairy tale heroes do, with a variety of obstacles which impede his goal, union with the fairy tale heroine Sophie. Not least amongst these obstacles are a series of rapacious women whose single-minded pursuit of their lustful designs on Tom are the subject of many comic interludes: the point is that the comedy derives from the unwelcome nature of their advances which Tom, for various reasons specific to the plot, finds difficult to resist. Both Lady Belleston (Joan Greenwood) and Sophie's cousin Harriet Fitzpatrick (Rosalind Knight), accustomed to conducting their affairs in the eighteenth century London society in which this part of the film is set, are vilified in the preferred reading of the text for their expression of sexual desire. The exception to this rule – the only one in all of the eighteen films analysed here – is the minor character Jenny Jones (Joyce Redman). The justly celebrated set piece of her lascivious meal at the inn with Tom and, as one reviewer[7] put it 'their subsequent rush to a bed [was] a catharsis new to British cinema': certainly it was a rare, if not unique example among the films of the post-war period of a woman indulging her sexual appetite with impunity. Even Molly (Diane Cilento) the first woman with whom we see Tom, though she is certainly depicted as expressing and satisfying her sexual desire relatively freely and with just as much enjoyment as Jenny, is implicitly condemned for her 'slatternly' behaviour and attacked by her own class when, heavily pregnant, she dares to 'show herself' at the Sunday service in the village church.

Thus in the vast majority of cases female desire is represented as a problem whose solution lies exclusively in the approbation of a particular man; the expression of desire in older and/or unattractive women is comic, tragic, or appalling – in any case unseemly – depending on the generic codes ordering the diegesis. Above all in every film it is a patriarchal view of female sexual desire which is inscribed in the narrative closure, as we shall see in the next chapter.

In the group of films from the mid-forties active and independent female desire *is* represented, albeit in characters who are in the end compromised for their temerity; in the mid-fifties – in this group of films at least – it is simply absent; by the mid-sixties the only central female character in the six films analysed, Marnie, is of interest precisely *because* she apparently experiences no desire. The dual project of the film is to discover the causes for this lack and to remedy it by showing that 'really' she must want the hero, her husband Mark (Sean Connery) *because* he wants her. The systematic onslaught on female independence in any expression of womanhood – of which the articulation of sexual desire is but one aspect – which is evident in the popular films of the mid-forties onwards would seem, by the mid-sixties, to have gone too far for its own good since Marnie's 'dormant' sexuality must, by then, be entirely reconstructed.

The sexual status of female characters, whether they are to be understood as young girls on the threshhold of adult life like Sophie, Abra and Judy, and therefore in search of the 'right' man (defined by whether or not the male character thinks they are the right woman) or, more rarely, as adult women negotiating the pitfalls of social conventions and their roles as wives and mothers like Laura and Maddalena, is by far the most important defining characteristic by which the audience is invited both initially to perceive and subsequently to understand the character.

A cursory glance at the dominant female characters in the eighteen films under consideration here might suggest that gender relations, desire and motherhood are the only motivating factors in life for women. It is nevertheless of interest to consider what other ways we are offered of understanding these fictional women. How many of them follow an occupation which contributes to our understanding of their characters? Do any of them express any aims in their lives, apart, that is, from those relating to sexuality and motherhood?

Occupations and Aims

In considering the range of female occupations and the aims of the fictional women represented on the cinema screen it is important to distinguish between those occupations and aims which are suggested to be crucial to the make up of the character (generally this would apply to central and major characters), and the simple range of occupations to be seen on the screen. During the post-war period many of the mass circulation women's magazines routinely carried features and series concerned with women's employment, training and careers opportunities. Since there was, arguably, likely to have been a considerable overlap between the readership of these magazines and the regular cinema audiences – and since also many of the women constituting the magazine readership and the cinema audience will have been working women – it will be interesting to compare the range of employments to which these two contemporary sources referred. The question informing such a comparison concerns the fit, or lack of fit, that female audiences may have observed between their own experience and that of their fictional counterparts. The answers to this question, in respect of our three historical moments, will be of interest in considering the reading activities of contemporary female audience members.

The absence of any diegetically significant occupations is remarkable amongst the central and major characters throughout the twenty year period, particularly given the steady rise in female employment and the gradual, grudging acceptance of the principle of equal pay during the period.

In the mid-forties Francesca's professional activity as a pianist is compromised by its disruption as a consequence of the major narrative problem, her relationship with Nicholas; Diana's duties as a Wren in wartime lead to her separation from her husband and the ensuing complications, as we shall see, require her death in the narrative closure for their resolution. In the mid-fifties the only major character whose *occupation* is crucial to the meaning of the film is the ambiguous figure of Kate whose successful business is affirmed by her as a preferable (and alternative) way of life to that of wife to Adam and mother to her twin sons. But her decision is compromised by the consequences for her husband and sons – all more central figures in the narrative than she is – and by the fact that the business she runs so successfully is a bar/brothel on the outskirts of town.

In the mid-sixties Mary Poppins presents an ideal, problem solving nanny – but she never expresses any desires of her own, though she does hold views and they are the ones upheld in the preferred reading of the narrative. In the end we must understand her as a cipher, a catalyst in the role of nanny whose task is to resolve the difficulties of the family she visits and thus, through her intervention, to offer to the audience a preferred set of values which, it is implicitly claimed, will reinforce that fundamental social unit, the nuclear family. The film's handling of the 'suffragette' Winifred Banks (Glynis Johns) is particularly interesting in this respect. Winifred's involvement with the 'Votes for Women' campaign is offered as an inherently frivolous activity which is an obstacle to the proper fulfilment of her duties as wife and mother. Thanks to Mary's intervention she comes to realise the error of her ways and in the closure of the narrative her 'Votes for Women' sash is put to better use as the tail for the children's kite. Marnie, the only other important female character in the group of films from the mid-sixties, is even more problematic. Though we see her at her secretarial work, and we are certainly privy to her entrepreneurial skills – albeit criminal ones – in the end these activities are explained as deviant consequences of the pathological repression of her sexuality.

Where female characters are of sufficient interest to occupy centre stage, as it were, it is not on account of their occupations or their professional aspirations that we are invited to attend to them. The only exception to this rule is the celibate Sister Mary Benedict (Ingrid Bergman in *The Bells of St Mary's*, Leo McCarey 1946), headteacher of the catholic school. Considerable screen time is devoted to her pedagogic aims and methods, but even this attention is compromised by its opposition in the hermeneutics to those of Father O'Malley (Bing Crosby). In the end it is the contest between these two characters which the audience is invited to enjoy, their pedagogic principles being relegated to the position of a simple pretext for the clash of their personalities.

The representation of aims and goals among these characters is similarly limited. Basically three aims figure: these are a desire for seclusion or solitude, for wealth and/or power, or for marriage. Maddalena in *Madonna of the Seven Moons* repeatedly expresses her desire for solitude – how far this is a consequence of her traumatic removal from her convent school which is shown to the audience in a preamble to the film, and how far it is a considered response to the social roles open to her is ambiguous but in this context immaterial. The point is that it is a wish she consistently expresses and one that is understood by other protagonists to constitute evidence of her unbalanced state. Her husband and her doctor are concerned with her mental health, her daughter understands her to be living in the past. But all agree that she must participate in the 'modern' world as they understand it. Their experience is privileged: the men's because they are men, her daughter's because she represents the future. Marnie, also traumatised in childhood as we discover during the narrative's unfolding, frequently begs Mark to leave her alone; apart from her mother Bernice and her beloved horse Forio she appears neither to have nor to want any other connexions. Her criminal activity, as far as she sees it, ensures the well being of these two. It is interesting to note that both these characters' clearly formulated desires for seclusion are presented to the audience as aberrant, something to be explained by reference to the discourses of popular psychology.

Wealth and power are the express aims of both Barbara, in *The Wicked Lady*, and Kate, in *East of Eden*. Their reasons for these aims, it is suggested in the two films, are closely bound up with a recognition that in this way they may ensure their independence. Barbara's route to her goal involves wielding her sexuality independently of the social conventions, and she is punished, in the resolution of the narrative, for both her aims and her means. Kate, ten years later, specifically announces her pleasure and skilfulness in the world of business and her recognition that in the past she had to choose between these and her domestic role: she is implicitly damned for her choice in the preferred reading of the film by the disparity between her assertions about her life and the visual representation of it in her arthritic hands, in the contrast between the crowded bar and her isolated office, and above all by the fact that her business itself – the bar/brothel known as Kate's Place – is both geographically and socially distanced from the life of the town. Both these characters are punished for their attempts at economic independence.

All the other central and major characters whose aims the audience is invited to recognise want marriage. This is the dominant female goal – not, interestingly, motherhood – but a reciprocal commitment to a particular man which, in popular film texts of this period, means marriage. Caroline in *The Wicked Lady* wants Ralph; Laurie Jorgensen in *The Searchers* wants Marty; Abra wants first Aron, and then his twin brother Cal in *East of Eden*; Judy eventually finds that Jim is the solution to her 'problem' in *Rebel Without a Cause*; Barbara Winters is far more satisfied by the prospect of marriage to the auto-mechanic turned tour operator Don (Cliff Richard) than in continuing with her apparently successful career as a popular singing star in *Summer Holiday* and Sophie Western in *Tom Jones* wants Tom. And they are all rewarded for the appropriateness of their goals by getting their men in the happy endings to the films.

Amongst the minor characters the question of aims doesn't arise since these characters are by definition marginal to the main thrust of the narrative – their primary function being as we have seen to motivate the narrative and to people the screen. After the examination of the major characters given above we might be forgiven for concluding that this *is* the dominant female social function in the post-war period – to motivate the social narrative and to people the social screen. However the minor characters and the mere figures, the 'diegetic furnishings', are of interest to us since they are the principal locus of screen images of women engaged in a variety of occupational tasks: here perhaps we will find evidence of the range of work which, conventionally, women were understood to perform. To some extent of course the range is prescribed by the particular qualities of the diegetic world: but our group of eighteen films includes both historical and contemporary settings in the USA and Britain as well as an assortment of film genres – war films, a western, musicals and melodramas – potentially the source of a good cross section of western society as it has imagined itself. But the range of occupations actually represented is, it seems, even more limited than that outlined in contemporary women's magazines which, during the forties and fifties, routinely offered features on women at work, careers and training advice and so on.

The relative paucity, not only of the overall numbers of women to be seen on the screen engaged in any kind of work outside their homes, but also in the range and variety of the actual female occupations depicted in popular cinema is striking. Among the minor characters and figures peopling the screen in the mid-forties group of films twenty different occupations are shown whereas a cursory glance at contemporary women's magazines shows nearly sixty different careers, jobs, training opportunities and so on discussed in reader's questions, feature articles and regular series. In the mid-fifties the gap is even wider: in this group of six films women are seen on screen in only fifteen different occupational roles while magazines addressed to women in the same period draw attention to over seventy. But, interestingly, by the mid-sixties while the number of occupations represented on screen is again about twenty, as in the mid-forties, in the magazines the number mentioned is enormously reduced – only about thirty – to less than half the numbers of different jobs for women noted in the mid-forties and mid-fifties.

Where the conventional (and not necessarily) limiting female roles of home-making and domestic maintenance appear on the screen – as for example in the case of Laurie Jorgensen in *The Searchers* (Ford 1956) or Jim Stark's mother in *Rebel Without a Cause* (Ray 1956), both of whom are shown performing routine domestic tasks skilfully and with evident pleasure – it is never the work itself which is foregrounded in the scene. This kind of work, it is implicitly suggested in such routine depictions, is not really 'work' but rather an automatic adjunct to 'being' a woman. On the rare occasions when the nature and range of the tasks summarised by the ubiquitous term 'housework' is the focus of our attention this formulation of the work as 'not-work' also comes into play. A celebrated example is the scene in the mid-fifties box office hit *Calamity Jane* (Butler, Warner, US 1943) where Calamity (Doris Day) and Katie

Brown (Allyn McLerie) perform the duet 'A Woman's Touch' while transforming the inappropriately 'masculine' and unkempt interior of Calam's cabin into a setting worthy of a women's magazine feature on home decorating. It is *because* they are women, the song and the scene tell us, that they are able, magically, to effect the transformation. The scene is, of course, delightfully susceptible to oppositional readings on the part of female audience members able to refer to their own experiences of the various tasks depicted – painting, sewing, baking, carpentry, horticulture and so on – nevertheless the preferred reading, which locates Calamity Jane's own narratively crucial transformation in this scene, urges that the audience in general accept the 'work' shown as forms of activity and skills 'natural' to women. There are other films in the 1950s which offer a different view of domestic labour – *Woman in a Dressing Gown* (J. Lee Thompson 1957), for example, but these did not generate box office success on the scale of *Calamity Jane* or the group of films under discussion here.

There are various propositions to be drawn out of the comparison, summarised above, between the routine representations of female occupations in popular cinema and the routine references to women's employment to be found in the pages of contemporary women's magazines, though none of these are based on a sufficiently systematic enquiry to do any more than suggest questions for further exploration. Nevertheless the disparity between images of women at work outside their homes on the popular cinema screen and those in the pages of the popular women's press is significant enough to prompt speculation about the role cinema may have played in reinforcing the marginalisation of women as active and independent citizens, which seems to have been required for the maintenance of patriarchal hegemony.

But what are the occupations represented on screen, and how do they match those routinely discussed in women's magazines?[8] In the films the largest single occupational group is that best defined as *maid* – these are housemaids, lady's maids and so on.[9] The next largest group is of *performers* of various kinds, actresses, singers, dancers;[10] there are the same number of *nurses*.[11] Then there are *waitresses*,[12] and *teachers*,[13] though the latter is by far the smallest group. In the women's magazines, though these occupational roles do appear, the emphasis is quite different. Here the largest group is the medical/caring professions: there are forty-five jobs mentioned which fall within this general category amongst which nurses are an important, but by no means the only group.[14] The next largest group covers various aspects of retail trade, of which there are thirty-two mentions amongst which work in shops and small business dominate.[15] (In the films examined here there are only nine, minor characters or figures, seen to engage in this type of work of which six are saleswomen in shops or street stallholders.) Next are various technically based jobs; twenty-four of these come up in the magazines whereas there are only nine in the films: of these three are pilots in *Goldfinger* and two are television production assistants in *A Hard Day's Night*. Catering and domestic jobs are mentioned twenty-four times in magazines,[16] whereas there are forty-six minor characters or figures performing such tasks in films.[17]

It is difficult to avoid the conclusion that the routine representation of women in popular cinema during the post-war period severely limited their career possibilities. As central or major characters women were of interest chiefly for their emotional state, and in minor roles they were most likely to be seen performing a limited range of more or less subservient tasks. The most striking example is probably that of the maids: though this is one of the most frequent female jobs seen on screen in all three periods it is *never* mentioned in the contemporary women's magazines sampled here. The nearest is one reference to work as a volunteer home help in *Woman and Home* in April 1945. Within the medical and ancillary professions film representations limit women exclusively to the role of nurse whereas in the magazines fourteen different medical specialties are dealt with such as radiography,[18] physiotherapy,[19] bacteriology,[20] health visiting,[21] and so on. Conversely, and perhaps not surprisingly given the cinema's perennial absorption with its own world as subject matter, the professional performer is rather over-represented in cinema[22] compared to her presence in women's magazines.[23] Teaching and related professions such as librarian, journalist, youth leader and so on are, perhaps surprisingly, rather low profile occupations in both film and magazines. Mentions of these professions are roughly comparable in numbers to those of technical jobs such as telephonist or bus 'conductress', cited in women's magazines, or as radio operator or TV production assistant represented in films, and with clerical/secretarial work which is rather more evident in cinematic representations than in women's magazines.

Female audience members, we can safely assert on the basis of this brief comparison, were likely to find their horizons more broadened in contemporary women's magazines than they were among the images of their celluloid sisters on the screen.

REPRESENTATIONS OF WOMEN IN POPULAR CINEMA

As far as the definition of women goes in these popular film texts, we have a far narrower view of women being routinely offered – with one or two noteworthy exceptions – than a panoramic study of social history might be expected to yield.

Though there are more central female characters than male ones – more heroines than heroes – in the popular films of the mid-forties, and these films are mostly about female experience, there is still a roughly equal gender balance amongst all the characters and figures appearing on screen in all of the six films we have been discussing. However during the mid-fifties and mid-sixties not only is there only one central female character, Marnie, in all of the twelve films, but also male characters outnumber females by about 2:1. In the whole group of eighteen films there is thus a remarkable imbalance in the representations of men and women which would seem to detract seriously from any claims the popular cinema may make for verisimilitude. On this score, at least, these popular texts do not conform to the realities of the world outside the cinema.

Central characters are introduced through complex visual means, often involving the fragmentation of their bodies, and the locations in which such characters are first glimpsed usually indicate something about the mental state of the character. Major characters, on the other hand, more often appear in full figure and their surroundings are more likely to indicate their role in the ensuing narrative than to offer details about their subjectivity. Minor characters, whose main function is to motivate the narrative, are generally seen first in full figure shots which emphasise their location. Typically the relation between the minor character and her location is an important indicator of narrative themes. Lastly the figures which people the screen are chiefly important for their reinforcement of verisimilitude – notwithstanding the gender imbalance noted above – and are consequently offered in shots which privilege the location over the 'character'.

Sometimes central and major characters are additionally introduced by another protagonist, often one already known to the audience and this introduction either problematises the audience's reading of one of the two characters concerned or affirms the reading the audience is being invited to make *à-propos* one of the characters. Such an introduction is most likely to be made by a male character, particularly when it is one designed to alert the audience to the preferred reading.

Definitions of characters, which are built up gradually through the course of the film, are more likely to refer to their class position than to their race or nationality, and, until the mid-sixties when a wider range of social classes was routinely represented, the middle class predominated amongst all characters in all the films. A far more crucial indicator of the social positioning of female characters than class, however, turns out to be their age and sexual status. Here we find an overwhelming preponderance of the young adult age group, with older women generally represented as inherently problematic and often disruptive. The sexual status of female characters is almost always carefully delineated and the conventional path from virgin to bride to mother is the lot of characters with whom the audience is invited to sympathise. Those few characters who attempt either sexual or economic independence are usually compromised in some way – either by events during the narrative or, as we shall see in Chapter 5, in the narrative's resolution.

There are three main aims expressed by the various central and major characters: these are seclusion, power, or marriage. The first two of these are implicitly condemned in the preferred reading urged on the audience through the construction of the narrative and the last is affirmed as an appropriate and praiseworthy goal for a woman. Finally we have discovered that central and major characters are unlikely to be of interest as a consequence of their occupations, and that the range of occupations in which minor characters are seen to engage is considerably narrower than that to which contemporary women's magazines routinely referred.

The variety of female characters represented on screen in these popular hits is, certainly, remarkably limited. But to understand more about the meanings such representations may have had for their contemporary female audiences we need to look more closely at the narrative resolutions of those female characters constructed as central to the narrative. We must examine the narrative development of central and major female characters and consider also the way audience understanding of this development may have been nuanced by factors external to the diegesis such as contemporary press responses or the personae of particular stars.

5

The Narrative Resolutions of Female Characters

WHAT IS THE NARRATIVE RESOLUTION?

Audience satisfaction, at the end of the film, is directly related to the degree to which the enigmas proposed through the systematic process of offering and withholding information, posing and answering questions, which constitutes the 'unfolding' of the narrative, have been resolved. The apparent validity of such answers and the degree of veracity perceived in films' representations of the world outside the cinema – the world inhabited by the audience – constitutes the routine material of critical responses to the films. Close attention to such contemporary responses, as we shall see, offers an extra-diegetic yardstick by which we may evaluate contemporary reception of the discursive propositions lodged in the resolutions of the film texts.

Reviewers writing about *Rebel Without a Cause* in the mid-fifties, for example, made much of the film's assertion of parental responsibility for the delinquent behaviour of adolescents, taking issue in particular with the proposition that such behaviour was by no means confined to the group of poor, low class or deprived young people but routinely to be found among the offspring of the 'comfortable' middle classes. The American journal *Films in Review* wrote in November 1955:

> Teenagers from decent but inharmonious homes are made to behave as though they came from crime infested slums . . . The purpose of this distortion, ostensibly, is to show that parental neglect can be as deleterious in comfortable middle class homes as can parental a-morality and criminality at the bottom of the social heap. This is debateable sociologically and melodramatic

on screen . . . Part of the film's power derives from endowing one social class with the vices of another.

British reviewers were able, conveniently, to distance themselves from this assertion by understanding it to be a feature of American society. Hence the *Monthly Film Bulletin*'s rather more appreciative comment:

> By setting him on the right side of the tracks, the facile expla-nations of poverty etc., are out of the question: instead some brilliantly written and directed scenes probe the relationship of his father and mother and . . . provide the sharpest and angriest comment on some patterns in American family life that has yet been seen in cinema.[1]

Nevertheless the 'message' of the film's closing scene where, for once, Jim's father 'stands up' and his mother is silent, is one pertaining to family dynamics rather than to national differences.

Similarly, in the mid-forties, reviewers of *Brief Encounter* not only applauded Laura's choice in relinquishing her lover, Alec, but also unanimously asserted the relevance of the tale to the experience of female audience members.

> There's not a woman in this or any other land of 25 or over who won't see in it some well-remembered long-hidden episode in her own life or who wishes that some such tremulous joy might likewise have been hers.[2]

> The skill with which it destroys the flavour of stolen fruit will bring a blush to the cheeks of more than a few.[3]

> Where the film succeeds almost uncannily is in the combination of the delicious happiness love brings to a respectable middle-aged woman, with her sense of guilt and humiliation over the shabby deception to which it leads. This is a real-life romance as many will recognise – a painful magic leading to a choice between the solid, safe, if humdrum values and the loss of self respect. Celia Johnson gives an absolutely perfect performance as the tormented heroine – an ordinary, nice woman who had never expected such an experience. You may feel with me that she deserved a less unsympathetic lover than Trevor Howard –

1. *Picturegoer* cover, 31.8.46. Alan (Michael Wilding) and Diana (Anna Neagle) in *Piccadilly Incident*.

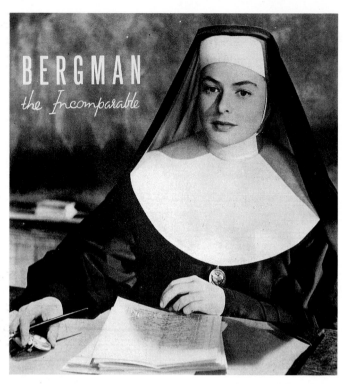

2. Sister Mary Benedict (Ingrid Bergman) in *The Bells of St. Mary's*. *Picturegoer* feature, 13.4.46.

3. Ingrid Bergman and her daughter Jenny. *Woman's Own* feature, 21.9.63.

4. (above) and 5. (below) Maddalena (Phyllis Calvert) is raped in the woods near the Convent School in the preamble to *Madonna of the Seven Moons*.

6. (above) Maddalena (Phyllis Calvert) and nuns in the garden of the convent hospital in *Madonna of the Seven Moons*.

7. (below) Maddalena/Rosanna (Phyllis Calvert) on her deathbed; her husband's cross and her lover's rose on her breast (*Madonna of the Seven Moons*).

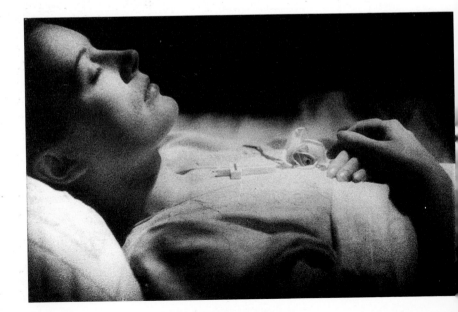

8. (above) and 8a. (below) Maddalena becomes Rosanna—Phyllis Calvert in *Madonna of the Seven Moons*.

9. (above) Ralph (Griffith Jones) and Caroline (Patricia Roc) ride through the landscape at the opening of *The Wicked Lady*.

10. (below) Barbara's death (Margaret Lockwood) in *The Wicked Lady*.

11. Barbara arrives at Skelton Manor. Margaret Lockwood superimposed on the couple, Ralph (Griffith Jones) and Caroline (Patricia Roc) in *The Wicked Lady*.

12.   (above) Dr Simon Sparrow (Dirk Bogarde) dining with his senior partner's family (daughter Wendy played by Joan Sims) in *Doctor at Sea*.

13.   (below) Miss Mallet nursing Captain Hogg. Brenda de Banzie and James Robertson Justice in *Doctor at Sea*.

YES—
Dors CAN
act without
her mink

Mary Hilton .... DIANA DORS
Macfarlane YVONNE MITCHELL
Jim Lancaster MICHAEL CRAIG
Governor .... MARIE NEY
Chaplain ...... GEOFFREY KEEN
Doctor .... LIAM REDMOND
Hill .... OLGA LINDO
Barker .... JOAN MILLER
Brandon ... MARJORIE RHODES
Mason ...... MOLLY URQUHART
Maxwell ..... MARY MACKENZIE

Fred .... HARRY LOCKE
ASSOCIATED BRITISH-PATHE.
BRITISH. X. 100 MINS.
PRODUCER: KENNETH HARPER.
DIRECTOR: J. LEE THOMPSON.
Photographed by GILBERT
TAYLOR. MUSIC: RAY MARTIN.
SCREENPLAY: JOHN CRESSWELL,
JOAN HENRY. BASED ON THE
BOOK BY JOAN HENRY. Re-
LEASE: SEPTEMBER 10.

YIELD TO THE NIGHT ★★★

DIANA DORS   YVONNE MITCHELL

MINKLESS and bleary-eyed, Diana Dors throws her all into the part of a vengeful murderess who kills the woman who did her lover wrong. And her all turns out to be quite a sizeable talent for sullen dramatics.

The story pads balefully around the condemned cell of the woman's prison, with Dors in focus most of the time. She broods, slouches, shudders—and re-lives her grimy love affair in flashback.

She whipped up my sympathies all right, helped by J. Lee Thompson's cunning French-type direction—and she did it in spite of the character she plays. So, I suppose, the film makes its point

that the death penalty is a jungle relic. But—apart from all the excitement of "can Dors do it?"—there's another performance in this film. It's given by Yvonne Mitchell, as the young wardress forced to live with the mounting hysteria of the condemned woman.

Michael Craig makes a nice impression as the scamp in Dors's life and there's an abundance of thumbnail acting—from players such as Geoffrey Keen, Marie Ney, Joan Miller and Liam Redmond.

Yes, here's fierce honesty that just misses the top grade by being rather too unvarying in mood. But I suppose there's not much scope in a cell. R. O.

Dors behind bars comes over as a sizeable talent

14. *Picturegoer* spread on Diana Dors in *Yield to the Night. Picturegoer,* 30.6.56.

THIS is a scene—in *Rebel Without A Cause*—with a history. The day after it was shot, Hollywood local papers headlined: "Dean terrorizes film set." It's the sequence where James Dean, playing a mixed-up teenager, fights with his weak-minded father (Jim Backus). It's a brilliant, hair-raising episode in the film. Sincere and frighteningly real. And a legitimate moment of any week.

's brilliant, it's brutal
d James Dean turns
a fine performance

REBEL WITHOUT A CAUSE ★ ★ ★ ★ JAMES DEAN NATALIE WOOD

CINEMASCOPE **I**T'S brilliant — but a brute of a picture. If you thought that *Blackboard Jungle* had said everything there was to say about juvenile delinquency, then you thought wrong. For here is an extra chapter on the theme. In many ways it is tougher, more searching, than anything in the *Blackboard* film.

The juvenile delinquents in this young tragedy aren't underprivileged youngsters from the wrong side of the tracks. They're mostly overprivileged boys and girls from the smarter set, whose parents either don't understand them or just don't care.

Jim (that's the late James Dean) is a teenager who is always getting into trouble. He's picked up drunk one night and taken to the police station. And why is he

drunk? Neither his bickering parents nor he can supply an answer. Then, at a new school, he becomes innocently involved in the death of one of the boys.

None of the young characters is normal. For instance, the girl whom Jim loves (Natalie Wood) has trouble "getting through to her father". It's fine film-craft and the acting can't be faulted, with James Dean towering over the film through an unforgettably moving portrayal. There's only one minor deficiency: I just didn't *like* it. **M. H.**

Jim .... JAMES DEAN
Judy .... NATALIE WOOD
Jim's Father .... JIM BACKUS
Jim's Mother .... ANN DORAN
Judy's Mother ...... ROCHELLE HUDSON
Judy's Father ...... WILLIAM HOPPER
Plato .... SAL MINEO
Buzz .... COREY ALLEN
Goon .... DENNIS HOPPER

Ray .... EDWARD PLATT
Mil .... STEFFI SIDNEY
                     WARNER BROS. AMERICAN.
CINEMASCOPE. "X." 110 MINS.
WARNER COLOR. PRODUCER:
DAVID WEISBART. DIRECTOR:
NICHOLAS RAY. PHOTOGRAPHED
BY ERNEST HALLER. MUSIC:
LEONARD ROSENMAN. SCREEN-
PLAY: STEWART STERN. RE-
LEASE: NOT FIXED.

15. *Picturegoer* spread on *Rebel without a Cause. Picturegoer*, 28.11.56.

Marriage–life's greatest joy

A husband and wife are friends seeking a unity that brings them happiness they couldn't find alone

whether his wife came smiling to the door to greet him.

Had they learned their lesson through spending the day in unhappiness created by themselves? Or was it possible that they were still foolish enough to be ashamed of weakening, to spend the evening in stony silence, and to commit the hurtful sin of letting the sun go down on their wrath?

I can never see where people get this idea that marriage is a mild form of warfare. Some husbands and wives waste far too much energy on thinking up smart retorts, trying to score off each other, struggling to put themselves in the right and their partner in the wrong.

If they want to conduct life the way countries conduct warfare,

16. (above) and 17. (below) Monica Dickens features in *Woman's Own*, 10.5.56 and 13.7.63.

MONICA DICKENS

. . . .

Top Secret— Be yourself

The Beatles' dream of stardom became a reality—through hard work, talent —and that most essential extra, originality.

it's living dolls for the under-15 class

On Thursday afternoons at Skelmersdale Secondary School, Lancs, 14-year-olds get classes in mothercraft—and their charges are real babies. Local mothers gladly lend their under-fives and get a rest, the pupils get a new interest and lessons in nappy-changing, washing and handling. "The girls get a real taste of motherhood," said headmaster Denis Wilson who thought of the idea

18. *Woman's Own* feature on education, 9.5.64.

NURSING

No! Some nurses do marry their patients but usually the infatuation fades when the bandages are removed! Doctors? You might find a Casey or Kildare but they're usually married already.

Selling's out too

You don't really expect to meet your dream man at that lingerie counter, do you? Because he'll be buying nylon undies for his wife's birthday. But if selling's in your blood, how about a transfer to the garden tools department?

Teaching — *that's no man-trapping profession either. But at a co-ed. school you may find a tweed-jacketed, leather-elbowed idealist who'll fall for a girl clever enough to catch him.*

Don't despair...

after a depressing list of non-starters, we're glad to report on numerous jobs that are *in* male-wise.

Advertising,

architecture, publishing— all bursting at the seams with smooth, artistic types. Or try an engineering firm for husky he-men.

Waitress — *excellent. According to taste, take your pick from beat coffee-bar to ritzy grill. But don't blame us if breakfast in bed is demanded as a conjugal right.*

Receptionist,

market researcher—highly recommended. So's petrol pump attendant. There's nothing more fetching than the feminine shape in a grease-stained overall. And this way you know in advance what kind of car he runs.

There it is—an up-to-the-minute guide to make your man-trapping career easier. Now you know where the Boys are — good hunting!

WHERE THE BOYS ARE

how to pick the jobs where they positively— repeat positively—can't miss you!

It's every girl's dream. An interesting job with prospects—romantic male prospects— where a bright girl has plenty of scope to make her choice—and then retire to be boss in her own home! Still dreaming? Then read on . . .
Marriages may be made in heaven, but a good proportion of them get their start in that nine - to - five period — 'working hours'. So, if all your colleagues are married and you long to find pastures new, we give, right, the results of research on where you will, and where you won't, find the boys.

First of all—out: *most of the so-called glamour jobs. As any model or hairdresser will tell you, these are crammed with lovely girls wasting the glamour on each other.*

Show business? *Don't put your daughter on the stage, Mrs. Worthington — not if you have wedding bells in mind. The stress and pace just aren't conducive to real romance.*

20. (above) James Bond (Sean Connery) in *Goldfinger*.

21. (below) Pussy Galore (Honor Blackman) and her flying circus in *Goldfinger*.

22. Sophie (Susannah York) in *Tom Jones*.

23. Mark (Sean Connery) and Marnie (Tippi Hedren) on their shipboard honeymoon in *Marnie*.

24. Mark attempts to discover the extent of Marnie's criminal activities. Sean Connery and Tippi Hedren in *Marnie*.

25. Tom and Mrs Waters dining at the inn (Albert Finney and Joyce Redman in *Tom Jones*).

but that, too, is like life.[4]

In addition to the near unanimous approval of the film's 'realism' in these testimonies, the *Woman* reviewer's reservations about Trevor Howard being the only qualification, the fanzines *Picturegoer* and *Pictureshow* drew particular attention to the minor character Fred – Laura's husband – to whom her 'silent' confession is ostensibly addressed:

> Celia Johnson is delightfully naive and feminine as a happily married woman who drifts into romance with a doctor and discovers before it is too late that her domestic happiness really comes first . . . Cyril Raymond is excellent as the homely husband who – I believe at least – suspected more than his emotions showed.[5]

> *Brief Encounter* is a picture of a romantic episode in an ordinary woman's life . . . It's a secure, placid, uneventful life, such as hundreds of Englishwomen lead . . . . Personally I think that the hero of that film was really the man in the background – husband Fred.[6]

In its claim that the 'real' hero of the film is Laura's husband Fred the *Pictureshow* review begins to displace Laura altogether from her textually central position and in so doing to assert, like the later film *Rebel Without a Cause*, the primacy of the man in the gender politics of the family.

Thus the consequence of characters' actions in response to narrative events is given in the films' resolutions and audiences, amongst whom the only members accessible now are the contemporary reviewers, are invited to evaluate these actions according to the nature of the consequence. In this way the audience is encouraged to engage in an evaluation whose meanings spill over into the world outside the cinema. Though Laura ends her diegetic existence in an embrace with her husband Fred we know that her future contentment has already been compromised, since in her voice over narration she has recognised the loneliness henceforward to be her lot: she cannot tell Fred about her affair with Alec.

Bernice is left, crying, alone in her armchair at the end of *Marnie*: a direct consequence of her 'misguided penitence' as one reviewer put it[7] and of the 'immoral' activities of her youth, characterised so severely by Mark:

I've read the transcript. The records of your trial for murder. In the records it states quite plainly that you made your living from the touch of men.

The resolution of this film requires that Bernice, the mother, be punished for the actions of her daughter, Marnie.

Both Caroline in *The Wicked Lady* and Francesca, in *The Seventh Veil* are, on the contrary, rewarded in the film's closures: when we examine the details of their values, motivations and actions through the narratives of their respective films we find a catalogue of obedience, self denial and silent sufferings. The concept of 'deserved' or 'undeserved' fate is at play here; the logic of narrative construction strongly supports a reading of causal relations between a character's behaviour and her narrative resolution, between her aims and her eventual fate. In short the character appears to be responsible for what happens to her in the end, despite any intra-diegetic protestations to the contrary. In the flashback scene near the end of *Marnie*, for example, the character Bernice is given the opportunity to explain both Marnie's illegitimate birth and her own prostitution and to demonstrate that she had always acted according to what she perceived to be Marnie's best interests, the protestation summarised as 'misguided penitence'. Despite the importance of this information the preferred reading of the narrative still consigns this character to the realms of the malevolent, those wrongdoers who have earned the punishment meted out to them at the end of the film.

In so far as a character has expressed her own aims or goals during the narrative, the resolution too is the last moment when the audience may know whether such aims or goals have been or are about to be realised. Caroline's marriage to Ralph, for example, to which she was looking forward with such pleasure at the start of the film, *will* finally take place – albeit after the film's ending. The audience has been in a position to compare the nature of this character's aim with her diegetic actions and behaviour and with the eventual 'happy ending'. Though we may not believe in the character Caroline we are nevertheless urged to perceive a direct relation between her understandings of love, committment and marriage and her 'reward', marriage to the man she loves, at the end of the film.

But is the ending important? We might argue that the demonstration, during the narrative, of successfully subversive behaviour and of independence from social conventions or constraints – such as that exemplified by Barbara in *The Wicked Lady* or by Marnie in *Marnie* – is in itself liberating, or at least pleasurable simply on account of its representation of subversion, its recognition of the constraints operative in the social world of the audience. However as we have seen films were routinely understood to be making moral, political or ethical assertions about the 'real' world, the world outside the cinema, and were evaluated by reviewers as much in relation to these assertions as in respect of the qualities of performance or the pleasures of spectacle they offered. It is in the ending of the film, in its narrative resolution, that the consequences of particular forms of behaviour, be they symbolic or exemplary, are demonstrated. *Brief Encounter*, in its depiction of a threat to the family, closes with an assertion of the primacy of family life. *The Searchers*, which drew on the codes of the western and of the melodrama, elicited comments from many reviewers about the problematic racism of the western hero who, at the end of the film, rides away into the empty desert leaving the family of the melodrama securely united and ready to embark on their 'multi-racial' future.[8] Ethan's racist distaste for the mixed race character Martin Pawley is not shared by Laurie Jorgensen who, simply, loves him. In the end it is they who are together, with Marty's 'sister' Debbie accepted in the symbolically extended family despite her 'defilement'; it is Ethan who is displaced, and racism which is problematised. The endings of films are important in revealing the preferred social codes, particularly when these codes are currently subject to re-evaluation as so many have been during the post-war period.

For female audience members then the aims, behaviour and resolutions of female characters must be of particular interest: as we have seen the aims of female characters expressed in the films under discussion can be summarised as marriage, power and solitude. The resolutions of central and major female characters are invariably marriage and the family, offered as a positive conclusion; solitude, if not actually negative then certainly problematic for the character; and death, an inescapably negative conclusion. No character achieves power.

MARRIAGE AND THE FAMILY

As we have seen in Chapter 4, amongst those female characters who express any aims at all the overwhelming majority want a reciprocal commitment to a particular man – sometimes already designated at the start of the narrative like Laurie Jorgensen's choice of Marty as her future partner in *The Searchers*, sometimes discovered during the course of the narrative as Judy finds her 'problems' solved by loving Jim in *Rebel Without a Cause*. In these popular texts marriage is understood to be the outcome of such a commitment, guaranteeing its permanence and affirming the seriousness of the feelings involved. In the semantic process whereby 'marriage' names such committed relationships there is an elision between the rather different propositions entailed in individual romantic love and in the social status, the motherhood and the unending domestic responsibilities invariably entailed in the marital partnership. In 'marriage' the bride is transformed into the wife.

It is interesting and possibly ironic to note that marriage – loosely standing as it does for both bridal fulfilment and the labours of wifehood – is *always* represented as a positive conclusion, a resolution with which female characters are rewarded. This is not just true of those characters who expressly wish for such a 'conclusion' to their fictional existence, but also of those characters whose behaviour the audience has been encouraged, through their sympathy with them, to applaud – such as Francesca in *The Seventh Veil*.

Francesca's aims are vague: as a child she appears to want to be a pianist, as an adult pianist she wants self-determination which she conceives as escape from the domination of her guardian, Nicholas – hence her ill-starred romances, first with the band-leader Peter and later with the painter, Max. But though her aims may be sketchily represented, her behaviour is not. Her dutiful obedience throughout childhood and early adult life is most carefully delineated: the two exceptions, two occasions on which she is disobedient, being the pretexts for important narrative developments. The first is in the flashback to her childhood where she is punished for lateness (disobeying the bell summoning her to her boarding school chapel) by a caning on the hands which results in failure in her music exam. The depiction of this incident strengthens the audience's understanding of the outrage and shock Francesca feels when Nicholas canes her hands, the incident which allows her the resolve to defy him. The second, in her adult life, directly results in the traumatic paralysis of her hands for which she is receiving treatment in the present time of the narrative. When she defies Nicholas to run away with Max their car crashes and her hands are burned – irreparably, she believes. But is it her hands or her disobedience that is being 'treated' by the psychiatrist Dr Larsen (Herbert Lom)? Her cure, at any rate, though it does result in her playing the piano briefly, off-screen, really concerns her 'free' choice of Nicholas as her life partner. The film ends with a deep focus long shot of their passionate embrace which obliterates the image of the piano behind them. In the flashbacks which punctuate this film it is Francesca's enforced alienation from the conventional routines of social life through her childhood and adolescence, to which audience attention is drawn. Similarly, in *Rebel Without a Cause* and *East of Eden* we are privy to the troubled adolescent yearnings and soul searchings of Judy and of Abra. Marriage, in its sense of committment, is the paradigm for the integration of female characters into the social fabric of the adult group.

More often, though, we can understand the character's 'achievement' of marriage as the direct fulfillment of her express narrative goal. When a character is 'rewarded' in the narrative resolution by having her aims achieved, we are encouraged to understand her achievement as the deserved consequence of her behaviour and actions, informed by her values. In considering her positive and successful narrative resolution, therefore, we are encouraged also to examine the exemplary behaviour which led to such a happy conclusion. In *The Wicked Lady*, as we have seen, Caroline's self denial may have guaranteed her suffering during the course of the narrative but it also ensured her a happy ending with Ralph. In conversation early in the film the two young women express their view of marriage:

> *Barbara*: When you're married you can have everything you want. You can fill this house with amusing people. You can go to London and become a famous hostess.
> *Caroline*: Oh, I don't think Ralph would care for that.
> *Barbara*: A clever woman can make her husband do as *she* likes.
> *Caroline*: But if a woman really loves her husband she'd rather do as he likes.
> *Barbara*: Still the same self sacrificing little ninny.

And it is Caroline's values, of course, which are affirmed in the narrative's close. This film, in its lascivious and spectacular depiction of Barbara's eventful life, offers images of female independence which are justly celebrated in contemporary reviews and were certainly enjoyed by contemporary audiences, as the following samples from a recent survey of women's recollections of their cinema going in the post-war period show:

> I quite liked seeing Margaret Lockwood as a thoroughly bold woman, rather than wicked. (P. Burgess)

> I liked it very much at the time. I liked rebellious, forceful women. (J. Astell)

> I liked the excitement of Margaret Lockwood getting back home unnoticed, and hiding her secret life. (V. Hamden)

> Enjoyed it, liked the contrast between the good and bad women, liked the bad one best. (D. West)

> Enjoyed it, even though she was evil, I enjoyed the woman scoring over the males. (R. Gardner)[9]

Despite her bad end Margaret Lockwood as Barbara was clearly a more charismatic figure than Caroline to contemporary female audience members, yet even oppositional readings centre on the colourful spectacle of Barbara and neglect the patriarchal instruction implicit in the dialogue quoted above. Barbara is *too* bad, and Caroline is *too* good: their underpinning by this clear exposition of the patriarchal requirement that it must be the women who put their partners' interests before their own is often lost in the denigration of Patricia Roc's performance or the celebration of Lockwood's role.

In the mid-sixties film *Tom Jones* the heroine sharing the embrace with Tom in the happy ending is Sophie. She has wanted Tom for most of the film, and she's got him, in the end. Unlike Francesca and Caroline though she has been neither obedient nor self-denying. In what ways, then, can we understand her behaviour as deserving of such a happy end? It is within the terms prevalent in the group of films from the mid-sixties that we can understand Sophie's behaviour as exemplary. She has resisted the inappropriate strictures of class and parental authority by defying her father and running away to find Tom, whom she loves. She has refused a marriage of convenience with Blifil, and rejected the advances of Lord Fellmer because she insists, like a good sixties heroine, on following her own inclinations and acting only out of 'genuine' desire. Thus it is idealism which informs her actions, in contrast to the pragmatism urged on her by the duplicitous and convention bound 'older' generation personified by her aunt Western, her cousin Harriet, her benefactress Lady Belleston. Perhaps even more important is Sophie's insistence that Tom, too, should defend himself more effectively than he does against the gratification of immediate (therefore not 'genuine' in Sophie's terms) desires. She refuses him when she finds him with Jenny Jones, or with Molly, and in so doing enables his gradual growing up. That is to say, by offering Tom a goal – herself – she enables him to begin to take responsibility for his own actions and to practice forethought in his dealings with the adult social world. Sophie may be disobedient and a tomboy but she is morally pure and prepared to take responsibility for ensuring Tom's 'purity' too: this is what the conclusion of the film rewards by deeming her worthy of its hero.

In many films the positive resolution of a female character whose values, actions and behaviour the audience is invited to consider and approve takes the form not of the moment of actual or implied marriage but of the resumption of family life. The 'happy ending' in these cases is the successful re-alignment or re-uniting of a family group in which the character has a central position and which has been disrupted as a consequence of narrative events at some point during the film – often, though not always, at the beginning. The disruption may be the consequence of the character's own actions, like those of Laura in *Brief Encounter*; in this case the major project of the narrative is to demonstrate the character's own awareness of the wrongness of her choices – during the film she must, and does, learn to mend her ways. Laura is rewarded for her eventual decision since in giving up Alec she put the family before her own desires and her reward is the continuance of her comfortable life with Fred and their children. Her trespass outside the family will, as we have seen, compromise her future happiness and this is her punishment.

The lesser character Winifred, mother of the disorganised Banks' family in *Mary Poppins*, must learn to put the interests of her children as well as those of her husband first and as we have seen in the narrative closure the family is happily united, the suffragette sash which she wore in the opening sequence being now relegated to the tail of the children's kite. Winifred has been portrayed as 'silly' rather than wicked and is therefore easily recouped for family life by the more fundamental change in her husband's attitude to his familial responsibilities – he is the primary object of Mary's ethical interventions. Winifred herself has never questioned his authority, as we have seen early in the film when she hurriedly removes the symbolic sashes at the hour when George is routinely expected home, saying to the maid as she does so 'Ellen, put these things away. You know how they annoy Mr Banks.' She has never actually posed a threat to the patriarchal harmony of the household, merely neglected its proper running, and can thus easily be 'reformed' by the simple expedient of removing the offending sash. In this deeply chauvinist film we are invited to presume that all that the sash implies is as easily removed. In the equally chauvinist mid-fifties film *Reach For the Sky* Bader's wife Thelma is rewarded for her self-effacing support of her husband by his safe return. In the mid-forties in *Piccadilly Incident* Joan Draper's loyal pleasantness to her husband's unknown female friend, in reality his first wife Diana, is rewarded by Diana's subsequent and convenient death in the air raid: Joan's future family life is assured.

In the details of such characters' fictional existence there is ample material defining the forms of female behaviour which will be rewarded, albeit ambiguously, with the assured position of wife and mother. Such 'happy endings' as we have summarised here are ubiquitous to the point of invisibility: it is when female characters refuse, for some reason, to conform to patriarchal dictats that the audience's attention is drawn to them. Hence the preponderance of problematic female characters in the immediate post-war period when women had become accustomed to a degree of economic independence and self-determination apparently incompatible with the smooth running of a peacetime market economy in patriarchal order. We find no comparably problematic characters in the group of films from the mid-fifties, and in the mid-sixties as we have seen the only central female character is Marnie. The project of this film, successfully achieved in its resolution by Hitchcock's celebrated directorial skills, is not only to correct Marnie's values and behaviour but also to show that her so-called independence is nothing but a pathological perversion resulting from an appalling childhood trauma. Marnie, the film asserts, is not really independent, she just doesn't know her own mind because she is ill.

> *Marnie*: Oh listen to me, Mark. I am not like other people. I know what I am.
> *Mark*: I doubt that you do, Marnie.
> *Marnie*: But I don't need your help.
> *Mark*: I don't think you're capable of judging what you need, or from whom you need it.

Mark knows better, and it his his meanings to which Marnie and the audience will subscribe in the closure of the narrative.

> *Marnie*:   Oh Mark, I don't want to go to jail. I'd rather stay with you.

Thus Marnie is excused her aberrant behaviour since she was sick; like Maddalena/Rosanna in *Madonna of the Seven Moons* she was 'in the dark, and could not see'. But in the sixties, unlike the forties, such aberrant behaviour is apparently no longer hreatening to patriarchal order and Marnie can be allowed to live, to 'stay with' Mark in contrast to Maddalena for whom the only possible resolution is death, as we shall see. Nevertheless Tipi Hedren's performance as Marnie, like that of Phyllis Calvert in *Maddona of the Seven Moons*, was evidently sufficiently unnerving to attract some severe censure in contemporary reviews.

> The film also suffers from the beautiful blankness of Tipi Hedren and her non-performance in the title role.[10]
>
> Tipi Hedren's cool, brazen, child-eyed exterior suggests the character's tensions alright, but avails the actress nothing when it comes to frenzied displays of desperation which are patently beyond her.[11]

'Beautiful blankness' and Hedren's 'child-eyed exterior' suggest a mannequin rather than an actor – the notion that Hedren *couldn't* perform invoking a connection, doubtless an unconscious one, between the fictional Marnie's frigidity and the professional actor Hedren's 'non-performance'. Just as sexual warmth is beyond Marnie, so 'frenzied displays of desperation' are 'patently beyond' Hedren. The American journal *Films in Review* (August 1964), after a swipe at Hedren herself referred to the much publicised fact that Hitchcock had originally offered the role to the hugely popular star Grace Kelly, and vilified the very concept of any successful performance of this subversive character with the suggestion that it would have destroyed Kelly's star persona.

> I personally do not react to Tipi Hedren , nor do the men of my acquaintance with whom I have discussed her. I was surprised to hear so many of them say the same thing women say so

often 'I don't see what he (Hitchcock) sees in her'. The Marnie character would have killed the 'image' Miss Kelly succeeded in creating before she retired to Monaco. I can't understand Hitch being willing to abet the destruction of that image.

ALIENATION AND SOLITUDE

Central and major characters under discussion here are rarely left 'alone' at the end of their films, thus the few whose narrative resolution does take this form are of particular interest. Although relative solitude is, as we have seen, a goal expressed by Maddalena in *Madonna of the Seven Moons* and by the eponymous Marnie these two characters are not resolved in this way. They do not achieve their aims. In our consideration of the evaluation of characters' behaviour and values, the ethical systems by which they order their fictional existences, the consequences of which are implicit in their narrative closures, we have paid careful attention to the various kinds of information offered to us, the audience, about the characters and the constraints particular to the diegetic worlds they inhabit. We are therefore in a position to understand whether or not a character is offered positively, as somebody we might admire or even emulate, or negatively, as a misguided person whose fate, deserved or not, may be perceived as a warning about the pitfalls ahead of those whose choices are not supportive of the status quo.

The more complex and central the character, we have seen, the more varied are the forms of information offered and the less straightforward any such evaluation becomes. Nevertheless the preferred reading constructed in the textual order invariably does suggest some particular form of audience response to the character – admiration, sympathy, censure and so on. This becomes particularly interesting in relation to contemporary published responses to the films and to the performances of the actors. It seems, on perusing quantities of such material, that there is a fairly stable relationship between the critics' assessments of performance and their approval or censure of the narrative path of the character. Frequently reviewers, in the apparently routine and uncontentious epithets with which they necessarily summarise both characters and plots, oversimplify characters whose narrative construction turns out to be far more complex and even ambiguous than the critical language allows. We can perhaps assume that where there is striking unanimity between a wide variety of critics their understandings may be taken as evidence of a wider contemporary reading of the role or performance, and, conversely, that where there is disagreement between them we are dealing with a character construction whose ambiguity holds some special relevance to contemporary struggles over ethical, moral or political questions.

Kate in *East of Eden*

Kate, in *East of Eden*, is just such a character. Critical language concerning her was far more damning and censorious than the more subtle visual representations of the film itself appear to be, and the positive aspects of her narratively important support to her son Cal are entirely neglected by reviewers summarising the main outlines of the film.

> To the basic themes of the various natures of love (distorting, blinding and satisfying) and the consuming loneliness of the boy who yearns for it, Kazan only ever offers a peripheral illustration.[12]

> Cal has never learned to love because he himself has never been loved. His father is a well-meaning but gauchely pious farmer. The mother turned her back on domesticity and motherhood years before and became a Madam.[13]

Yet at the same time Jo Van Fleet's performance as Kate was frequently singled out for special praise:

> Jo Van Fleet as the rebellious wife who becomes a Madam seethes with appropriate discontent and frustration.[14]

> I liked Jo Van Fleet best, as the bad mother who caused all the trouble.[15]

> Somewhere about the middle of East of Eden (Warners) there is a scene when the boy Caleb, played by James Dean, visits his mother whom he has discovered to be the proprietress of a brothel, in the hope of borrowing money for a business venture. This scene, in which Jo Van Fleet as the mother gives the best supporting performance of the year, is handled with such meaningful economy, and seems the result of such cogent understanding,

that it contrasts strongly with the empty show of much of the
rest of the film.[16]

It would seem then that Kate's choice, to abandon her husband
and sons and pursue an independent career was not one that
found favour with contemporary critics and that Jo van Fleet's
performance was admired because of its representation of the well
deserved sufferings of the character. By the end of the film she
has disappeared from the narrative but we can infer from Cal's
re-union with his father that her solitary and ostracised existence
will continue and it is thoroughly ambiguous whether or not this is
an existence that is satisfying to her – she is, after all, a relatively
minor character but one of particular interest to female audience
members since she is both an independent woman and an older
woman, both rare on the popular screen. What was it, in detail,
about this character that attracted such vociferous censure from
critics?

Kate is a paradoxical and in many ways an inconsistent figure.
She is independent, by her own choice. She is a successful business
woman. Like the businessman Will Hamilton (Albert Dekker) and
the personification of the law, Sam the Sheriff (Burl Ives) but unlike
Adam and Aron, she is prepared to accept Cal at face value. Yet
she is also a mother who deserted her children; a wife who shot
at her husband; a brothel and bar owner whose profits are based
on exploiting the moral weakness of 'half the stinking city hall'
who 'sneak in at night'. Her history is as vague as her desires.
We learn from Sam that she had been exceptionally beautiful as a
young woman, that she was one of the legion of rootless drifters of
the '90s. The implication is of a morality unacceptable to bourgeois,
settled America; the reference is to the frontier towns, railheads and
mining camps of legendary American history known, by the 1950s,
chiefly through filmic accounts. Kate left her baby sons and shot at
her loving husband because, as she tells Cal:

> Because, because he tried to hold me.
> He tried to tie me down on a stinking little ranch
> keep me from seeing anybody
> keep me all to himself.
> Well, nobody holds me.
> Love. He wanted to own me.
> He wanted to bring me up like a snot nosed kid and

tell me what to do.
Nobody tells me what to do.
Always so right himself.
Reading the Bible at me.
Your father. He's the purest man alive, isn't he.
He wanted to tie me up in his purity.

She is shunned by the townspeople, feared by her employees and always alone. Money and power in the form of her successful business appear to satisfy her – there is certainly considerable satisfaction in her voice and demeanour when she respond's to Cal's request for a loan. Yet the encounter with Cal is constructed in such a way that the audience is invited to perceive the distress that conventional morality expects, in the clenching of her fists, in the way she turns to the wall and the camera lingers on her, alone after Cal has left the room. This is the scene, above all, upon which contemporary reviewers appear to have drawn in their summaries of Kate, in which she gives, according to the *Sight and Sound* reviewer 'the best supporting performance of the year'. Yet later, when Cal in his jealous rage forces Aron into Kate's room she appears to empathise with Aron's distress as she reproaches Cal for the outrage. So although at the narrative's opening we are invited to share Cal's simple view that Kate is the embodiment of all that is bad, by the end of the film it is Adam's position that is in doubt and we can understand and even sympathise with Kate's past actions since we now know that they were provoked by Adam's excessive rigidity. The price of her freedom, however, has been and will continue to be exclusion from society and a solitary life – the very things with which she had reproached Adam when she told Cal 'he tried to keep me from seeing anybody'. Her independence can be exercised in the world of business but only at the cost of social isolation. She is elegant but no longer beautiful and her hands, of which, as Adam tells Cal, she had once been so proud, are now crippled with arthritis. She is a figure of authority, and 'nobody tells her what to do' but only in 'Kate's Place' on the outskirts of 'rough and tumble' Monterey.

Bernice in *Marnie*

A figure comparable with Kate, also the mother of a young adult child whose distressed state is the main focus of the narrative, is

Bernice in *Marnie*. We see even less of her than we do of Kate, but unlike Kate she is crucial to the narrative's resolution since it is she, prompted by Mark, who 'explains' Marnie's perversity. In accordance with the thriller structure adopted in this film we are offered a view of Bernice when Marnie visits her early in the narrative; this is all we have to refer to on the numerous occasions during the subsequent unfolding of the plot when Marnie's mother is mentioned. The scene is thus a crucial one since it is here that disparities between Marnie's and the audience's view of Bernice must be initially located – even if they are not developed until later in the narrative. We do not see Bernice again until the denouement in which she is, effectively, tried and found guilty by Mark; held to be culpable for both Marnie's antipathy to men and her life of crime. Yet the flashback scene and Bernice's court testimony, to which she and Mark refer, both show clearly not only that the sailor's death was in fact a tragic accident but also that Bernice acted subsequently in what she understandably felt were the best interests of her beloved daughter. Like Kate, Bernice is a site of paradox: susceptible like Marnie to alternative reading but, unlike Marnie, unable to be recouped in the narrative closure. When Mark and Marnie drive away in the 'happy ending' of the film Bernice is left alone with her culpability.

What are the oppositions contained in this paradox? They are indicated in Bernice's physical presence; in her major (and only) function as mother; and over the issue of knowledge – a vital consideration in many aspects of the film. In Bernice's first scene Marnie pays one of her random and unannounced visits to her mother. Little Jessie Cotton, a neighbour's child, is with her – a routine occurrence since Jessie's mother is out at work till six. Marnie's jealousy of Jessie is evident and of hermeneutic importance for the insights it offers into Marnie's own character. Yet Bernice's obvious pleasure at Marnie's visit and her initially amused dismissal of Marnie's jealousy as inappropriate is also of importance. As the scene unfolds two different aspects of Bernice are developed. Firstly she is maimed: she limps and walks with a stick, and this is the subject of a classically Hitchcockian piece of nastiness when, after waking Marnie from her rest Bernice slowly descends the ill lit stairwell, the sound of her tapping stick echoing the tapping of the tree on the windowpane which had precipitated Marnie's nightmare. Here it is suggested to the audience that Bernice is a sinister character; a suggestion which is in direct opposition to the indulgent fondness evident in her treatment of Jessie. Secondly she has, we discover, brought Marnie up alone – thus she has usurped the place of the father in the socialisation of the child. Not only that but she has taught Marnie to distrust men, if not to dispense with them altogether:

> *Marnie*:   Oh we don't need men, Mama.
> We can do very well for ourselves.
> *Bernice*:   Decent women don't have need for any man.
> Look at you, Marnie.
> I told Mrs Cotton, look at my girl Marnie.
> She's too smart to go getting herself mixed up with men.
> None of them.

Yet although she has usurped the patriarchal place she is also, as Marnie retorts in anger later, dependent on her daughter for financial support. The paradoxical nature of Bernice as mother is suggested in this scene but only fully evident at the end of the final scene of the film. Initially we are shown Bernice freely handling and cuddling Jessie, yet unable to touch her own daughter Marnie.

> *Marnie*:   Why do you always move away from me,
> Why?
> What's, what's wrong with me?
> *Bernice*:   Nothing, nothing's wrong with you.
> *Marnie*:   No, you don't think that.
> You've always thought there was something wrong with me,
> haven't you?
> Always.
> *Bernice*:   I never.

Later we learn that Bernice went to considerable lengths, including perjury, to protect her daughter and her assertion 'Why, you're the only thing in this world that I ever did love' is utterly convincing. Bernice loves Marnie, but she cannot be loving to Marnie. She is the good mother (she loves and provides for her child) and she is the bad mother (she withholds love from her child). Finally *à-propos* knowledge Bernice tells us in the final scene that she alone is in possession of the 'truth' of the traumatic event which is then revealed to the audience by means of the flashback insert. But she also implies in her speech to Marnie directly after the inserted flashback when everything is out in the open, 'unlocked', to borrow one of the film's own recurring metaphors, that the disastrous events were in some way a consequence of her youthful ignorance. So Bernice is maimed, yet she has a stick (and a poker in the flashback scene); she has usurped the position of the patriarch yet she is dependent on her daughter's support; she is the good and the bad mother at the same time; and she is the possessor of vital knowledge yet she is ignorant.

She pays the price of her unfixity by being made the victim at the end of the film. Marnie's rehabilitation will not make it any more possible for Bernice to touch her, and she loses 'the only thing I ever did love' to the man, Mark.

Although the narrative sequence of the film indicates quite unequivocally this reading of Bernice there are sufficient moments of fluidity in the images of her – particularly the last one where she sits alone in her chair by the window, the tears still wet on her cheeks – to generate questions in the attentive reader. The transgressive Marnie can be recouped because she is desirable, yet the tragically mistaken Bernice, the 'misguided penitent' as reviewers summarised her, is doomed to suffer for ever. The uncompromising severity of this prognosis seeps out in the interstices of the film, undermining in the process the 'happy ending' by revealing it for the myth making fiction it is.

Kate and Bernice are, in their construction and resolution, negative or at least ambiguous characters, both of whom attempted at some stage to 'take the law into their own hands' for purposes ultimately subversive of, or threatening to, patriarchal order. In their different ways they are abandoned at the end of the films.

Sister Mary Benedict in *The Bells of St. Mary's*

Sister Mary Benedict in *The Bells of St Mary's* and the eponymous Mary Poppins, on the other hand, though also abandoned at the end of the films, are both constructed, and responded to in the contemporary press, as thoroughly positive characters. Both achieve their narrative goals; Sister Mary saves the school and Mary Poppins successfully alters George Banks' values thus ensuring a subsequently happy family life for the children Jane and Michael. The fact that they end the films either actually alone, like Mary Poppins, or about to be alone like Sister Mary, indicating that they are henceforward dispensable, is a consequence of the selflessness of their aims. We don't know or care what happens to them 'next' because they've done their job.

Sister Mary Benedict is the main female character in *The Bells of St Mary's*; the narrative's major concern is the relationship between her and Father O'Malley (Bing Crosby). Many reviewers, whether they liked the film or not, noted this feature and insisted on dealing with it as a love story despite the convent setting:

> Religion is used as a cloak, and a titillating one, for what is in effect a long abortive love-story between Bing Crosby as a Roman Catholic priest and Ingrid Bergman as a seductive looking Mother Superior.[17]

> For *The Bells of St Mary's is* a love story. It is the story of the love of a nun for the city slum school she is running, and of the deep affinity that grows between her and the pastor of the parish.[18]

In this film Bergman was seen to personify certain moral and ethical positions, rather like Mary Poppins did twenty years later and, ostensibly at least, it is these which are at issue rather than her own personality or narrative path. Although she is an important point of identification for the audience we have little sense of her beyond the dedicated professional persona, the immigrant Swedish headteacher of a catholic school in a run down New York Irish neighbourhood. The same is true of the central character in the film, Father O'Malley himself, though the narrative privileges his position; the film opens and closes on him and the audience shares knowledge with him of which Sister Mary remains in ignorance, crucially in the important scene near the end of the film concerning her impending departure from St Mary's. She is loved by all and described by fellow protagonists with such epithets as 'a remarkable woman', 'perfect', 'impractical', 'full of vitality and stamina'. A central element of the plot is her belief in the magical efficacy of prayer, a belief which is vindicated in the fairy story ending to the film. Her wish that the school should be saved from a dreadful fate (being demolished to make way for a carpark for the neighbouring, newly built office block) is granted and so is her final prayer, that bitterness be erased from her heart, when Father O'Malley decides to ignore the doctor's advice and tell her that her unwelcome transfer away from school is not a consequence of their professional disagreement but is because she has tuberculosis. Ingrid Bergman attracted near ecstatic reviews for her performance in this fable:

> I am taking a chance early in the cinema season and have awarded my Oscar for 1946. It goes to Ingrid Bergman for magnificent acting in *The Bells of St Mary's* and it will have to be something really sensational to relieve her of the honour.[19]

> Bergman brings humanity, dignity and a delightful sense of humour to the role.[20]

> Yes, Ingrid Bergman is the loveliest woman on the screen. She is the sort of girl every man falls for, every girl wants to be like. For loveliness comes from the heart, and Ingrid acts from the heart, too.[21]

These reviews offer an indication of the uncomplicated satisfaction enjoyed by audiences in contemplating the spectacle of this beautiful, amusing and 'impractical' celibate woman 'full of vitality and stamina' selflessly dedicated to the care of others and thoroughly obedient to the dictates of her superiors.

It is interesting to note that the two most thoroughly satisfactory female characters, as far as reviewers were concerned, in all of the eighteen films under discussion here, were both women selflessly dedicated to ensuring the smooth and harmonious running of those institutions fundamental to society's future stability, the school and the family.

Mary in *Mary Poppins*

The mid-sixties film *Mary Poppins* opens with Mary, in an extreme long shot, seated on a distant cloud as the camera pans slowly across an idealised version of London's skyline, while the film's credits are shown. As the titles disappear the film cuts into a medium close-up of Mary Poppins and the audience is offered a brief but adequate visual summary of her character. She is sitting on a cloud with her carpet bag at one side and her parrot headed umbrella at the other, powdering her nose as she looks in a small compact mirror. She is neatly dressed in Edwardian costume. While she looks in the mirror we note that first her bag, then her umbrella are gradually slipping down into the (presumably) fluffy cloud. At the last moment and without altering her gaze she retrieves each item. This introduction informs the audience that we are in the Edwardian period; that Mary Poppins has unusual powers; that she is neat and careful of her appearance; that she is observant and reliable. The summary thus offered is expanded during the course of the subsequent narrative but we learn very little more about Mary: the film, despite its title, is not *about* her. She does, however, dominate a considerable proportion of screen time and is a consistent character within the parameters noted above. She is also, importantly, the first character to be seen on the screen. Mary's importance in the film lies in the fact that we are invited to understand subsequent characters by reference to our already established, albeit limited, knowledge of Mary herself. She is not affected by her contact with other inhabitants of the diegesis but offers a steady yardstick by which we, the audience, may measure the changes in other characters – principally of course in the central character George (David Tomlinson). In addition she is understood by other characters in different ways; the juxtaposition of these various understandings is the principal means through which the audience is invited to evaluate the moral and ethical themes of the film, and to subscribe to the preferred reading. The principal characters with whom Mary interacts are George Banks, her employer; Jane and Michael, her charges; and Bert the sometime chimney sweep, sometime narrator, the representative of indigenous 'Londoners'.

Mary's initial interview with George offers a delightful contrast, for the audience, between the subservient women of the Banks' household and Mary, in her refusal to recognise his superiority. Her arrival throws him into a confusion which is in marked contrast with the self-satisfied control of the world articulated in his songs 'How pleasant is the life I lead' and 'A British Nanny must be a general'. This confusion reiterates the central enigma of the narrative which concerns their differing philosophies of education.

The connection between Mary and Bert (Dick van Dyke) is the most ambiguous and inconsistent element in the film. In fact, just as Bert himself 'stands for', that is to say he signifies a whole gallery of London characters, so the relationship between Bert and Mary is made to signify many different models. The underlying connection between them is that they are both the agents of the story – they control and direct both the audience and the protagonists and step in and out of the various levels of reality proposed within the diegesis as well as occasionally stepping outside the diegesis altogether as in Bert's direct address to the audience. Mary, it seems, is all things to all people. She makes things happen, her presence acts as a catalyst for all sorts of pleasurable developments, and she is responsible for the major change in George's view of the world which will ensure his family's future happiness. She is dependable, reliable (to the children, to Bert); she is subversive, uncontrollable (to George); she has no desires of her own. While we may enjoy the examples she offers we must also acknowledge that, above all, she is a fiction. This crucial aspect of her character is indicated in the nursery sequence when, preparing to take the children out, Mary looks in the mirror. Mary and her mirror image sing 'A Spoonful of Sugar' in duet and, as the 'real' Mary leaves the frame the camera stays on the reflected Mary. Mary doesn't exist at all; her appeal, like that of the fairy godmother or the lucky sweep in the myths described by Lévi Strauss,[22] is that she is the embodiment of desires about the relations between people, rather than being the embodiment of a potential individual. Like Ingrid Bergman's representation of the dedicated pedagogue in the mid-forties, Julie Andrew's film debut in *Mary Poppins* attracted fulsome praise, even from those who had criticisms to make of the film as a whole.

Julie Andrews floats into stardom on an impeccable performance.[23]

Julie Andrews is perfect in the role . . . Disney's Fair Lady has a pure sincerity that no amount of sweetness can cloy.[24]

She is quite enchanting: unspectacularly pretty with a charming singing voice.[25]

She is a very dream of a nanny, a pretty grown up doll in Edwardian costume and sensible shoes.[26]

Julie Andrews glows like a tree full of twinkling stars . . . sings like a lark.[27]

Both the role and her performance were celebrated – clearly reviewers and, we may assume, the audiences who flocked to see the film, found the spectacle of the 'pretty grown-up doll' Julie Andrews selflessly dedicated to the well being of others a profoundly engaging one, a representation of precisely the kind of female behaviour generally thought to be most appropriate. Her subversion of the patriarch George Banks, after all, did not challenge his ultimate authority but rather re-negotiated his executive methods, bringing him into line with the consensual views of the sixties. As the *Financial Times* reviewer put it (18 December 64) Mary Poppins 'opens the parents eyes to their children . . . leaving a wiser and more loving family behind her'. At the end of the film Mary, shutting the door of no. 17, Cherry Tree Lane behind her, looks across to the park where the 'wiser and more loving family' are flying their kite. Her parrot-headed umbrella, like the questioning child at the end of a story read aloud, articulates possible audience objections to this solitary ending:

> *Parrot*:   That's gratitude for you, didn't even say goodbye.
> *Mary*:   No, they didn't.
> *Parrot*:   You know, they think more of their father than they do of you.
> *Mary*:   That's as it should be.
> *Parrot*:   Don't you care?
> *Mary*:   Practically perfect people never permit sentiment to muddle their thinking.
> *Parrot*:   Is that so? Well I'll tell you one thing, Mary Poppins, you don't fool me a bit.

Nevertheless, the umbrella is opened and Mary flies away over the unexplained sunset, noticed only by Bert.

DEATH

The group of films from the mid-forties is remarkable not only for the unusually large number of central female characters but also for their suffering. Two of the six attempt suicide because of their unhappiness, Francesca in *The Seventh Veil* and Laura in *Brief Encounter*, and three die at the end of their films. Barbara's death at the close of *The Wicked Lady* is offered, according to the preferred reading, as thoroughly deserved, but both Diana in *Piccadilly Incident* and Maddalena in *Madonna of the Seven Moons* die 'tragically'. That is to say that though their deaths are inevitable, within the terms set up by the narrative, they are not 'deserved' in the sense that Barbara's is. It is therefore interesting to note that both characters speak, from their deathbeds, words that suggest their own approval of this resolution; these words allow the audience,

through the tears induced by the tragedy, still to enjoy the satisfaction required of the narrative closure. Maddalena ambiguously
refers to her 'sins' in the deathbed absolution, though the audience
knows more about these than she herself does, having been privy
to the details of her dual existence, and Diana unambiguously
welcomes her own death as the solution to her husband's unwitting
bigamy.

Diana in *Piccadilly Incident*

The narrative of *Piccadilly Incident* takes the form of a long, chrono-
logical flashback interrupting the short courtroom scene which
opens and closes – frames, in effect – the narrative. Thus although
the final image of the film as a whole is the judge delivering his
verdict concerning the legitimacy of Joan and Alan's son, the final
image of the narrative is Diana's death in hospital, reunited with
Alan, after the fatal air raid. The story is overtly given as a tragedy
– as the lawyer informs us at the opening of the film 'this is an
unusual case, though unfortunately not unique'. Diana and Alan's
whirlwind romance is suggested as unexceptionable to the heightened perceptions of the disrupted wartime context, a suggestion
confirmed in the *Motion Picture Herald*'s nostalgic review:

> In the way we had those days the two young folks marry, indulge
> in an ecstatic two day honeymoon, whereafter Neagle is drafted
> to Singapore.[28]

Her responses and deportment are exemplary: she falls in love
with Alan but they undergo the marriage ceremony before com-
mitting themselves sexually; she obeys her service orders to go
overseas; she contributes to the morale and survival of the shipwrecked group and on her eventual return to the UK three years
later seeks to join her husband. She finds, however, his new wife
and their infant son: a close-up of the two women's faces as they
gaze at the infant in Joan's arms allows the audience plenty of time
to interpret Diana's expression when Joan, in passing, mentions
to her 'anonymous' guest that she and Alan have been married
for eighteen months. Implicitly Diana accepts Joan's greater claim
to Alan: she herself may have been first, we can almost see her
thinking, but what is two weeks compared to eighteen months

and a son? She continues to conceal her identity from Joan and when she finds Alan himself pretends that their marriage was of no consequence and suggests that he divorce her. Neither the institution of marriage nor Alan himself, however, is to be taken so lightly and in order for Alan's marriage to Joan to have any future the narrative requires the intervention of chance. This comes in the form of an air raid in which Diana is fatally wounded. Thus she and Alan can be reunited safely, if momentarily, before she dies, and Alan and Joan's marriage can be sustained. In other words she is required to uphold the institution of marriage by validating, if retrospectively, the widowerhood which enabled Alan's second marriage. As if that wasn't enough Diana, with her dying breath, not only accepts her death but also congratulates Alan on his son and asks for reassurance that he is making his new wife happy:

> I'm happy to go, Alan.
> It's so much easier than any other way.
> Your baby's so sweet, like you.
> Oh Alan, you are making her happy?
> Kiss me, darling.

No matter what the cost, a good woman will sustain the institutional structures: Diana upholds the legal order by enabling, through her death, the bigamous marriage of Alan and Joan to be legitimated; she obeys the military order by going overseas to serve her country; and she sustains the family by ensuring, through her death, the stable future of Alan's son and, by implication, of the Pearson 'line'.

Maddalena in *Madonna of the Seven Moons*

The final image of Maddalena/Rosanna in *Madonna of the Seven Moons* is of her corpse with the ivory cross placed on her breast by her husband Giuseppe and the red rose beside it, a last offering from her lover Nino. These two objects are clearly intended to symbolise and summarise the tragic fracture of her existence which resulted in her untimely death. The audience has been offered, by means of the opening flashback scene and through the voice of the doctor, an explanation for her 'split' personality. The film's claim to verisimilitude rests not only on the substance of the text but also on a written preamble which claims that the ensuing ficticious events are based on fact and that there was indeed a 'real' Maddalena. Looked at dispassionately her death may be understood both as the ultimate climax of her tragedy, begun by her rape when still a schoolgirl, and as a punishment for her betrayal of her marriage. She betrayed her marriage by periodically abandoning her husband, by living with another man and, though the film is somewhat reticent on this point, by bearing another man's child as her husband's. Close attention to the inscriptions in the prayerbook, the device used to link the flashback to the main action of the film, reveals a mere eight months between the birth of her daughter Angela and her marriage to Giuseppe, a marriage which closely followed her rape by the peasant in the woods.[29] It can also be argued that the plot is irreconcilable without her death. In all cases, however, it is also clear that she cannot be held responsible for her actions, yet must still be punished. Hence the device of mistaken identity is used to represent the intervention of chance. The concept of chance in this film, as in many others, functions like a quasi divine retribution: an implicit 'day of judgement' which is more persuasive than the theatrical *deus ex machina* since its logic is embedded in the events and value structures of the preceding narrative. In detail, Maddalena dies because, as Rosanna, she mistook Sandro for her lover Nino: seeing him with an unknown woman she jealously stabbed him. Before he died Sandro threw a knife at her and she dies, later, from this wound. But the chance mistake also saved Angela who is the unknown woman: unknown because she comes from Maddalena's and not Rosanna's world. Thus Angela, the modern girl, the 'future', is saved and Maddalena/Rosanna, the old and troubled 'past' is sacrificed. The message of the cross and the rose, then, would seem to be that in order to survive women must reconcile these opposing forces.

What are these forces? The cross symbolises devotion to the church, culture, history, the sanctity of marriage, the law of the father and so on; the rose symbolises nature, the eternal present, sensuality and desire. Two models of woman-as-sign are operative here: the woman as an essential social bond, the primary object of exchange between men validating the structures of society; and woman as 'the other', forever outside language and the social order, powerful and threatening to this order precisely because of its irrelevance to her. As Rosanna said 'I live in the present, the past and the future mean nothing to me'. Maddalena/Rosanna had to die because she failed to confine her sexuality within the institution of marriage and she failed to maintain the social institution of the family. She failed, as a woman. This is the preferred reading implicit in the textual structure, but the film's many ambiguities and inconsistencies make it particularly susceptible to alternative readings, as is frequently the case with films which attempt to engage with the contradictions between woman-as-sign and 'real' women. As the *Kinematograph Weekly* reviewer put it 'the story wants a little swallowing':

> Phyllis Calvert plays the dual role of religious yet inhibited Maddalena and wild hot-blooded Rosanna, but her performance is sound rather than inspired . . . The story wants a little swallowing. In the first place it is hard to imagine one being containing two such vastly different personalities, and in the second, it is equally difficult to believe a person of position could disappear so easily . . . With all its novelettish fundamentals, it is a compelling woman's picture.[30]

The 'novelettish' plot was thought to be 'unconvincing', 'crude' and, simply, 'bad':

> Persons of critical standard may look upon the whole endeavour as a slightly phoney adventure. They simply won't be convinced of the odd happenings.[31]

> Artistic settings beautifully photographed are a pleasing feature of this lavish production, but they cannot disguise the crude melodramatics of the story.[32]

> Within a week the best and worst English film of many months have made their appearance. *Western Approaches* brought home to us how far we have advanced in film making since the war; with *Madonna of the Seven Moons* we slip back almost as far as it is possible to slip. It is notably bad.[33]

Running through all this criticism is the thinly veiled disgust of an aesthetics based in realism for the unashamed melodrama of the film. On the whole this was recognised and the film consequently banished to the despised realms of the 'weepy', a category reserved not for 'persons of a critical standard' but for the evidently alternative category 'masses of women' as the *Motion Picture Herald* review goes on to suggest:

But the picture will have an undoubted appeal to masses of women in Britain's industrial towns, as was clearly evidenced by its reception on the opening night.[34]

The distaste for the film evident among many contemporary reviewers not only shows the pervasiveness of a realist asthetic but also, implicitly, reveals the importance attached to the radical contradictions in the definition of 'woman' in the mid-forties, as well as the failure of the film's attempt to locate such contradictions in 'the past' and to offer the 'modern' Angela as evidence of a problem solved. At worst the reviewers simply characterised the film as embarassingly inept, at best they treated it with a kind of cynical scepticism, a refusal to accord it the 'serious' attention bestowed on films like *Brief Encounter* or *The Seventh Veil*.

It will, I feel, reassure intending visitors to this handsomely produced novelette to know that in spite of a drugging and backroom sequence, the matron's daughter, played by Patricia Roc, is still an honorable girl. So are they all, all honorable girls.[35]

The reviewer in the American publication *Time and Tide* seized on the chance to locate the film's melodrama within a specifically English tradition, perhaps in a kind of unspoken revenge for the habitual scorn expressed by British reviewers for the melodrama that they considered to be a typically American form of excess:

Whether this film is being religious or sensual it remains the purplest production English cinema has yet achieved. It's the sort of dream dreamed in the last century by a lonely governess sipping her cocoa over 'Jane Eyre'. See it anyway to delight your sense of the ridiculous and to feast your astonished eyes on some of the ugliest and most expensive sets ever contrived.[36]

Barbara in *The Wicked Lady*

British or American, the reviewers writing in the mid-forties gave melodramas a hard time, reserving their deepest scorn for pictures they felt were 'aimed at' female audiences. As we have seen this did nothing to diminish the popularity of such films at the box office, and it seems unlikely that the huge audiences implied by box office success in this period were entirely composed of women. This review from one of the national papers when the film *The Wicked Lady* was released in late 1945, is typical of the exasperated response of critics to the Gainsborough costume dramas:

> It is an artfully compounded bromide: the lines never aiming higher than the readership of *Mabel's Weekly*, the smutty quips and bedroom byplay, the Tottenham Court Road 'Restoration' costume and setting (on which I cannot trust myself to comment), with Margaret Lockwood, Patricia Roc, James Mason and Michael Rennie doing their turns with the embarrassed gravity and hesitant timing of participants in a family charade.[37]

Though the film came in for its share of critical opprobrium, the role played by Lockwood is one of the most celebrated of the period. The film is set entirely in the distant past of the seventeenth century, though it is the bourgeois morality of the latter part of the 1940s which is upheld in its preferred reading. Lockwood's character Barbara is constructed as a disruptive influence, her intervention in the Skelton household causing considerable suffering to the worthy couple Ralph and Caroline. As the narrative unfolds she goes from bad to worse so that her horrible and lonely death must be understood, in the preferred reading of the film, as the well-deserved retribution for her callous and amoral behaviour.

The Wicked Lady is unusual in having two central female characters: like the 'split' personality Maddalena/Rosanna each of the two represents an alternative conception of the term 'woman' as one of the crucial signifiers in patriarchal order. But whereas in *Madonna of the Seven Moons* the impossible co-existence of these alternatives in one body, as it were, necessitated not only the therapeutic destruction of 'the other' but also the tragic end of the necessary, bonding woman, in *The Wicked Lady* we have two separate 'bodies', Barbara and Caroline, so the film can have it both ways. The threatening 'other' personified by Barbara can be held responsible for her unacceptable behaviour, and the figure represented by Caroline, crucially important to the stability of patriarchal order in general and post-war reconstruction in particular, can be rewarded for her patience, loyalty and self-effacing devotion.

There are inevitably serious problems in this filmic construction – principal among them being that Barbara has so much more compelling a screen presence than Caroline. Many reviewers noted this anomaly in the film's 'message' and attempted to account for it in a variety of ways: the film elicited greater disagreements amongst the published responses than any other in the mid-forties group under discussion here. To a certain extent, of course, such disagreement can be accounted for by the different readerships to which the various publications addressed themselves. Hence the mass circulation national newspaper, the *Daily Sketch*, welcomed the film:

> Gainsborough have spread themselves on *The Wicked Lady* (Gaumont, Sunday), a gorgeously dressed and mounted, and admirably photographed piece about the days of Charles II.[38]

The left-wing *Tribune*, on the other hand clearly deplored its very existence:

> And yet only one of the four films in my mind is inept to the point of exasperation. This is *The Wicked Lady* . . . In short, if the future of the British film industry hangs, as some say, on the success of *The Wicked Lady*, then let us dispense with that future.[39]

Kinematograph Weekly, the trade paper addressed to distributors and cinema managers, was rather more ambiguous:

> The staging is more convincing than the hearty and salutary tale, but, although its talk is ocassionally cheap, its twists novelet-tish and its moral obvious, it has glamour, rousing action and considerable feminine appeal . . . It does not overestimate the intelligence of the Kinema-going public. Its appeal to the Dick Turpin in every woman – and youngster – alone guarantees its commercial success.[40]

It was the character of Barbara, however, that elicited the most specific comments. *Today's Cinema*, a British trade magazine, was admiring:

> Not within our recollection has the screen given us so choice a specimen of feminine malignity as does this Gainsborough picture . . . Such happenings are larger than life, of course, but they are presented with such a surge and sweep of realistic byplay that they should be keenly relished by the populace.[41]

The American trade publication *Motion Picture Herald* was rather more sceptical:

> Fortunately, maybe, for her myriad admirers none can believe that Miss Lockwood's winsome charms, that demure blush which inevitably seems to suffuse her cheeks, might ever be associated with the very odd behaviour she is called upon herein to affect. Fortunately, on the other hand, for such verisimilitude as the film possesses, Mr James Mason is around to play the highwayman.[42]

The final image of Barbara, often recalled as the final image of the film, which it is not, is one of the most memorable images from the popular cinema of this period. It is a high angle long shot through the opened centre of a window: the rectangular grid of the mullions and panes evoking the bars of a prison. From this vantage point we see the dying Barbara, framed in the open centre of the window and slumped to the floor with her back to the window as she fell, trying in vain to follow her beloved Kit (Michael Rennie) who, in the preceding shot, had recoiled in horror from her deathbed confessions. In contrast the final image of Caroline, which *is* the last in the film, is a long shot, similar to that with which the narrative opened, of her and Ralph riding together into frame through the pastoral landscape. Thus Barbara is alone, enclosed, dying; Caroline is with her lover, in the open, moving towards the centre of things. This shot follows a medium close-up of the pair as Ralph tells her:

> When she came a dark shadow crept over our lives. Now she has gone we shall know laughter and happiness again, and love.

Thus in retrosect we can perceive the narrative of Barbara as inserted into the narrative of Caroline, a nuance expressed in the first image of Barbara superimposed between the couple Ralph and Caroline. Barbara, then, is in the end merely an interesting digression in Caroline's story – but one so interesting that she dominates most of the narrative. Caroline embodies the virtues of all our 'heroines' it seems, rolled into one: she is devout like Maddalena, self-effacing like Diana and capable of controlling her own desires just as well as Laura in *Brief Encounter*, as her remark to Ralph testifies: 'The things we stand for are more important than us'. She is also the only one of all the central female characters to be rewarded with an unequivocally happy ending. Barbara, on the other hand, is the only really villainous character: utterly amoral and scornful of social institutions and conventions she wants wealth, power and attention. Nothing is sacred to her – even her mother's brooch is staked, and lost, in a card game and the villains' code of honour by which her highwayman lover, Captain Jerry Jackson (James Mason), operates has no meaning or value for her. She is thus outside all the social codes (she is 'other') and her punishment is death. The device of mistaken identity is wielded here to ensure a fitting retribution. Barbara, in her highwayman's guise, holds up the coach in which she expects to find Ralph alone, intending to kill him so that she may marry Kit. However Kit himself is aboard the coach and takes advantage of her momentary hesitation to take aim and fire, unaware of course that the assailant is in fact Barbara. Not only does she die violently, she dies at the hands of the man she loves. When later, on her deathbed, she tells him the truth about herself he abandons her and she dies alone.

Not only is the threatening 'other' thus conveniently disposed of but she is also to be held entirely responsible for her transgressions. Though Barbara personifies one of the recurrent patriarchal signifiers it is not patriarchy which is implicated in her downfall, in this way the contradictions implicit for women in patriarchally determined language and, hence, social codes, are displaced from the institution itself onto the single figure of one aberrant woman.

THE SIGNIFICANCE OF ENDINGS

It is clear from the foregoing discussion that the range of narrative closures deployed to resolve female characters is limited. It is moreover invariably related more to gender, to the fact of 'being' a woman, than it is to the particular contours of each diegesis. Thus, whether we are considering a tale set in seventeenth century UK or nineteenth century USA, in Edwardian London or contemporary America, it seems that the denouement, for female characters, must always turn on the degree to which they can be shown to have conformed to specific meanings of the signifier 'woman' in patriarchal discourse. Broadly this implies either the summary 'woman = other', or 'woman = servitor'. Either women maintain, through the subjugation of their own interests, the fabric of patriarchal order (or they accept this maintenance as being in their own interests which, in terms of gender politics, comes to the same thing) – they put society's needs and well-being before their own or they identify the two – or, if they must express their inner selves, their own desires, they are relegated to the realm of the dangerous since they threaten the dominant order simply by virtue of their refusal to put it first.

Now it is of course a commonplace that films such as those we are discussing here are fictions: entering the cinema the audience gladly suspends disbelief and prepares to be entertained by spectacle and story, age old social pleasures. It is possible to take pleasure in the fiction without swallowing every suggestion it makes about what the world is like. Yet the means employed in constructing filmic fictions – moving images often drawn from places and events in the 'real' world combined with a linguistic form common to both players and spectators – are powerful ones whose effects are strengthened the closer they suggest correspondence with the lived reality of the world outside the cinema. This commonplace informs much film criticism which often, in its dependence on a realist code of aesthetics, evaluates films by measuring them against lived reality. It also informs most of the legislative attempts to control cinematic representations such as, on the one hand, censorship of various kinds, and on the other hand the trade regulations by which the industry is organised.

In the modern period, certainly since the counter-reformation when the term 'propaganda'[43] described positively the activities of the catholic church in its attempts to control the multiplicity of non-conformist, breakaway religious groupings, the notion that 'cultural' forms of various kinds are instrumental in ensuring conformity with prescribed patterns of thought and behaviour has been universally subscribed to. Examples abound in both the international and the domestic spheres from the times of the renaissance in Italy, the Tudor dynasty in Britain or the first European colonists of the Americas.

In any social group the dominant means of exchanging ideas are central to individuals' recognition of their own place in the order of things. In mass society the forms loosely grouped together under the catch-all phrase 'popular culture' are an important way, not the only way but a central one, of both representing and maintaining consensual views. Thus, though representations which could be considered subversive of the dominant order may appear, even frequently, in the texts and objects of popular culture, this by no

...means implies their dissemination as models. On the contrary, it is necessary for the dominant group, in the struggle to maintain its hegemony, to demonstrate its ability to control potentially subversive elements. In the contemporary patriarchal society of western capitalist democracies the politics of gender is one locus of hegemonic struggle. This is an uncontentious truism borne out by the histories of the suffrage movements, by the gradual acceptance of such principles as equality in property owning rights or equality of pay in employment and by the ubiquitous celebration of 'firsts' – the first woman to fly the Atlantic, the first woman in space, the first woman cabinet member, congress delegate, national leader and so on. Hence the representation of women in the dominant form of popular culture in the post-war period, cinema, is of particular interest for the way it reveals details of the negotiations between men and women, between the dominant and the dominated, over their roles in and expectations of contemporary society. Cinema, between 1945 and the late 1950s when audiences had declined so much that it could no longer be regarded as a dominant cultural form, showed men and women their places in the order of things, in the post-war social order.

For female protagonists in the struggle between the genders over the meanings of 'woman' cinematic representations are clearly of vital concern. Hence the celebration of actors routinely associated with the performance of strong and assertive fictional characters, such as Bette Davis, Joan Crawford and, to a lesser extent in UK of the forties, Margaret Lockwood. But though we may take pleasure in Bette Davis as Margot in *All About Eve* (Mankiewicz 1950), or in Joan Crawford as Mildred in *Mildred Pierce* (Curtiz 1945), or in Margaret Lockwood's Barbara we must also consider whether the dominant order succeeded in exerting its control over these fictional figures. In the narrative resolution the consequences of female assertiveness or compliancy are fixed and the meanings of 'woman' functional to the dominant order are re-instated. Bette Davis' speech as Margot is one which can stand for the successful re-imposition of patriarchal dominance, following the bitter struggles which, as we have seen, resulted in the misery or death of so many forties heroines:

> One career all females have in common, whether we like it or not, is being a woman. Sooner or later we've got to work at it no matter how many other careers we've had, or want, And in

the last analysis nothing's any good unless you can look up just before dinner, or turn around in bed, there he is. Without that you're not a woman. You're something with a French provincial office or a book full of clippings, but you're not a woman.

And the dearth of such heroines in the top box office films of the next fifteen years is further evidence of this success.

Two film genres, above all the rest, are celebrated for their habitual foregrounding of female characters – these are film noir and melodrama. The strong women of film noir have been the subject of numerous studies by recent film theorists and historians and it is true that they are of interest for the ambiguity of their female characterisations as well as for the often unwitting foregrounding of the dictats of patriarchy in their narrative resolutions. These strong women, however, are always and only offered as threatening figures whose interventions into plot events are, if not clearly motivated by evil intent, certainly disruptive. The narrative closure must entail either their destruction or their recoupment, that is to say their transformation into compliant figures: often the latter is followed by the former, in which case the character can be understood as tragically misled rather than wilfully perverse. They are typically represented through film noir's characteristically nocturnal, shadowy *mise-en-scène*; they are usually constructed as alluring, provocative figures whose apparent sexual promise ensnares the hero rather like Circe or the sirens of Greek myth.

Melodramas, on the other hand, are characterised by the even clarity of full sunlight and typically concern intrigues and power struggles within the family unit, often conceived rather broadly and acting as a metaphor for society in general. The distinguishing feature of melodramas, also the subject of much recent attention on the part of film historians, is the pivotal position occupied by female characters in the dynamics of the plot. But we are not dealing with 'woman as other' here, rather with patriarchy's preferred model, the compliant woman: the conflicts and contradictions that arise from her attempts to comply are, in brief, the substance of the narrative. Such films, despite their frequent popularity at the box office during the forties and fifties, were routinely denigrated by contemporary reviewers precisely *because* of the centrality of female characters: they were dismissed with such epithets as 'woman's picture' or 'weepy'.

In both cases, film noir and the melodrama, we should note that the familiar designation of 'woman' as *either* 'other' hence subversive and threatening *or* 'pivotal' hence compliant and self- sacrificing underlies the resolution of the narratives. Frequently the substance of the plot entails a female character's passage from one of these designations to the other – the film *shows* what patriarchy expects. This is particularly true of the melodrama, the genre *par excellence* conventionally understood to be 'addressed to' a female audience. It is precisely in such revelations that an understanding of gender politics from a woman's point of view may begin – hence the interest for female readers (and contemporary feminist theorists and historians) in such films. Nevertheless it is a complex task to unravel the polemics of hegemonic struggle from the satisfaction manufactured through film form's processes of giving and withholding information, posing and answering questions and in this way positioning the audience so that they are most likely to subscribe to the film's preferred reading.

6

The Film Audience and the Female Reader

READERS AND THE AUDIENCE

It is a truism to assert the synonymity of readers and the audience, since the latter necessarily comprises the former, yet the important distinction between the two terms is often elided in such an assertion. In general when 'the audience' is invoked we are engaged in a consideration of the wider social field in which popular cinema, amongst other cultural forms, is situated, whereas if our attention is directed to the 'the reader(s)' of the (film) text we may expect discussion to focus on the detailed workings of the text in respect of its apparent address to the individual reader.

However, though the object of these discussions, readers' and audience's understandings of popular cinema, is the same, in practice the two discussions tend to lead in quite different directions: it is often difficult to keep them in mind simultaneously despite their interdependence.

The Audience

When we speak of the cinema audience, certainly during the period following the Second World War when cinema admissions reached their peak, we are talking of large numbers of people occupying darkened auditoria in cinemas up and down the country. This was the dominant form of mass entertainment: cinema-going for many was a routine pleasure, a social activity punctuating with greater or lesser frequency the other routines of work, domestic responsibilities and family gatherings. At the beginning of the period going to the cinema was for many the only available form of entertainment; by the mid-sixties, as we have seen, it was one form amongst many. We must therefore consider not only the fragmentation of the cinema audience into specialised groupings with particular tastes and loyalties – a fragmentation mirrored in the move to break up the large cinemas themselves into multiscreen facilities capable of attracting these different audience groupings at the same time – but also that the cinema audience as a whole was, by this time, a 'specialised' audience amongst other audiences or spectatorial groups.

This process took place gradually between 1945 and 1965, gaining momentum during the latter part of the fifties as television ownership increased and the broadcasting network spread throughout Britain. Thinking of the period as a whole, and of the 'cinema audience' as an identifiable part of the population despite the qualifications noted above, we may note the changes in audience tastes evident in the characteristic narrative themes of the top box office hits and consider the implications of these changing themes as 'markers' of the generalised pre-occupations of the day. We should remind ourselves that it is audience choices, by definition, that generate the box office hit so sought after by the producers and distributors; the corollary is that it is the mass audience to whom the attendant discourses such as publicity, fanzines and reviews are addressed – albeit in a variety of different groupings which cut across, intersect the mass audience in its entirety.

So the audience is a practical fact: we might say the *raison d'être* of the commercial cinema, but it is also a theoretical problem since we are always, inevitably, talking about a probable audience, a putative audience, a statistically predictable audience. The elusiveness of the actual audience leads us to deal with the (arguably) more controllable concept of the individual reader when we wish to consider the reading activity of 'the audience'.

The Readers

Perhaps if we attend to the activity of individual readers we may get closer to understanding the audience, composed as it is of large numbers of individual readers whose proximity to each other in the darkened auditorium is an element of the 'conditions of viewing'. What does the reader do? What is this 'activity' summarised by such phrases as 'reading the text' or 'producing meanings'? A variety of interactive processes are at work, and these processes are each the proper subject of differing theoretical frameworks, differing academic disciplines: hence the notorious difficulties inherent in conceptualising the reading process satisfactorily. Confronted by the elements of performance, *mise-en-scène* and narrative united on the cinema screen the reader or spectator attempts to make sense of the totality and to derive pleasure from the endeavour. A sociological account of the reader's endeavours would draw on the references she or he makes to extra-diegetic experiences, highlighting his or her conscious evaluations of the text's degree of verisimilitude measured by the yardstick of these experiences and thus privileging the empiricist basis of the realist aesthetic. A semiotic analysis of the reader's task, while still emphasising the conscious activity of the alert reader, would accord greater importance to the intra-diegetic relations of the multiplicity of signs constituting the text, distancing itself from the simpler equation between the sign and its referent which characterises a sociologically based perception of verisimilitude. A psychoanalytical account of spectatorial activity, in contrast to both of these, would attend to the unconscious processes of the reader's mind, drawing on a variety of propositions about the individual's formative apprehension of the relation between him/herself and language, culture, authority and so on in their original positioning of the individual as a social subject. In addition such an account would invoke the mechanics of the subjective experience of desire in explicating the various and often contradictory forms of pleasure (voyeurist, fetishist, exhibitionist) yielded by the text.

The problem with an exclusively sociological framework is that it fails to account adequately for the psychic mechanisms of individual readers, as well as ignoring the epistemological plurality of the world outside the cinema. The referent of any sign may itself be unfixed, its significance the subject of struggle. The problem with both the semiotic and the psychoanalytical models of 'reading' is that, in their detailed and labyrinthine complexities they tend to slide into a consideration of the ideal reader implicit in the construction of each text, ignoring in the process the unknown and possibly unknowable attributes of each or any real reader, the audience member sitting in the darkened auditorium. Theoretical accounts of the reading process, on the whole, are concerned with ideal rather than real readers.

The Differentiated Audience

If we want to consider both the activities of real readers confronted with particular film texts, and the contours of the mass audience which they collectively form, whose tastes changed so markedly during the twenty-year period chronicled here, we must confront the notion of the differentiated audience. The term 'audience' refers, we note again, to large numbers of discrete individuals differentiated from each other by age, gender, class, race, nationality and, importantly, by their own experience both of cinema-going and of the various life events from which both films and stories draw their narratives.

For our purposes it is the differentiation of the audience by gender which is of interest, though we should keep in mind that this is merely one among many factors likely to contribute to the variety of meanings produced from any given film text. The films we have been discussing here were the outstanding box office successes of their day. This means that, relative to all the films produced and distributed within the same two-year period, these films attracted exceptionally large audiences. Though the composition of a particular audience for a particular performance may have varied, in the absence of satisfactory evidence we may also assume that, overall, the gender balance of all the audiences for all the performances of all the films bears some resemblance to national demographic profiles in the same period. Thus we can assume that the representations of women in these films were 'read' by mixed gender audiences to whom the meanings of such representations were likely to provoke radically different experiential references depending on the sex of the reader.

The relative importance of the elements of film form – *mise-en-scène*, performance, editing – which together construct the narrative, differs in explications of the reading process according to which model of the text:reader interface informs the account. Thus a sociologically based account would privilege *mise-en-scène* and performance in its perception of the narrative; the semiotic model would pay greater attention to such formal elements as camera angles, lighting and cutting in their ordering of both *mise-en-scène* and performance; and an account drawing on the insights of psychoanalytic theory, while referring to all these elements, would accord more importance to the psychic processes of each reader and the ways in which these might be invoked by the sequence of images and events constituting the diegesis.

Though current theorisations of the reading process may throw some light on these differences they cannot, on their own, adequately account for the variety of meanings produced by an heterogeneous audience. Bearing this in mind we will now consider a little more closely the details of some theoretical models: firstly those which take the individual reader as their starting point, and secondly those which begin by considering larger spectatorial groupings.

THEORIES OF READING

Leaving aside the problematics of the mass audience for the moment, it will be useful to our speculations about female readers' possible responses to their celluloid sisters to consider in rather more detail some current propositions about spectatorial processes. The two main issues here are, firstly, the status of the text itself and secondly the strategies which readers/spectators do or might employ in formulating their understandings of the text.

The Status of the Text

One way of dealing with the problem of conceptualising the relation between the text and its putative readers is to 'discover' the reader in the evident textual address: that is to say the almost insuperable difficulties of speaking with any assurance about actual readers are overcome by recourse to the notion of the 'ideal reader'. This has the great advantage of allowing extremely detailed attention to the internal mechanics of the text, to the relations between performance, *mise-en-scène*, and narrative authority in the unfolding of the diegesis. By concentrating entirely on the reader thus 'imagined' in the textual construction we can not only evaluate the internal consistency of the film's fictional world but also we can, apparently, draw conclusions about the moral, ethical and indeed the epistemological features of this world. By accepting the reader as theoretically embedded in the text it is possible to conceive of the duality 'text and reader' as a united whole – a convenience which allows the illusion, at least, of thorough and complete study of the text's meaning.

But this ideal, imaginary reader is a rarified creature, not to be encountered in the cinema queue or the crowded auditorium. A model of the cinema audience which depends on such a conception of the readers constituting the audience is likely to slip into a position where, the text itself being the sole arbiter of its meanings, the audience is understood to be entirely and perfectly passive in its reception of textual meaning. Alternative readings, unless they are already present within the textual structure, in which case they must be understood to be the product of an ideological contradiction within the text itself rather than the product of readerly activity, are theoretically impossible because the independence of the readers from the text is denied. An example of this problem inherent in the semiotic model is that of a structural analysis whereby an oppositional reading of a film text is generated through attention to the absences in the text.[1]. But the 'reading' generated here is still a product of the text, whereas 'readings' must always be understood to be the product of the momentary and always shifting point of contact between the reader(s) and the text. Thus in the semiotic model the real reader still remains a *tabula rasa* with no past and no future on which each text encountered can freshly inscribe its meanings – with or without their internal contradictions.

The intriguing ambiguities and uncertainties with which, as we have seen, many popular film texts are studded can offer no evidence of social or ideological struggle based on the materiality of the text, within such a framework. Where ambiguities are unarguably present they cannot be conceived of as invitations to the reader but must simply be understood as a failure in the text, an incoherence of the diegesis. Such an incoherence may indeed be significant, indicative of contemporary ideological struggles, but it remains a function of the text alone and as such offers insights into the processes of production rather than the process of consumption we call 'reading'.

A different model for the study of film draws on the pervasive aesthetics of realism with their fundamental dependence on an empiricist epistemology. This model accords less importance to the text, since filmic constructions are evaluated by reference to extra-diegetic realities and judged to be more or less 'truthful' depending on the degree to which they deliver convincing representations of the world inhabited by the readers, outside the text. Here the context of cinematic constructions finds a place in the relation between the film and the readers. At first sight this might seem to be a more satisfactory way of understanding this relation but on closer consideration we find a kind of leapfrog from the film to the extra-cinematic world in which the actual spectators of the film, the audiences, are ignored: this happens because the extra-cinematic world is falsely presented as an homogenous and

stable totality. Textual ambiguities are still understood as failures
– in terms now not of the internal coherence of the film text but of
the film's failure to reproduce the assumed coherence of the 'real'
world outside the cinema. Further, according to this model not only
ambiguous texts but also entire genres such as the melodrama and
the musical tend to be dismissed, to be deemed unworthy of any
'serious' consideration because of their deliberate distancing from
the supposedly homogenous 'real' world. Here again the independence of the reader is denied. In its place the critic or historian
substitutes his/her (invariably his) authoritative reading of reality;
in the period we have been considering this authoritative reading
is almost always one which subscribes to, thus serves to maintain,
the dominant social discourse. An empiricist epistemology must by
definition always claim the fixed and palpable materiality of the
real, including social relations, thus is always liable to confirm
the status quo through naming deviations from it as inadequate,
irrelevant or, simply, meaningless.

Where these two models of the film-reader relation converge
is in their denial of the independent, discrete social experience
of individual readers. The first substitutes an imaginary reader
perceived within the text, the second usurps the real readers'
experiential histories by claiming the right to sole interpretation
of extra-cinematic experience. Thus both demean the individual
reader's own activity in respect of the text, by implicitly asserting
the passivity of the audience. For our purposes, that is an exploration of the relation of female readers and representations of women
in popular cinema, this is a particularly grave matter since, in a
patriarchal society, both the concept of the imaginary reader and
the dominant interpretation of extra-cinematic reality will privilege
male understandings rather than female ones, thus contributing to
the hegemony of the masculine.

Spectatorial Strategies

In recognition of this problem for women in gender politics many
feminist theoreticians have paid close attention to the ways in which
individual readers, particularly though not exclusively female readers, actually make sense out of the filmic representations typically
offered through the institutions of cinema. This has entailed consideration of the early psychic formation of the unconscious subject,
the acquisition of language and its role in the social positioning of

the conscious subject, and, importantly for discussion of what is generally understood to be 'entertainment', substantial examination of the mechanics of pleasure and the associated concept of desire.

In contrast to the two models of the reader outlined above, this model concentrates on the psychic activities of the individual, proposing a variety of spectatorial strategies which might be employed by the reader in the dual processes of deriving pleasure and producing meaning from the text. The emphases here tend to be on the unconscious operations of the reader's mind and the insights of psychoanalytic theory have been called on and variously adapted to elucidate these processes. Given the basis of this work in feminist scholarship it is not surprising to find that the central concern is with the female reader and the strategies she might employ to derive pleasure from texts that invariably offer patriarchally determined representations of women.

There are problems associated with this model of the reader too, principally associated with the marginalising of the subject's conscious experience and personal history: the psychic mechanisms of the individual, illuminating though these certainly are, are foregrounded at the expense of the experiential trajectory of discrete individuals. Though all women share the fact of being 'not-men' they do not consequently share equally in the experiential consequences implicit in the status 'Woman': the differentiation of the audience, as we have noted, extending beyond the obvious one of gender difference. However many of the psychic mechanisms described in feminist accounts of the spectatorial process are most useful in conceptualising the heterogenous activity of the audience. Chief among these are the related concepts of 'identification' and 'disavowal'.

The idea of 'identification' and its associated terms 'sympathy', 'empathy', 'imitation', and 'projection', has been central to most discussion of spectatorial activity, particularly in attempts to account for the reader's experience of pleasure and desire. Though these are not necessarily problematic concepts when we are thinking about an imaginary reader since she or he can also be assumed to conform to psychoanalytic theory's propositions about individual psychic formation, for a real female reader there *are* problems. Either she identifies with a female character, sharing in the course of the identification the patriarchally determined resolution of the narrative or, as Laura Mulvey has suggested may sometimes be the case, she identifies with a male protagonist, suspending temporarily her own, feminine, subjectivity. In her important article 'Visual Pleasure and Narrative Cinema' (1975) which, as she has more recently written 'has taken on a life of its own',[2] Mulvey proposed that the spectator position, in relation to classical narrative films such as those we have been discussing here, was inevitably a masculine one; that to consume the spectacle, to engage with the narrative, the female spectator must identify with the male protagonist. This is a debateable proposition and one which, subsequently, she herself has qualified considerably. Most recently[3] she has used it to demonstrate the extreme dificulties of any adequate theorisation of the spectator position, taking this as further evidence of the intangibility of women's position outside not only the dominant discourses but even of the language possible within a patriarchal order. It is for this reason that none of the theoretical models outlined here can, on its own, offer an acceptable account of the ideological struggle which must be central to female readers' perceptions of an ultimately repressive representation of women.

Insofar as the process of identification operates across differentiated spectator positions, then, the female spectator must 'oscillate between a feminine and a masculine position', as Doane characterises it.[4] Within psychoanalytic theory there is a further refinement of the concept of identification – that of 'identification with the aggressor'. This is a

Defence mechanism . . . : faced with an external threat (typically represented by a criticism emanating from an authority), the subject identifies himself with his aggressor. He may do so either by appropriating the aggression itself, or else by physical or moral emulation of the aggressor, or again by adopting particular symbols of power by which the aggressor is designated . . . [5]

It is an aspect of the psychic processes of identification which may well throw additional light on female spectatorial activity. Confronted with the spectacle of aggressive masculinity on screen the female spectator might identify with the male protagonist or the male narrational authority, such as the authoritative medical figures discussed by Doane[6] not only to share the pleasure of the protagonist's prowess, special qualities, superior knowledge and so on but also in order to defend herself against the extra-diegetic implications of such masculine aggression rather than to accept her own 'disempowering'.

'Disavowal' is, in psychoanalytic terms, another form of defence. Though this term, in Freudian discourse, refers to the concept of sexual difference, specifically the moment when the little boy first perceives the anatomical difference in the little girl's genitals, a difference which according to Freud, he reads as a castration and thence disavows, yet it is applicable by extension to the experience of the film spectator. As Jacqueline Rose puts it:

> while the spectator is more duped in the cinema than in any other art form, she or he is nonetheless aware of that process and is therefore strictly in a position which psychoanalysis would call one of disavowal. 'I know (that what I am seeing is not real) but (I will pretend whilst I am here that it is)'.[7]

This allows an opportunity, admittedly a fragile and tenuous one, to the female reader to both 'see' and 'not see', to 'know, but' what passes before her eyes on the cinema screen, to recognise her marginality or the conditions of her centrality to the social discourse represented before her *but* to refuse its interpretation in terms of her subjective experience outside the cinema.

The question of what the female spectator does with the multiple positions potentially available to her as a consequence of her look at the screen is an absorbing one: it is, for feminist spectators, a political matter. It is here that the politics of gender and ideology intersect the politics of gender and culture: as a consequence of this intersection popular cinema is, to borrow Teresa de Lauretis' phrase (*Technologies of Gender*, 1987), a technology of gender. The cinematic apparatus is one of the means by which the patriarchal definitions of gender are routinely regulated, even 'policed'. Her argument draws attention to two terms in the equation film/reader. Representations *constructed* by means of the technologies of cinema are *addressed* to the films' spectators. The second term, then, concerns spectatorship:

> the crucial notion is the concept of spectatorship, which feminist film theory has established as a gendered concept; that is to say, the ways in which each individual spectator is addressed by the film, the ways in which his/her identification is solicited and structured in the single film, are intimately and intentionally, if not usually explicitly, connected to the spectator's gender.[8]

Once we are enabled to regard 'spectatorship' as an inevitably gendered concept the crucial relationship between the film's address, the way in which it apparently attempts to position its readers, and the necessarily differing histories of the subjectivity of male and female readers, is revealed. Hence the references to psychoanalytic theory and other speculative accounts such as Foucault's *History of Sexuality* (1976) which propose functional relations between individual subjectivity, language and the discourses through which society is ordered. The special problem for the female spectator is that the dominant discourse, the language controlling and informing the representations on the screen, is a masculine one. And as de Lauretis points out, not only is the discourse which constructs cinematic representations male, but also

> sexuality, not only in the general and traditional discourse but in Foucault's as well, is construed not as gendered (as having a male form and a female form) but simply as male. Even when it is located, as it very often is, *in* the woman's body, sexuality is an attribute or property of the male.[9]

In this politicised intersection between gender, culture and ideology which certainly characterises the work of the feminist reader, if not of all female readers, there are several issues at stake. Not only patriarchal instruction about women's social functions, but also highly problematic assertions about the subjective experience of womanhood are routinely delivered in these popular fictions. Popular film tells us what women (must) do, how they (should) behave *and* what women are, but does so with a masculine voice. The issue is at its clearest in films which are, apparently, addressed specifically to women, the so-called 'woman's film'. Writing in detail about a group of such films made during the 1940s, Mary Ann Doane[10] suggests some of the positive strategies with which female readers might recognise and thence revise the representations of women offered in the texts:

> it is only through a disengagement of women from the roles and gestures of a naturalised femininity that traditional ways of conceptualising sexual difference can be overthrown. Mimicry as a political textual strategy makes it possible for the female spectator to understand that recognition is buttressed by misrecognition.[11]

In the woman's film, she argues, the signs of femininity are enacted by the female protagonist in such a way that it is possible to detach them from 'the natural' and recognise them as mythic constructs.

> In the woman's film, the process of re-mirroring reduces the mirror effect of the cinema, it demonstrates that these are poses, postures, tropes – in short, that we are being subjected to a discourse on femininity.[12]

In other words if, as female spectators/readers, we understand patriarchal structures and language represented on screen not in terms of the content of their instructions but rather in terms of the fact of an instruction, that is to say that in the course of our enjoyment, our pleasure in the cinematic spectacle, we also recognise that we are being 'instructed' it follows that through the readings we construct we may subvert the limiting definitions of women within which patriarchal order attempts to confine us. At the least, we may imagine such a subversion.

THEORIES OF THE AUDIENCE

The theoretical constructs summarised above are, however, simply theories. Audiences do not habitually draw on such constructs in their understanding of film texts any more than they do in recognising their gendered subjectivities. These theoretical propositions aim to elucidate the complex relation between texts and readers in order to uncover the workings of ideology in its relation to individual subjects. There are serious problems associated with these propositions, particularly in their application to the mass audience and to the historical audience, neither of which are susceptible to the clarification which can accompany the concept of the individual, probable but never actual, reader. A focus on the individual reader tends to ignore, if not to deny, interaction between audience members in the formation of their readings: attention to the interactions of actual audiences may throw some light on this interesting consequence of the practice, habitual in the cinema, of viewing *en masse*. The historical audience is even more difficult – we can never 'know' such a group but we can engage in conjecture about its activity using studies of more recent audiences as a basis. Contemporary scholars interested in the mass audience have tended to look at the audiences for television and for popular fiction since, following the decline in cinema audiences which we have noted, these are more properly representative of mass culture than popular film now is. Bearing this qualification in mind it is still of interest to consider such studies since they offer insights of a quite different order than those yielded by speculation about the psychic functions of the discrete individual. An understanding of the mass cinema audience requires attention to both forms of exploration. Within the relatively recent field of audience studies a variety of approaches to the tricky problem of defining both the audience(s) and the text(s) have been employed.[13] At one extreme a particular *text* is taken as the starting point for study of various audience groups and their responses whereas at the other extreme a discrete *audience* group is studied for its uses of a succession of different, though similar, texts.

These extremes are exemplified in the work of David Morley in the UK and Janice Radway in the USA. But both Morley, investigating the British television audience,[14] and Radway, exploring the reading activities of a specific group of women romance readers in the American mid-west,[15] assert the substantive link between the experiental world of the audience group and their recognition of the signifying systems particular to the form under discussion. Morley insists on the need to consider the socio-economic differentiation of audience groupings, while Radway's study attends to the conventional patriarchal ordering of female experience which is the uniform context of her group of respondents. What is interesting for our purposes, the common feature which we may claim is also likely to be characteristic of cinema audiences, is their concurrence in the notion that textual readings (of television or of romance fiction) operate simultaneously, in respect of dominant ideology, in contradictory ways.

> As ideologies arise in and mediate social practices, the 'texts' produced by television must be read in their social existence, as televisual texts but also as televisual texts drawing on existing social representations within a field of dominant and preferred ideological meanings. For this reason a concern with the level of social connotations must remain as a central part of the analysis.[16]

While the content of the televisual representation is important, it is also crucial to recognise the unfixed, negotiable meanings of its referents: a two way process of negotiating the meanings of the text accords more importance to the social experience of the audience than a focus on the text alone would allow. A similar process, though differently articulated, is at work with the romance readers.

> Because the [reading] process must necessarily draw more or less on the language she uses to refer to the real world, the fictional world created in reading bears an important relationship to the world the reader ordinarily inhabits. The activities of reading and world construction, then, carry meaning for the reader on a purely formal level in the sense that they repeat and reinforce or alter and criticise the nature of the world as the reader knows it.[17]

The reference to the experiential reality of the audience in its 'de-coding' of representations of an apparent (but possibly fictional, certainly reconstructed) reality tends to confirm the dominant discourse's naming and ordering of experiential reality. Yet at the same time an understanding of the meanings and consequences of experiential reality as oppressive or limiting to the audience group can also be extended, consolidated and even fortified through their ability to distance themselves from the representation because of their recognition that it is, indeed, a representation.

> I want to argue . . . that by participating in a fantasy that they are willing to admit is unrealistic in some ways, the Smithton women are permitting themselves the luxury of self-indulgence while simultaneously providing themselves with the opportunity to experience the kind of care and attention they commonly give to others. Although the experience *is* vicarious, the pleasure it induces is nonetheless real.[18]

Here is another version of 'I know, but'; this time conceived in terms not of the psychic activity of the individual but of the day to day lived realities of functional groupings whose negotiations of their social positioning are conducted as much through their interactions with each other as through their isolated interaction with any particular cultural artefact. 'I know' that this is how things are conventionally ordered in society 'but' I understand that these are conventions: it need not necessarily be so, this order is not 'natural' despite the fact that we conduct our lives *as if* it was.

It remains a moot point whether or not such a dual recognition of ideological constraints is, in the end, a 'safety valve' ensuring the maintenance of the status quo, thus a conservative feature, or whether the pleasure generated in such recognitions can develop into a subversive force likely to produce actual social change. Maybe both can happen: the social processes implied in the notion of 'ideological struggle' are, after all, unevenly experienced, sporadic and contradictory. It is a point on which, understandably, Morley and Radway are unwilling to commit themselves, both claiming the necessity for further research along the lines of their own interventions before the question can be approached, let alone answered.

However Radway's propositions about the use value generated in the act of reading romances (repeatedly) by their almost exclusively female readership are of particular interest for our consideration of what female audience members might do with their readings of popular cinema. Firstly she finds that the heroines, their descriptions, their fictional experience and their narrative paths are the prime focus of interest to the readers: despite their recall of the narrative functions and special features of the male protagonists, the heroes, it is always via the woman's narrative path that readers identify a particular story. The readers invariably empathise (a form of identification) with the heroine's narrative obstacles, frequently comparing these to their own extra-textual experience, and finally, while vicariously enjoying the satisfactory narrative resolution of the heroine's fictional experience also always maintain their distance from this resolution, perceiving it to be an improvement on the reality with which they are familiar, but nonetheless a fantasy.

The whole process of reading these romances has its own use value too, in that it signals a private space, separated from the routine domestic responsibilities which are the lot of this particular 'audience' group: hence many readers consciously understand the very act of reading as subversive since during their reading they are, as far as they see it, *not* fulfilling their patriarchal functions of nurturing and servicing their families. Perhaps the habit of romance reading in the America of the eighties (cinema-going in the forties and fifties?) is in itself productive for female emancipation, despite the monotonous repetition of patriarchal requirements that constitutes the staple diet of such fictions. Routine participation in the escapist pleasures to be had in popular fiction or popular cinema or popular television soaps constitutes an assertion of the right to individual pleasure on the part of female audience members whose habitual role is to identify self interest with the interests of others. By their participation, also, they engage in a community of interest with other audience members – hence perhaps the film fan magazines of the forties and fifties and the more recent soap fan magazines: not only is the repeated act of viewing or reading in itself a repeatable and dependable pleasure but also the interaction with other audience members contributes to the sense of self denied to many women because of their positioning in patriarchal society. Ann Oakley's study of the woman's role in patriarchal order[19] succinctly summarises female experience in a way distinctly reminiscent of the definitions of women we have encountered in our examination of the representations in popular cinema through the post-war period.

> In the housekeeping role the servicing function is far more central than the productive or creative one. In the roles of wife and mother, also, the image of women as servicers of men's and children's needs is prominent: women 'service' the labour force by catering to the physical needs of men (workers) and by raising children (the next generation of workers) so that men are free *from* child-socialisation and free *to* work outside the home.[20]

Though it is true that there are plenty of female characters in popular films whose narrative paths do not conform to this description we must also remember that such characters invariably come to a 'bad' end: positive narrative resolutions being reserved for those characters who wholeheartedly accept such a definition of their reason for existence. But female audience members, in claiming for themselves a space outside such continuous commitments to others' needs also, inevitably, win the space to reflect on, to consider the terms of their existence through their exposure to fictional representations of a congruent (fictional) world sharing many features of their own (real) world.

Thus in a variety of ways readers and audiences draw on their own experience to 'make sense of' to read, the film text – or any other fictional text. But the converse is also the case: audiences may draw on texts in order to construct meanings out of their experience. This possibility is implicit in all of the institutional constraints, such as censorship, trade regulations and so on, which regulate the exchange of popular fictions. A current oral history project aiming to research the film viewing recollections of female audience members from the forties and fifties[21] has generated some intriguing reminiscences which corroborate the proposition that at least some audience members, while fully recognising the fantasy status of screen representations, also routinely drew on them in ordering their daily lives. The narrative experience and fates of fictional characters were used to shape and/or validate the extra-cinematic experience of the audience members.

Ann Todd – the concert pianist with James Mason as her jealous guardian and Herbert Lom the hypnotist. I learnt to play Beethoven's Pathetique Sonata and made myself a dirndl skirt from a cretonne curtain.

M. Scruby on *The Seventh Veil*.

We all *hated* him after this, not believing how she could take it all. She began another hair fashion of course. But even *then*, I didn't accept any woman could be so cowed and under the power of that P-I-G.

R. McWiggan on *The Seventh Veil*.

Ann Todd ideal as Francesca and James Mason all brooding and cruel 'cos he loves her really. I identified totally with the heroine, which must have set development of my feminism back several years.

A. Smith on *The Seventh Veil*.

Even then James Mason was a man you couldn't like, and Margaret Lockwood's beauty spot was something new, we all started to add them with eye pencil.

R. McWiggan on *The Wicked Lady*.

. . . her adventurous role made every woman feel she would like to be a wicked lady. My mother, like many others, bought the fashionable 'Wicked Lady' style hat.

A. Morrow on *The Wicked Lady*.

It was very natural, a romance that could have happened to the ordinary housewife where incidentally she visited the cinema

every week when she had finished her shopping. Good entertainment. One could imagine oneself in the part of the housewife.
                                    J. Finlayson on *Brief Encounter*.

Celia Johnson came across as ordinary – not as a glamorous Rita
Hayworth type. Therefore, there was hope for all the ordinary
girls like us – for romance to be around the corner.
                                    E. Sewell on *Brief Encounter*.

Though these recollections are made with hindsight, more than forty
years after the event, yet they reveal a range of responses whose ability to remain, albeit in summary form, in the respondents' memories
can be taken as evidence of their importance in the contemporary
experience of the respondents, all members of the female audience
during the forties. The influence of the fictional representations on
visual style – Lockwood's beauty spot, her hat, Todd's dirndl skirt
– on moral or ethical formations – whether or not Mason's cruelty
was unacceptably overbearing or simply evidence of his 'loving
her really' – and on the expectations audience members were
encouraged, through their readings, to have of their own future
experience – going to the cinema every week after the shopping,
the hope that romance might be 'around the corner' – all point
to the substantive negotiations made by audiences between their
active readings of films and their own behaviour outside the cinema.
There is clearly a relation between the audiences' understandings
of all aspects of the representations of women from dress styles to
gender politics, and their own, real life management of these issues:
this relation is close to that observed by Radway in her study of the
Smithton romance readers.

There is no way that we can glean the details of historical audience's responses with any accuracy, but it is worth considering,
briefly, what kinds of of evidence we might reasonably call on in
speculating about contemporary meanings. This endeavour is an
important one for feminism because it aims to reveal the relation
between ideology and gender construction, a relation which popular
texts routinely attempt to make invisible through their assertions
about the 'natural' and 'inevitable' social positions of women. It
is important, drawing on theories of audience activity and the
recollections of audience members such as those cited here, to allow
for the possibility of a more distanced, varied and independent
negotiation of these fictions by audiences, in order to refute the

possibility of social history being constructed out of the filmic representations themselves. *Brief Encounter* or *The Seventh Veil* may well offer veracity in their visual representations of the forties in Britain but we must not understand this veracity to extend beyond the simple surface of things – as these excerpts from audience recollections indicate.

We can accord some significance to a marked disparity between the critical reception of a film and its box office performance: a film that does particularly well at the box office, whatever reviewers say about it, is clearly one that has some use value to contemporary audiences. Thus *The Wicked Lady*, though vilified by many reviewers, pulled in enormous audiences who were clearly able to enjoy it despite supposed historical innacuracies, over-stagey or wooden acting and so on. In other cases, *Brief Encounter* and *The Seventh Veil*, for example, there was a greater unanimity between critics and audiences as to the 'worth' of the film, but the case of *The Wicked Lady* should alert us to the possibility that there may still be important differences between the reasoning of audiences and that imputed to them by reviewers. Our consideration of the ways in which both theories of reading and theorising of audience activity throw light on the multiple processes simultaneously operating between the readers and the text should allow for the possibility of a more sophisticated, more knowledgeable management of textual representations on the part of audiences. Critical discussion published at the time of the film's first release remains, however, our only trace of the discursive context in which the film circulated, and is thus a valuable resource provided we keep in mind both its limitations and other contextual factors. Such discussion is of particular interest in two distinct ways. Firstly, when there apppears to be unanimity between disparate critical sources we may hypothesise that the subject of the unanimity is an uncontentious one; and secondly, when there is marked disagreement between reviewers about some character or aspect of the narrative in a film which was also highly popular at the box office, we may take the subject of the disagreement to be one with particular significance to contemporary social struggles.

7

Female Readers
and the Film Text

If the audience draws on their own experience to make sense of the text and, at the same time, draws on the text in evaluating their own experience, forming expectations or images of themselves, it is of particular interest in a consideration of the special activities of female audience members to consider filmic representations of experiences which are specific to women. In perusing, as it were, such representations in all the films we have been discussing from the twenty-year period following the Second World War we have two distinct concerns. One is the nature and frequency of representations of particular aspects of female experience, that is to say how many mothers are represented, or how often are we presented with a depiction of an authoritative woman possessing important knowledge, or how many representations are there of significant friendships between women, and so on. The second concern is with the usefulness of the various theoretical models outlined in the previous two sections on reading and the audience, in illuminating the ways in which any particular representation might be understood by its female audiences. Thus the first concern is straightforward, though nonetheless interesting, while the second is speculative and necessarily schematic.

Within these popular fictions we may ask, then, what specifically female experiences are most frequently depicted or, to put it another way, what general experience is routinely offered from a female point of view. In considering specific representations we must also bear in mind their diegetic contexts: as we have seen in Chapter 4 the overall numbers of screen women diminished, in relation to men, between the forties and the sixties. Whereas a character in a forties film inhabited a world composed of roughly equal numbers of men and women, in the sixties films women were significantly outnumbered by men. We might suppose, then, that female audience members' attention to representations of women in the sixties would be likely to be more acute since there were far fewer women with any narrative importance to be seen on the screen.

Representations of female experience, or representations constructed from an (apparently) female point of view, in the group of films which we have been discussing, can be roughly grouped into five categories. These are mothers and motherhood; female understandings of love and marriage; friendships between women; female knowledge and power; and the rape or assault of women by men.

Mothers and Motherhood

This is the largest of the representational groups – but of twenty-eight 'mothers' in the eighteen films only two, Maddalena in *Madonna of the Seven Moons* and Laura in *Brief Encounter*, are central characters, the majority (11) being minor characters whose chief function is to motivate the narrative. Six of the twenty-eight, though unarguably present in the diegesis since they are referred to in both dialogue and *mise-en-scène*, are never actually seen on the screen: they are either dead or absent. The other observation to be made here is that although the general group 'mothers' is clearly an important one, and though as we have seen in Chapter 6 marriage and family was a preferred narrative resolution for positive female characters, yet there is not one representation of a pregnant woman in all of the films. The only images of a mother with a small baby are of the bullion guard Ned Cottrell's wife in the christening scene in *The Wicked Lady*, and of Joan Draper in *Piccadilly Incident*. As we have seen, Joan's main narrative function was to represent that which Diana had lost: our attention, in the two scenes in which mother and baby appear, is drawn to the Pearson family group (the christening party) or to Diana herself (the scene where she discovers that Alan has remarried). Those characters whose function as mother is represented as a positive aspect of their experience are invariably subjected to some narrative event which compromises their contentment with the role. Thus in *Brief Encounter* Laura's fantasy on the train ride home after her romantically satisfying meeting with Alec is brutally followed by the news of her son's accident.

Maddalena in *Madonna of the Seven Moons* is, simply, unable to 'mother' her child. Though she loves her daughter she cannot comprehend her, nor can she communicate with her. The relationship between Maddalena (Phyllis Calvert) and her young adult daughter Angela (Patricia Roc) is one of the more compellingly ambiguous features of this film. Though in the fictional world of the film there is eighteen years between them, yet the two actors are much closer in age. This feature of the intersection of film and star texts allows a reading of their interactions as much in terms of female rivalry as of mother and daughter. The rivalry concerns their status as sexually desirable to men: it is significant here that Maddalena's alter ego Rosanna is the mistress of Nino Venucci, and that it is Nino's brother Sandro who attempts to rape Angela. On this carnival night Nino and Sandro are identically dressed in harlequin costumes, hence Rosanna's mistaken attack on Sandro, fatal to them both. The preferred reading of the film attempts to suggest that the fatal mistake, while sacrificing the troubled Maddalena/Rosanna (the past), also ensures the survival of Angela (the future). The context of the mid-forties in Britain encourages such a reading as an optimistic approach to the post-war period.

Yet it also true that Angela's sexuality, in a more detailed examination of the film, can be seen to be just as problematic as that of her mother, Maddalena. Early in the film, on her arrival in Florence with her boyfriend Evelyn, Angela has a small but precious object stolen from her by Nino. Evelyn, as he tells her parents, slept in their Florence hotel with the key to her room under his pillow. Despite Angela's frequent assertions to the contrary she is not able to take care of herself: she is robbed by the Venucci gang when Sandro has lured her to the Seven Moons cafe and drugged her, and she is about to be raped when Rosanna jealously knifes Sandro, mistaking him for Nino. In the end Angela will marry Evelyn thus ensuring for herself not only male protection but also that of a member of the British diplomatic service. The survival of the future is, clearly, not to be entrusted to an autonomous woman but to one whose social status is unequivocally underwritten by a reliable man. Maddalena's efficacy as a mother in this representation is, despite the care and anxiety for her daughter which is carefully described in the first part of the film, deeply compromised.

In *The Searchers* there are three mothers: Martha Edwards, Mrs Jorgensen and Martin Pawley's dead mother – though all we actually see of the latter is her scalp on Scar's stick of trophies.

The opening scene of the film describes the Edwards' domestic life, disrupted firstly by Ethan's arrival and secondly by the Indian attack: Martha may have been a satisfied and satisfactory mother but she doesn't survive long enough to develop the point. In a sense Mrs Jorgensen is another version of Martha: she is an important character, an almost paradigmatic representation of the acceptable face of Woman. She keeps things going (the Jorgensen household, the wedding, the care of Mose Harper); she doesn't answer back (when Ethan rudely repudiates her well meant plea 'If the girls are dead, don't let the boys waste their lives in vengeance'); she gives good advice and she is philosophic about the disasters befalling the settler's community:

> someday this country's gonna be a fine good place to be. Maybe it needs our bones in the ground before that time can come.

She is a variant of Martha, and she is what Laurie will become. In the preferred reading of the film she is the melodrama's resolution of the western. But we know nothing about her beyond the fact that she was once a teacher; we can only understand her desires and fears in terms of her family and her country – she has no 'self'.

Winifred Banks in *Mary Poppins* is a devoted mother, yet her incompetence in running the household has led to the chain of events in which Mary intervenes. It is her inappropriate concern with women's rights, with the suffragette movement, which has contributed to the sorry state of the family. There are some compelling moments, particularly those in which Winifred questions her husband's severity with the children, in which the warm, supportive aspect of mothering can be glimpsed: but, the film suggests, Winifred is so scatterbrained that she cannot sustain her function as mother satisfactorily without her husband's practical involvement, achieved in the end through Mary's intervention. These aspects of Winifred's character and the well-being of the family are summarised in the motif of the kite. It is the runaway kite which leads the children astray in the first place; it is George's mending of the kite which signals his transformation into a caring father and it is Winifred's suffragette sash which forms the newly mended kite's tail as the happily united family group fly the kite together in the last scene of the film.

These characters, Laura, Maddalena, Martha, Mrs Jorgensen and Winifred Banks, are the most positively represented of all the twenty-eight mothers; in every case, though, there is a price to be paid through the narrative experience of the character. Another group, all much less important characters in their respective films, is composed of women who, though seen to be caring for their children, are also shown as incompetent in some way.

Barnes Wallace's wife in *The Dam Busters* is clearly unpeturbed by the minor illness of her daughter, but needs the assistance of the doctor to monitor the health of her husband:

> I wish you'd have a talk with him, I think he might listen to you.

Douglas Bader's mother in *Reach For The Sky* must give her permission for the amputations that may save his life. Having done this, with great misgivings ('I'm so afraid Douglas will hate me for ever after this but I couldn't let him die, could I?') she can, evidently, be of no further support to him in the struggle he faces: she disappears from the film. Mrs Gallagher takes her daughter Patsy to the school in *The Bells of St. Mary's*, putting her in the care of Father O'Malley because

> she's getting to be a big girl now, Father, and she's beginning to think I'm no good. I want to put her in your care before she finds out she's right.

These three all profess themselves inadequate to the tasks they face, turning to male professionals to help them out. But the group of mothers to whom the audience is invited to pay the closest attention are those whose mothering is in itself harmful. For various reasons ranging from egoism to ignorance these characters' attitude to their offspring has damaging consequences for the children – generally young adults in the time of the film – and the narrative dwells on these consequences. Not only are we invited to pay closer attention to the business of mothering as it is represented by these characters, but also they are the largest group – there are eight mothers whose performance of their role is constructed as at best deeply flawed, at worst downright malevolent.

We have already seen, in Chapter 5, how Bernice in *Marnie* and Kate in *East of Eden* are blamed for the tortuous paths followed by Marnie and Cal respectively, which, the preferred readings of the films suggest, are a direct result of the mothers' mistaken (Bernice) or unfeeling (Kate) mishandling of their maternal responsibilities. In *Rebel Without a Cause* Jim Stark's mother (and grandmother too, for good measure) are the prime cause of Jim's alienation from his peer group:

> *Jim*: You are not going to use me as an excuse again.
> *Mother*: I don't.
> *Jim*: Every time you can't face yourself you blame it on me.
> *Mother*: That isn't true.
> *Jim*: You say it's because of me, you say it's because of the neighbourhood. You use every other phoney excuse. Mum, just for once, I wanna do something right. I don't want you to run away for me again.

The narrative also suggests they are responsible for his father's spinelessness. Jim's father is so 'hen-pecked' that he is no use as a role model for his son. This is the film in which the mid-fifties 'problem' of teenage delinquency is laid at the door of their parents. Though it is Jim and his parents who are the central focus of the narrative there are other youngsters experiencing, like Jim, difficulties in their passage from childhood into the adult world. Chief amongst these are Judy (Natalie Wood) and Plato (Sal Mineo). Judy's mother fails to intervene or to support her daughter in the problems she has with her father, and Plato's mother leaves him in the care of a nanny/housekeeper for whose authority he clearly has no respect. In the mid-sixties film *Summer Holiday* the major female character, Barbara Winters (Lauri Peters) is temporarily on the run from her grasping and manipulative agent/mother who, we are informed, has been milking her daughter's success as a singing star. Stella Winters' (Madge Ryan) machinations are offered as a motivation for various complications in the film's basically simple travelogue plot but are also meant to be a source of comedy. Like many other sixties films this comedy looks, to the attentive female reader, pretty savage – yet another example of the misogyny which lies close to the surface of many popular films of the period.

Thus motherhood is more often than not represented as a negative force, an obstacle to the narrative path of another character. Mothers are more likely to be minor characters and are frequently un-named – nameless. When a character is shown to be positive in at least some aspect of their maternal role there is invariably a price to be paid during the unfolding of the narrative. Given the conventional acceptance of a causal relation between the concepts (and the real social experiences to which they refer) of love, marriage and motherhood, and given the unquestionably desirable state of marriage as it is generally represented in these popular fictions, it seems odd that the state of motherhood itself should get such a consistently 'bad press'.

Though the extra-cinematic experience of many female audience members is re-presented via these images of mothers, the narrative construction rarely situates such characters in a central position where the psychic mechanism of identification is, by virtue of film form, most strongly encouraged. It seems more likely that, where the female reader does pay particular attention to such a character, the process of disavowal will be at work. 'I know' (that a proposition about the nature of mothering is being offered) 'but' (I will temporarily forget that I too am a mother). Thus the female reader may detach herself from recognition of the unpleasant connotations of the screen representation of motherhood. Perhaps the semiotic techniques of analysis are more useful here. A convenient way of dissociating from unsympathetic representations of the reader's own social or familial role would be to understand the representation only in terms of its strategic function within the diegesis.

Yet our glimpse of audience theory should remind us that the reader does habitually draw on her own extra-diegetic experience in making sense of the narrative. Thus she will either be encouraged to devalue herself by accepting the negative representation of mothering, or she will escape the problem by disavowing the representation and choosing another character with which to identify. The Smithton women studied by Janice Radway, whether they were mothers or not (and most were) invariably identified with the (young and as yet unmarried) heroine of the romance. However, whatever means different female audience members employ in their reading strategies, whether they recognise and deplore the negative representations of mothering, whether they (temporarily) deny their own maternal experience, or whether they accept the proposition apparent in so many of these films that there is something intrinsically suspect and potentially damaging in being or having a mother, in the end there seems to be one overriding proposition linking both fictional women and female audience members. That is that female autonomy ends at marriage, and that preferably this should take place as early as possible in adult life.

Love and Marriage

Representations of romantic heterosexual love in popular films are ubiquitous to the point of invisibility: the absence of any depiction of romance at the centre or at the periphery of the narrative is more striking than its presence. The films which we have been discussing in detail, all selected because of their huge contemporary popularity, are no exception. Only two films, *The Dam Busters* and *A Hard Day's Night*, lack any heterosexual romance in their plot: and the latter substitutes the extra-diegetic fantasy romance between the Beatles and their fans. In these representations of romance a distinction is frequently implied, if not overtly drawn, between love ('good') and lust or desire (mistaken if not actually 'bad'). This distinction is at the basis of Laura's dilemma in *Brief Encounter* where she must choose between Alec whom she 'desires' and Fred, who she 'loves' and, at the other end of our historical period it is by means of this distinction that the audience is invited to distinguish between Sophie Western's 'love' for Tom in *Tom Jones* and the lascivious 'desire' of other female characters such as Molly, Jenny Jones or Lady Belleston. Romantic heterosexual love is *always* consummated by the legal/religious contract of marriage, either within the time of the narrative or implicitly, following the narrative closure as, for example, in *The Wicked Lady*, *The Searchers*, or *Tom Jones*. Marriage is the point at which the private experience of heterosexual romance is transformed into a public asset. Though in popular films of the forties there is some exploration of female experience after the marriage contract, by the sixties the mythic simplicity of the 'happy end' has been restored. This is not to suggest that no films were made which took marital problems as their central subject matter – there are numerous examples[1] throughout the twenty-year period – but the fact remains that on the whole these were not films which proved to be the major box office successes of their day.

Given the frequency of love and marriage as a plot element and a constituent of the narrative closure it is somewhat surprising to find how infrequently any serious discussion of the implications of marriage, its possibly various personal meanings, is accorded any narrative prominence. When such a discussion does take place its narrative function is invariably to indicate to the audience how they should evaluate particular characters: thus the audience's complicity with a particular definition of love and marriage is assumed. In *The Wicked Lady* the conversation between Barbara and Caroline early in the film in which Barbara asserts that 'a clever woman can make her husband do as *she* likes' is countered by Caroline:

> But if a woman truly loves her husband she'd rather do as he likes.

And through their exchange each woman defines herself for the audience, by referring to the assumed audience recognition of the validity of Caroline's position, the iniquity of Barbara's. The problem in such a clear exposition of patriarchal requirements is that audience members who already recognise the inequity of conventional gender politics within marriage have a powerful incentive to identify with Barbara's position rather than with Caroline's. It is clear from recollections of individual audience members[2] that many contemporary female readers did indeed respond in this way.

> I liked it very much at the time. I liked rebellious, forceful women, I was also interested in history and seemed to think there was a grain of truth in it. (J. Astell)
>
> Every growing girl must have wanted to be as wicked and devil-may-care as Margaret Lockwood in this film . . . yet our moral training told us she must get her 'come-uppance' in the end. (M. Brassett)
>
> I did see this and enjoyed it at the time. I quite liked seeing Margaret Lockwood as a thoroughly bold woman rather than wicked. (P. Burgess)

Thus female readers *identify* with Barbara's intra-diegetic experience of pleasure and power, while at the same time drawing on their recognition of popular fictional structures in distancing themselves from the consequent fate of the heroine. Here are examples of the simultaneous operation of the sociological, psychoanalytic and semiotic models of spectatorial activity. Transgression of, or compliance with, the patriarchal codes governing love and marriage are, however, more often exemplified through generalised plot development than by means of specific utterances by individual characters, though the combination of both modes as in *The Wicked Lady* constitutes a particularly forceful invitation to the audience to consider the ethics of the case. In *The Searchers*, the romance between Laurie and Marty is a minor plot element, though nonetheless one to which almost every reviewer referred in their characteristically and necessarily schematic summaries. Neither Laurie nor Marty ever discusses either the terms or the consequences of marriage, but Laurie's mounting exasperation with Marty's repeated absences, and her narrowly averted marriage to the buffoon Charlie Corey, both assert the importance of marriage *in itself* to women. Laurie *must* marry in order to assume fully her place in the adult world: marriage to the man she loves, Marty, is her choice but in the absence of this possibility any marriage is preferable to none. It is also of interest in this context to note that, in the typical symmetry of the classical Hollywood narrative, both Laurie and Marty must experience the narrative obstacle of an invalid 'marriage' during the unfolding of the plot.

A comparison between the two is illuminating. Laurie's potential union is invalid because she doesn't love Charlie, but nonetheless since any husband is preferable to none she nearly does marry him, the ceremony being only just averted because of Marty's return. Marty's 'accidental' marriage to the Indian squaw Look is contracted according to Indian customs of which he is ignorant: nevertheless from Marty's point of view it is a misunderstanding the consequences of which are appalling and unacceptable. For Ethan (and the audience, invited in these scenes to share Ethan's point of view) it is merely comic. For female protagonists (for women) marriage is an essential pre-requisite to participation in the collective of adult society. For male protagonists it may be comic, appalling or it may be desirable but it is *never* essential.

A close reading of the implications of this uneasy and often ambiguous text shows that the meaning of the marriage contract is variable according to context and point of view. Context in this case refers to ethnicity, point of view is a function of gender politics. Laurie, apart from being a member of the narratively dominant white settlers community is, of course, a more important character than Look. Few reviewers referred to the 'marriage' of Marty and Look while all referred to Laurie's romance with Marty and one, at least, appeared to concur with Laurie's own recognition of her unavoidable destiny as a wife:

> its heroine, a nubile gal named Vera Miles, looks and talks like someone who could not only make a man an attractive consort,

but could also cook him a good meal. She is an admirable mixture of sex appeal and no-nonsense.[3]

One of the ways in which the audience is invited to subscribe to the definition of Marnie as sick and in need of psychiatric help in the sixties film *Marnie*, is through her 'perverse' rejection of Mark (or any other man) as a husband. Reviewers concurred with the diegetic proposition that her behaviour is perverse, drawing on Sean Connery's star persona to make the point:

> though lady customers may feel that any heroine who can hold off Sean Connery for approximately 120 minutes deserves to have her head examined . . . [4]

> the only suspense rests on whether or not a frigid bride will ever succumb to her husband. James Bond never had troubles like this.[5]

Goldfinger and *Marnie* were on release in UK at the same time and it was doubtless irresistible to many audience members who saw both films to make comparisons between the ultimate capitulation of both Marnie and Pussy Galore, to the charismatic sexuality of Sean Connery/Mark Rutland/James Bond. In this way the representation of Marnie as a perverse woman is consolidated through intertextual references. But the perversity of her rejection of Connery also attaches to her other utterances. Thus her articulation of many contemporary observations on the real nature of the marriage contract, which bear more than a passing resemblance to some of the insights of the emergent women's movement in the sixties, are also characterised as 'perverse' and so refuted. In her furious confrontations with Mark, Marnie draws attention to the economic and legal aspects of the marriage contract:

> *Mark*:   Oh, and Marnie, when we get home, no cute ideas about absconding with the family silver. Just get a grip on yourself for one short week and after that, well, you can take legal possession.
> *Marnie*:   Like you? Like you take legal possession?
> *Mark*:   Yes – if you want to put it that way. Somebody's got to take on the responsibility for you Marnie, and it narrows down to a choice of me or the police, old girl.

The problem for a female reader for whom Marnie's articulation may have some experiential resonances is that, no matter how sympathetic she may be to Marnie's analysis, in the end it is Mark's meanings to which she must subscribe as a consequence of the inexorable logic of Hitchcock's narrative construction. In case the reader should be left in any doubt on the matter there is the tragic spectacle of Bernice, old, tearful and alone, to suggest the fate of the abandoned, unmarried woman. Many of Marnie's utterances were clearly too close for the comfort of contemporary reviewers who devoted a considerable amount of column space to demolishing Hedren and her performance – thereby attempting to undermine even oppositional readings of the character.

> What I resent most about this trumped up load of nonsense is its contempt for the intelligence and sensitivity of people who go to the pictures.[6]

> Tipi Hedren plays a compulsive thief whose larcenies . . . provide her with the kicks her frigidity denies her . . . She's fixated on a horse; she has a thing about keys and locks; she fondles a pistol like a lover.[7]

> the film also suffers from the beautiful blankness of Tipi Hedren and her non-performance in the title role (would it have seemed less wierd with a better actress?)[8]

> The Marnie character would have killed the 'image' Miss Kelly succeeded in creating before she retired to Monaco. I don't understand Hitchcock being willing to abet the destruction of that image.[9]

The reference to Grace Kelly is of particular interest since, in a blaze of publicity, this hugely popular star had recently abandoned her screen career for an illustrious marriage to Prince Rainier of Monaco. The subtext of these and other reviews suggests that not only was Tipi Hedren inadequate as a performer – she couldn't act – but also that the role of Marnie was in any case offensive, a role that would have 'tainted' the hitherto impeccable persona of Grace Kelly.

So Marnie's resistance to the institutions of both love and marriage was reviled: but a similar dismissal is accorded to the opposite case – those screen women who, though eager for marriage, are themselves so undesirable that their ambition can only be regarded as comic, the fate of a man entrapped by them a frightful one. The case of Marty and Look in *The Searchers* is an instance of this plot device which, however, is substantially developed in other popular hits of the periods: the device usually signals adherence to the codes of comedy. Hence the film *Doctor at Sea* details the atrocious pursuit of the young hero, Dr Simon Sparrow, by his senior partner's 'homely' daughter, Wendy Thomas (Joan Sims), offering this incident as the uncontentious motivation for his decision to go to sea. During the course of the SS *Lotus* voyage the same 'gag' is recycled, this time in the form of Miss Mallet's (Brenda da Banzie) pursuit of the fiercely misogynist Captain Hogg (James Robertson Justice). It is not only Captain Hogg's avowed misogyny that produces the comedy, but also Miss Mallett's age and inappropriately girlish behaviour. This comic theme of an undesirable but nevertheless predatory woman, is developed into a routine constituent of many of the films in the successful Carry On series, the woman in question often being played by Hattie Jacques. It appears in the musical comedy *Summer Holiday* in the Yugoslavian sequence where the hero, Don (Cliff Richard) inadvertently acquires a bride (rather than the bread he thought he'd asked for): the ensuing feast and chase motivating both spectacle (the barbaric wedding dance) and comedy (the boys' narrow escape from a fate they clearly considered close to, if not worse than, death). But where such narrative devices concerning marriage are required to produce comedy, it is interesting to note that we are always offered the incident from the point of view of the male protagonist. Thus, in such popular fictions, marriage can be a joke for the men: for the women it is invariably a more serious matter – it is their chief reason for existence.

Female Friendships

The representations of love and marriage, in their ubiquity, assert the universal nature of this life experience. It is only on close examination of the details of individual narrative constructions, and in consideration of the female reader's possible spectatorial strategies – of the 'use value' of such representations to her – that we can begin to recognise the ideological functioning of such representations: in de Lauretis' phrase, here is a 'technology of gender' at work, moderating the gender specific meanings of the universal experience of heterosexual interaction. But no such importance is accorded the equally universal experience (for women) of female friendships. Representations of *any* friendships between women are rare; friendships carrying narrative significance are almost entirely absent. There are, however, a few exceptions in the group of films discussed here, and these fall clearly into two groups.

The relationship between Barbara and Caroline in *The Wicked Lady* is central to the development of the plot and the construction of both the film's preferred reading and its ideological 'message'. Less important but nonetheless clearly evident within the overall diegetic construction are friendships between Angela Labardi and Millie Fitch in *Madonna of the Seven Moons*, Diana Fraser and Sally Benton in *Piccadilly Incident*, and Sophie Western and her cousin Harriet Fitzpatrick in *Tom Jones*.

In the first case, though the friendship is of obvious importance to both protagonists, yet it cannot survive disruption as a consequence of the rivalry between the two women for the affections of a particular man. Thus the relationship is construed, in the end, as an adversarial one. Though the concept of loyalty is introduced, it is never strong enough to compete with the force of an heterosexual attraction. Barbara is one of the two people Caroline loves best, and despite Barbara's callousness she remains caring and loyal to her throughout the film: this friendship is a onesided one though since Barbara doesn't even recognise the interpersonal ties that characterise it for Caroline. The 'friendship' is finally shattered by the revelations concerning Barbara's double life, and by her death in the penultimate scene.

The second group comprises contacts between women which are so circumstantial and tenuous as scarcely to merit the term friendship. In the absence of any more satisfactory representations, however, it is worth considering them. All these contacts depend on an initial acquaintance which generally precedes the time of the narrative, and an opportunist and temporary interaction in the pursuance of some plot specific narrative goal. Thus Angela Labardi is 'friends' with Millie Fitch: they have travelled from London to Cannes together, but their various chance meetings merely serve to motivate the narrative in allowing contact between Sandro, with whom Millie is infatuated, and Angela, in whom Sandro is interested. Millie never says anything except to imply her jealousy of Sandro's interest in Angela, and Angela only refers to Millie in the most disparaging terms. In *Piccadilly Incident* Diana Fraser and Sally Benton are colleagues in the Wrens, meeting by chance at

Waterloo station when Diana, accompanied by Alan, boards her train back to the barracks after her first meeting with him. Sally's reaction to Alan alerts the audience to the narrative significance of the meeting. Subsequently Sally is marooned with Diana and the small group of sailors after the evacuation of Singapore and they support each other in that long ordeal, but on their eventual return to the UK (once again in the form of Waterloo station) they separate, returning to their respective men – or in Diana's case, to the search for Alan. Similarly in *Tom Jones* we are invited to believe in the friendship between Sophie and her cousin Harriet, but only when Sophie, already on the run from her father, accidentally meets Harriet who is running away from her red-haired husband. Harriet befriends and protects Sophie in London, but has no qualms about deceiving her once the desirable Tom appears on the scene. Sophie's approach to this friendship is thus shown to be opportunist and naïve, while Harriet's is opportunist and duplicitous. A long term committment of affection and loyalty clearly has no place in the 'friendship' demonstrated by these two characters.

In these highly popular films of the mid-forties, mid-fifties and mid-sixties, there are *no* representations of any sustained alliance or friendship between women which is of importance in either the narrative development or the construction of individual characters. Such representations as do exist are frequently adversarial, certainly inconsequential alongside the altogether weightier business of securing a husband. We may well wonder what the consequences of this glaring absence might have been for contemporary audience members. Do we have here an example of a kind of patriarchal strategy of divide and rule? How would female audience members have understood this repeated marginalisation of the importance of their relationships with each other? The 'network' of female friends, which in many western urban centres has substituted for the extended family of previous epochs and which can provide essential support for women in the multiple tasks inherent in their social and familial roles, is in these films not so much an ambivalent presence, like representations of motherhood and of marriage, as a striking *absence*.

Female Knowledge and Power

Though on the whole major female protagonists can be characterised by their lack of knowledge and power within the framework of the diegesis, a few noteworthy minor characters, those whose function is to motivate the narrative, do possess either knowledge or power – rarely both. Given the crucially important position patriarchy accords to women in the maintenance of its structures (as Ann Oakley reminds us,[10] women service the labour force by catering to the needs of men and by raising children), albeit at the expense of any fully autonomous exploration of the interface between self and society, it is worth considering these 'vestigial' representations more closely.

In *Madonna of the Seven Moons* there are two minor female characters, both in their old age and both occupying a relatively subservient position in their respective households. They are Tessa (Amy Veness), housekeeper to the Labardi family, and Mother Venucci (Nancy Price), mother of Nino and Sandro. Of the two it is Mother Venucci who has the more power, but both are clearly indicated at various points during the narrative as the possessors of knowledge relevant to the unfolding of the plot. What is interesting for our examination is that, though their knowledge is offered to the relevant protagonists, they cannot act on it themselves. In Tessa's case her insights are ignored. When Maddalena faints after seeing Sandro (unknown to her as Maddalena but well known to her alter ego Rosanna) at Angela's birthday party, Giuseppe and Dr Ackroyd take her up to her room and put her to bed. It is Tessa who demurs at the prospect of leaving Maddalena alone, but she is brushed aside: during the night Maddalena awakes and, assuming the persona of Rosanna, leaves the house. The narrative construction and *mise-en-scène* make it perfectly clear that Tessa's warning is a timely one, and subsequent events prove her right: neither her insight nor her knowledge is valued, however, and she does not act on them herself.

Rather more attention is paid to the insights of Mother Venucci, the only character in the film who appears to have any recognition of the mystery surrounding Rosanna's inexplicable appearances and disappearances. But her insights and her advice, sought by her son Nino, are couched in the cryptic form of gipsy lore, and she is devalued as a potentially authoritative character by her position in the petty criminal Venucci clan, opposed as it is to the wealthy bourgeois Labardi family at the centre of the narrative. There is however sufficient information for the reader to empathise with the knowledgeable status of these two women, and to sympathise with their powerlessness. Both these psychic mechanisms, we should remind ourselves, can be subsumed within the general term identification. A reading which draws on the structural analysis prompted by the semiotic model of the text:reader interface would, however, recognise that the narrative obstacles which motivate audience attention would be subverted, should other characters choose to value the knowledge of Tessa or Mother Venucci more highly. In other words the narrative structure itself requires that they be ignored.

In the sixties film *Tom Jones* two minor characters are in possession of crucial information which they never reveal: it is only as the plot unfolds that the audience is enabled to deduce that they must know more than they have said. These two are Squire Allworthy's sister Bridget and Jenny Jones, both present in the pre-history of the narrative, the segment chronicling the appearance of the 'foundling' in Squire Allworthy's bed. Jenny is the presumed mother of the baby and is consequently banished for her indiscretion; Bridget is the real mother. Both these women could avert Tom's being disinherited, yet neither speaks. It is not a question here of their being ignored since they effectively silence themselves by their collusion with the rigid moral codes which inform the film's depiction of social relations.

Pussy Galore in the sixties film *Goldfinger* is a rather different case. She has power (over James Bond) by virtue of her position as the villain Goldfinger's accomplice, and she possesses both skills and information: she is proud of her aeronautic expertise, and she is privy to the details of the master plan, Operation Grandslam. Yet she has been, apparently, unable to understand the wider implications, hence the meaning of either her (qualified) power or of the criminal plot. Thus she has power without knowledge. Bond recognises Goldfinger's madness and is able, in his inimitable eleventh hour manner, to communicate all this to Pussy who promptly changes sides, enabling Bond to avert the disaster. The point here is that neither Pussy's limited knowledge nor her (qualified) power are of any practical use to her until directed by masculine intervention. Like Marnie she is, simply, wrong: Sean Connery puts her right.

The representation of women as possesors of knowledge or power are few in number and, where such a representation does figure in the mechanics of the plot, it is severely circumscribed. Either the woman's knowledge cannot be used because of her lack of access to power – she is disempowered – or her power can be overturned because of her lack of knowledge. Both her knowledge and her power, insofar as they impinge directly on narrative events,

are, precisely, use-less. In her reading of this frequently reiter-
ated pattern the female reader's own knowledge and/or power
is problematised. If she identifies with 'knowledgable' women
like Tessa or Mother Venucci, she must accept powerlessness; or
in disavowing powerlessness she must also disavow knowledge;
or in choosing to identify with the powerful and knowledgeable
male protagonist she must disavow her femininity. As Doane points
out in her discussion of the group of forties films she classifies as
belonging to the 'medical discourse', the woman must concur with
the view that her way of looking is in itself 'ill':

> If female spectatorship is constituted as an oscillation between
> a feminine and a masculine position, the films of the medical
> discourse encourage the female spectator to repudiate the femi-
> nine pole and to ally herself with the one who diagnoses, with
> a medical gaze . . . The doctor/patient relation is a quite spe-
> cific one, however, which unrelentingly draws together power,
> knowledge, the body, and the psyche in the context of an institu-
> tion. Therein lies its force in convincing the woman that her way
> of looking is ill.[11]

The relationship between power and knowledge is well known;
for the female reader their articulation around representations of the
body and the engagement of the psyche in reading such representations is of especial significance, a significance not confined to films
of the 'medical discourse' though particularly clearly exemplified
in such films. This is because the position of the narrator, or of
narrative authority, participates to a greater or lesser extent in the
medical 'authority' of the fictional doctor. The doctor is licensed to
'read' the body, just as the narrator is licensed to urge the preferred
reading of the film text. It follows from this that it is of the utmost
importance, in speculating about the activity of the female reader,
to recognise the plural and simultaneous activity of the reader:
she may identify with, say, Tessa in *Madonna of the Seven Moons*
in her recognition of the danger to Maddalena in leaving her unat-
tended, while *at the same time* disavowing Tessa's powerlessness.
This process implies a degree of sophistication in the reader which
is not generally assumed by reviewers but which is essential to the
possibility of deriving pleasure or use from the text. Underlying the
pleasure in the text is the recognition, validated by the sociological
model of the text:reader interface, of patriarchy's disempowerment,

its disabling, of women. That the text was pleasurable and/or useful is guaranteed by its position as a contemporary box office hit.

Rape and Assault

Whereas the female protagonist is more or less discredited as a source of authorial power or knowledge, and there are far fewer representations of friendships between women than we might perhaps expect given both the routine pre-occupation with heterosexual relationships and the frequent delineations of male friendships of narrative importance, overt depictions of the extreme forms of male power and domination over women in the form of assault or even rape are surprisingly common.

The opening scene of *Madonna of the Seven Moons*, a scene which takes place almost twenty years before the time of the main narrative and is supposed to explain, for the audience, the reason for Maddalena's precarious mental state, details her rape in the woods near her convent school. Near the end of the same film her daughter Angela is subject to a violent sexual assault, her actual rape being narrowly averted by the intervention of Rosanna who mistakes both the identity of her assailant and the nature of the event she witnesses.

In *The Wicked Lady* Barbara is raped by her erstwhile partner in crime, Captain Jerry Jackson, in revenge for her betrayal of him which almost resulted in his death on the gallows. In the mid-fifties film *The Searchers* the Edwards family is murdered by Scar's Comanche band: we don't know exactly what fate befell Martha at the homestead and her daughter Lucy, later, in the mountains, but whatever it was it so shocked and upset Ethan that he forbade Marty to look at Martha's body and later prohibited questions about Lucy's corpse. No such horror nor attention surrounded the deaths of Ethan's brother, nor of the Edwards' young son: the audience is specifically invited to speculate about the fate of the women, not the men who, simply, were killed. In *Marnie* the eponymous heroine is raped by her husband on their honeymoon. In *Goldfinger* Pussy Galore is forcibly kissed by James Bond.

In *Tom Jones* Lord Fellemer (David Tomlinson), acting on the suggestion of Lady Belleston, attempts to 'take' Sophie by force – an attempt which is unsuccessful because of the unexpected appearance of Sophie's father, Squire Western. The contrast between the two men – the foppish urbanite and the bucolic countryman –

encourages a reading of the scene as comedy, despite the attack on Sophie and the almost equally violent resolution where Squire Western literally carries Sophie off, over his shoulders like the proverbial sack of potatoes. Sophie is a possession – not to be 'taken' by one with no legal right to her.

Now these are, clearly, all assaults of a different order whose meanings are substantially modified by the details of their respective diegeses: they are, however, all assaults on women by men and must inevitably generate different spectatorial responses in male and female readers. Male readers may deplore such assaults but they cannot identify with the victim, neither can they draw on personal extra-diegetic experience in considering the connotative resonances of such representations. The filmic construction, preferred reading and discursive responses associated with these depictions are of particular interest to our examination of popular texts as 'technologies of gender'. The assaults on Maddalena, Angela, Martha and Lucy are all unequivocally deplored in the preferred reading urged in the textual construction and in particular in the case of Maddalena the audience is strongly invited to empathise with her terror, anguish and remorse: we are invited to share Maddalena's point of view of the event in the medium close up of her after she returns to her convent room.

The cases of Barbara, Marnie and Pussy Galore are, however, quite different. All three women have been constructed as 'bad' in some way, that is to say they are undeserving of audience sympathy because of their narrative actions. Barbara is callous, amoral and murderous. Marnie, though 'sick' is also perverse and transgressive: she breaks the law (she steals from her employers and uses false identity cards) and she refuses the sexual attentions of her husband ('if you touch me again I'll die'). Pussy Galore is an accomplice of the arch villain Goldfinger, and Bond is their prisoner. In all three cases the filmic construction suggests that these women are 'fair game' and the assault is presented to the audience either from the ('objective') point of view of narrative authority (Barbara, Pussy Galore) or from the point of view of the male agressor (the extreme close up of Marnie's eyes as, following the medium close shot where he disrobes her, Mark pushes her down onto the bed). Barbara, then, 'asked for it' by betraying her lover to the authorities, but the point is laboured in the scene itself where Jerry Jackson, following her refusal to continue their liaison, picks her up in his arms and, advancing towards the left hand side of the frame beyond which is Barbara's bed, laughs as he tells her:

> It will be a new experience to take you against your will.

The implication that violence can be a pleasurable constituent of sexual activity is a disturbing one, for the female reader at least.

Lady Belleston in *Tom Jones* goes even further. In her discussion with Lord Fellemer about the lack of progress in his courtship of Sophie she suggests that rape is an acceptable strategy to employ in 'winning' her:

> Fie upon it, are you frightened by the word rape? All women love a man of spirit. Remember the story of the Sabine ladies? I believe they made tolerably good wives afterwards. Come this evening at nine. I will see she's alone.

The case of Marnie is even more disturbing since she has already been constructed as a mentally unstable character, and Mark has not only been offered as an exemplar of intelligent, responsible and caring authority but has also given Marnie his promise that he will not 'touch her again'. Though no reviewers went so far as to applaud his action, many clearly felt that it was understandable:

> When Mark cannot restrain himself any longer he puts into effect the answer which will have occurred to most of the audience . . . Huge close-ups of him pressing her down on the bed quickly kill our identification with him by making us see the meaning of the experience for Marnie.[12]

> We identify with him when, on his shipboard honeymoon, he finally decides to take his marital rights, even though we know that the only possible method is effectively rape.[13]

But the grudging acknowledgements that, in this case at least, 'marital rights' equals rape are developed as evidence of the film's unsatisfactory and somehow unfair teasing of its audience by problematising the hitherto clear invitation to empathise with Mark. For the female reader the assertion of male marital rights, present in the film *and* in its reviews, lends additional credence to Marnie's earlier, angry, outburst about Mark's 'taking legal possession' of her following the marriage he proposes. Less obviously problematic is the case of Pussy Galore: this is not a violent assault, and within the terms of the thriller fantasy Bond films anything which enables the hero's survival is legitimate. But the disturbing aspect of this representation, for the female spectator, is the close-up shot of Pussy's resistance melting as she experience's Bond's initially violent kiss. Here is a case where 'no means yes' is graphically described on screen: in many ways the most unacceptable of all the cases cited here since unwanted kisses are a far more widespread experience than marital, or any other kind of rape. It is hard to imagine what strategy the female reader might employ in order to derive pleasure from the spectacle of these extreme representations of male violence to women, other than an identification with the male protagonist, which seems unlikely in these cases, or, simply, a rather un-pleasurable recognition of the extra-diegetic referents.

THE SOCIAL EXPERIENCE OF THE FEMALE READER

Looking through the pages of popular magazines – both those addressed specifically to women and those, such as *Picture Post* (until 1957), aimed at a more general readership – and at social histories of the period,[14] it is clear that there were several issues at the forefront of popular discussion which had particular relevance to women. In our consideration of the interaction between popular film texts and female audience members we may wonder whether, and if so how, such issues appeared on the screen. Broadly speaking the major social issues pertaining specifically to the experience of women in Britain concerned the question of working, wage-earning women and the attendant adjustments to family structures and state provision for maternity and child care; the often related issue of divorce, and the question of women's access to education on the same terms as their brothers. Most of the detailed debates of the day can be subsumed under these three headings: they all, at base, address the problem of whether or not, in the post-war democracy which Britain claimed to be, men and women had equal rights, as well as equal responsibilities.

The implications of this debate for gender politics began to surface in the women's movement of the sixties, fuelled by the recent access to philosophical speculation such as Simone de Beauvoir's *The*

Second Sex (first published in translation in 1953) and sociological accounts of women's lives such as Betty Friedan's *The Feminine Mystique* (1963). The real import of these studies was however, for many young women, easily dissipated in the twin forces of economic growth and a new moral permissiveness, both summarised in the terms 'swinging London' or 'the swinging sixties'. Before concluding our discussion of popular cinema in the twenty year period following the upheavals of the Second World War, then, it may be instructive to ask how, or whether, these issues were represented – bearing in mind of course the decline in cinema audiences and the spread of broadcast television which, by 1965, was the place where we would expect to find the most reliable evidence of contemporary social pre-occupations. We have examined the representation on screen of what we might understand to be specifically female experience, taking the films themselves as our starting point. Here we shall take the actual experiential context of female audience members in Britain, asking how far it is offered as a constituent of popular cinema's fictional worlds. Our terms will be working women; divorce; education; and the women's movement.

Working/Wage Earning Women

As we have seen in Chapter 5 the female protagonists in popular film tend to be defined by what they *are* rather than by what they *do* and the narrative resolutions of important characters invariably concern the outcome of a relationship with either a male partner or a family member. Few characters are engaged in work which predominates in their (fictional) lives. We might assume, from these filmic representations, that women rarely engage in paid employment and that when they do it is merely a means to some other end. Such an assessment would be confirmed by a look through the pages of contemporary women's magazines. In the mid-forties there are frequent references to employment and training opportunities, often linked to the issue of demobilisation and post-war reconstruction: thus women were urged to consider work in manufacturing, particularly where goods were in short supply – such as, for example, the footwear industry. At the same time facilities in the ATS,[15] in sixth forms and in various youth organisations which during the war had prepared young women for entry into the services were, as a *Picture Post* feature noted (8 December 1945) being modified to meet the demands of peacetime society:

several of these home-making courses are now being tried out. The ATS gives a practical course to girls who have been cut off from home life for six years. Arranging flowers, making cusions and curtains, and cooking for four instead of four hundred, will turn their barrack trained minds to a softer domestic scene. Several LCC schools have fully equipped flats attached to their cookery department and youth organisations are rapidly turning their pre-service instruction into courses for brides and future mothers.

The strategies employed to move women 'back' into the home were clearly successful since by 1950 there were already far fewer references to employment in the magazines, and the range of employment referred to was much narrower. In general features about work or training opportunities focused on the fashion and beauty industries and services, with occasional stories about 'exceptional' women's jobs – for example *Woman* (25 March 1950) carried a feature on 'radio's only girl reporter'. The latter half of the forties is thus characterised by a narrowing of the range of career opportunities for women, their central importance to industrial production being constantly marginalised. In February 1951 the BBC reduced the number of its news readers from nineteen to eight, excluding women (as well as anyone with a regional dialect), and claiming that:

> people do not like momentous events such as war and disaster to be read by the female voice.[16]

So the wartime 'consensus' in which differences of class, region and gender were subsumed into a national unity was, despite the Labour electoral victories of 1945 and 1951, abandoned. In the popular films of the mid-forties, as we have seen, the overriding thematic emphases are to do with women as problems, but there are nevertheless more working women to be seen on screen in these films than in those of the mid-fifties. Though, in *Brief Encounter*, Laura herself does not work outside her home yet the world she inhabits includes many women who do. In *Piccadilly Incident* the plot revolves around the consequences of Diana's conflict between her duties as a Wren and her desire to be with her new husband: in the narrative resolution she is punished for her inevitable choice. Thus the film's message to women suggests that leaving home may have dire consequences for them. The only working women whose dedication to their employment is thoroughly acceptable are the nuns, teachers in *The Bells of St Mary's*, teachers and nurses in *Madonna of the Seven Moons*. However this is a group of celibate women, by definition never likely to encounter conflicts between domestic and professional commitments.

During the fifties there is a striking decrease in women's magazines' attention to paid work: features and articles which did focus on employment tended to stress the problems inherent in combining the roles of housewife and/or mother, and worker. *Woman* (24 June 1950) for example, ran an article on 'Running a Job and a Home', and a feature (29 December 1956) on a couple running a public house together put its main emphasis on the effect of this work on their marriage. On the whole feature articles dealing with female employment were addressed to school leavers, or to the mothers of school leavers – it being generally accepted that young women would engage in paid employment before marriage, if not after. *Woman*, in the mid-fifties, carried a regular feature called 'Young Success' in which the details of various charismatic 'careers' were offered. Not even this limited recogntion of female participation in the labour force is evident, however, in the popular films of the mid-fifties in which women who put 'work' before 'the home' were by definition problematic – such as Kate in *East of Eden*.

Yet women did, routinely, work outside the home as well as within it in increasing numbers through the decade. It is during the fifties that the principle of equal pay was accepted, though considerable time elapsed before legislation endorsed the principle: the Equal Pay Act was finally passed in 1970. In March 1955, for example, the Burnham Committee recommended that equal pay for teachers be introduced 'in stages', and in September of the same year the Conservative government announced that it would 'gradually' introduce equal pay in the National Health Service. But there is no reference to this momentous principle and the debates surrounding it in popular film of the period. The gap between women's actual experience and media representations of it widened considerably between the mid-forties and the mid-fifties: maybe this is another reason for the decline in cinema audiences which characterised the same period?

By the mid-sixties when, as we have noted, the mass cinema audience was already a thing of the past, popular cinema again included representations of women at work – though still a limited range of work with minimal narrative importance. The offices where Marnie conducts her criminal activities are peopled by female employees in conventionally subservient roles; so are the various locations through which the Beatles, in *A Hard Day's Night* and Cliff Richard, in *Summer Holiday*, pursue their narrative paths. These are fictional worlds in which female characters are not so exclusively contained within the home as are those of the forties and fifties and in which there is some acknowledgement, however ambiguous for the female reader, of her life outside the home. But, as we have seen, the sixties films are primarily addressed to a youthful audience and are typically more concerned with pleasure and consumption than with the negotiations between different interest groups characteristic of the themes of earlier popular cinema. This emphasis on youth is also evident in the women's magazines' references to employment. A typical feature in *Woman's Own* (20 June 1964) headlined 'Where the Boys Are' categorised various kinds of employment according to whether or not they offered access to men 'jobs where you do meet men' and 'jobs where you don't': thus even in the sixties work, for women, was suggested to be a temporary and peripheral affair, a route to the more important business of finding a husband and making a home. The most bizarre representation of women at work is the group of female pilots in *Goldfinger*. Here there is some reference to the possible range of women's skills, but one that is seriously compromised by the title of the group 'Pussy Galore's Flying Circus', by their costumes – they look more like Barbie dolls than pilots – by the implication, picked up by several reviewers, that they are lesbians, and, not least, by the fact that they are on the 'wrong' side in the conflict between good (James Bond) and evil (Goldfinger). Few female readers would be tempted to identify with such exemplars, and most would probably concur with the film's preferred suggestion that the group of pilots is ridiculous, comic, and unlikely.

The fact that women did routinely combine domestic and wage earning roles was, despite the absence of much serious discussion in women's magazines or positive representations in the cinema, widely acknowledged, and the ensuing problems were also the subject of debate. But the problems, on the whole, were conceived as problems for children or for men. An unusually weighty series of three articles in *Woman's Own* (February 1965) was announced as 'A challenging report which affects the lives of eight million women'. It begins:

More women in this country are going out to work than ever before. In a changing Britain the role they play is vital – but it brings both benefits and problems . . .

The two subsequent articles deal with 'problems of child care' and 'what the men think': even when women's participation in the work force is acknowledged to be the norm we still find, as Ann Oakley did in her study of housework in the late sixties/early seventies, that women's primary and sole responsibility for the maintenance and reproduction of the national labour force is assumed, despite the fact that in 1966 five million married women had a job.

Divorce

The subject of divorce was of major public concern throughout the post-war period. During the forties the number of divorces rose, and at the time this was generally understood to be a regrettable though understandable consequence of both hasty wartime marriages and unavoidably prolonged wartime separations. The House of Lords debated the subject in November 1946, and in October (15 October 1946) *Woman* ran an article entitled 'Is Marriage a Mockery: Woman readers debate the question of easier or harder divorce'. In line with the widely held desire for a greater democratisation of society, expressed at the ballot box in 1945, access to divorce, it was felt, should not be dependent on income. Thus the 1949 Legal Aid Act accorded such access to many previously denied it because of its cost. The terms on which divorce was granted, however, remained the same as those laid down in the acts of 1923 (Matrimonial Causes) and 1937 (Divorce), namely insanity, desertion, proven cruelty and adultery. Though the divorce rate dropped during the early fifties, the debate continued with reformers urging that separation and consent be allowed as grounds for divorce while conservatives argued that the sanctity of the family would be irreparably damaged by such a change in the law. In a *Picture Post* feature (10 March 1951) Claud Mullins, a former Magistrate and the first chairman of the Marriage Guidance Council, pointed out the economic dimensions of the problem:

You must realise that our economics, as well as our morals, are based on monogamy.

Thus marriage was recognised as the fundamental economic unit of society, as well as its ethical base. But though during the fifties and sixties the institution of marriage came increasingly to be regarded as a partnership, the terms of the 'contract' were only ever addressed in the divorce courts. It was not until 1969 that the Divorce Reform Act acknowledged the already existing social practice and allowed that 'irretrievable breakdown' should be the only grounds for divorce, thus effectively legalising 'divorce by consent'.

References to divorce in the most popular films of the period, though rare, nonetheless do conform to the general contours of these developments in the divorce reform debates. We find though that they are always, in the preferred textual reading at any rate, allied to the conservative position. In the mid-forties the question of divorce is more or less explicit in several of the films we have been discussing. In *Brief Encounter*, though the word itself is never mentioned yet the possibility of Laura and Fred divorcing is implicit in her dilemma: as we have seen she shied away from even the recognition of this possibility and was warmly applauded both in the film's preferred reading and in the discursive material surrounding it, for the 'rightness' of her judgement:

> *Alec*: We know we really love each other
> That's all that really matters.
> *Laura*: It isn't all that matters.
> Other things matter too. Self respect matters, and decency. I can't go on any longer.
> *Alec*: Could you really say good-bye, never see me again?
> *Laura*: Yes, if you'd help me.

Caroline, in *The Wicked Lady*, expresses a similar sentiment to Ralph ('the things we stand for are more important than us') when she refuses a liaison with him despite the 'mockery' that his marriage to Barbara has turned out to be. Yet near the end of the film, when Ralph, Caroline and Kit discover together that they are each coupled with the 'wrong' partner, Ralph, clearly speaking here for and to the twentieth century rather than the seventeenth century in which the film is set, proposes that the problem facing them is soluble:

> *Caroline*: How do you think we can arrange things?

> *Ralph*: I don't know yet. There's no reason why four people
> should pass their lives in misery when they could be so
> happy.

But these are two couples on the threshhold of family life: in
Piccadilly Incident there is already a child, thus a family, involved.
When Diana finally catches up with Alan whom, as she has discovered, now has a (bigamous) second wife and a new baby, she
attempts to belittle her own marriage to him:

> I'm afraid our marriage was just excitement – fireworks that
> went up.

Neither the audience nor Alan believe her and, as we have seen,
fate intervenes in the form of an air raid and a falling wall which
kills her – though not before she and Alan have had time to 'reunite':
though reviewers found this ending strained belief none, of course,
had another solution to the unwitting bigamy and illegitimacy
supposedly central to the plot. It is interesting to note that, with the
exception of Ralph's proposition at the denouement of *The Wicked
Lady*, it is always the female characters who are given responsibility
in the matter of divorce. The only person in any of the films who
is actually divorced is the minor character Mrs Fitch in *Madonna
of the Seven Moons*, and she is a figure of ridicule embodying and
justifying, in the scene at the dress shop, Maddalena's fear of and
distaste for the 'modern' world in which her daughter is urging her
to participate.

There are far fewer references to divorce in our group of films
from the mid-fifties: in most of them the question is, simply,
irrelevant to the concerns of the film. In the two instances where the
subject is implicit, albeit tangentially, we are invited to understand
the problem from the point of view of the child and in thoroughly
negative terms. We never know whether, in *East of Eden*, Kate
is actually divorced from Adam, but as we have seen the film
chronicles the consequences of her absence for her children, Aron
and Cal. In *Rebel Without a Cause* the unhappy and disturbed child
Plato is offered as a sad example of the consequences of divorce.
His only happy moment, in the film, is in the scene at the deserted
mansion where he, Jim, and Judy are 'playing house' and he is
'child' to their 'parents'. Plato fantasises about his father, of whom
the only evidence is a maintenance cheque in his mother's drawer

and has nothing at all to say of his mother (with whom he lives, but who we never see) except that she doesn't care about him.

> *Plato:*   I used to run away a lot but they always brought me back. Mum and Dad. Now that I don't have them anymore I wish I'd never run away. I'd lie in my crib every night and I'd listen to them fight.
> *Jim:*   Can you remember back that far? I can't even remember what happened yesterday. How do you do it?
> *Plato:*   I had to go to a headshrinker. Boy, he *made* me remember. Then my mother said it cost too much so she went to Hawaii instead.

When Plato dies from the mistaken gunshot at the end of the film it is the negress housekeeper who cradles his head, crying 'Poor baby, got nobody, just nobody'. Plato's sad end, the film suggests, is the consequence of his 'broken' home, the responsibility of his uncaring, and thus irresponsible, parents.

By the sixties there are no such overt references to divorce in our group of six top box office hits, yet the increasing expectations of the individual for personal fulfilment and pleasure, the continuing rise in female employment, and the general increase in affluence which, as we have noted, were characteristic of the decade, all contributed to the increased economic independence of women and their consequent claims for autonomy, exemplified in the emergent women's movement. Though the issue of divorce is not treated directly in any of these six films, the question of female independence within marriage is. Once again it is a treatment which justifies the worst fears of those who opposed divorce reform, fearing its implications for the family (and, implicitly, for the state). Thus Marnie must be persuaded that marriage to Mark will, eventually, resolve her deviance; Winifred in *Mary Poppins* must give up her suffragette sash to the family kite; and Barbara Winter's dreadful mother Stella in *Summer Holiday* is probably an example of (to the British public in the sixties) the hideous stereoptype 'the American divorcee'.

The most savage attack on female independence from, or within, marriage, appears in *Tom Jones*. Here the age old opposition between the (good) country, repository of tested and reliable values, and the (bad) city, source of mistaken if not reprehensible innovation, which has been familiar to cinema audiences from the time of D. W. Griffith onwards, is re-presented. Sophie's cousin Harriet is running away from her husband; she is going to London where her 'protector' has taken a flat for her. The point is developed *à-propos* Harriet's friend, Lady Belleston. The film details the machinations through which she manipulates Tom and Sophie in order to satisfy her own lust for Tom. Tom's escape from her clutches, suggested by the faithful Partridge (already established as worthy since he comes from the 'country' world), is achieved by his supposedly ingenuous proposal of marriage: Lady Belleston instantly relinquishes him, telling her maid she will 'not receive' Mr Jones if he calls again. In case we are in any doubt as to the extent of her depravity we are also offered her activities as a (virtual) procuress – of Sophie for Lord Fellemar. Thus the awful consequences, albeit disguised by their eighteenth-century dress, of women's sexual and economic independence, are described for the contemporary audience.

To summarise we can say that in the forties divorce was represented in popular film as an unacceptable threat to the stability of the family; in the fifties its tragic consequences for the children was described; and in the sixties the spectre was raised of legions of licentious women, liberated only in order to satisfy their selfish and/or immoderate desires.

Education

The democracy and ensuing equality of citizenship which was so widely desired at the close of the Second World War implied, for women, the promise of gender equality as well as that of class and opportunity. The Education Act of 1944 was initially designed to ensure this but during the fifties developments in curriculum content in fact resulted in a very different experience of education for girls and boys. Just as the relatively rare references in popular cinema to divorce always privileged the conservative over the reforming forces in society so the even more meagre attention to female education in popular films confirmed the regressive notion that, somehow, education was a different matter for girls, of less importance than the education of boys.

In the forties, despite the fact that the themes of films in our group had in common a particular attention to women, that the 1944 Education Act was a piece of current legislation and that the Labour electoral victory apparently evidenced a widely held concern for the future quality of British society, there are only the most minimal of references to schooling. In *Madonna of the Seven Moons* Angela

Labardi has just left her London school where though her education had, apparently, fitted her to drive across Europe with a girlfriend it had hardly equipped her, as a closer examination revealed, to 'look after herself' despite her own assertions to the contrary. In *The Seventh Veil* the flashback references to Francesca's childhood experience of education reveal it to have been as repressive and authoritarian as the treatment she subsequently received at the hands of her misogynist guardian, Nicholas. Her schooling was a poor substitute for the care of her mother, and her pathological response to the injuries to her precious piano playing hands, which is the ostensibly central matter of the plot, initially derives, the film suggests, from a punishment received at school: thus her education, insofar as the film depicts it, was dis-abling rather than en-abling. In *The Bells of St Mary's* the film's action concerns, and takes place in, a catholic convent school in a run-down Irish neighbourhood of New York. The central subject matter concerns the differing approaches to education of the headteacher, Sister Mary Benedict (Ingrid Bergman) and the newly arrived pastor to the school Father O'Malley (Bing Crosby). However the real pre-occupation of the film, the narrative motivation for such discussion of pedagogic techniques as does exist, is the relationship between the two central protagonists who were both hugely popular stars at the box office: it is this, rather than the film's apparent concern with education, which would appear to account for its popular success.

In the fifties Launder and Gilliat's popular comedy cycle concerning the infamous St Trinian's[17] lampooned the education of girls. In the group of films in our sample there is only one reference to education which has any significance, and this again is one which asserts the relative unimportance of female education. In *East of Eden* Aron and his sweetheart Abra are first seen walking hand in hand in the sunny Salinas landscape. As far as we know they are about the same age, and as childhood sweethearts have been at school together. They plan to marry, and Abra wants to know when. Aron's reply is 'As soon as I get through with this darn school' The status of Abra's own education in this context is, clearly, irrelevant; there is no mention of it. In *Rebel Without a Cause* the high school which Jim attends is of interest principally as a meeting place; for the problematic young adults with which the film is concerned it is clearly as inadequate to the task of fitting them for entry to the adult world as their parents are. This is despite the thematic summary of the film offered allegorically in the lecture at the planetarium:

Jim's imagination is, temporarily at least, caught by the idea of
the awesome insignificance of 'Man' in relation to cosmic forces,
but Judy, along with the other students, is blissfully unconcerned
with such matters. In the sixties too, academic education is absent
as either a thematic or a visual concern; the single exception is
the group of schoolgirls in *A Hard Day's Night*, recognisable as
such by their uniform, who are on the same train as the Beatles,
travelling from Liverpool to London. But their narrative importance
lies entirely in their exemplification of the generation of Beatle's
fans: the school uniform functions simply to inform the audience
that the girls are in their mid-teens.

Thus although during the sixties the debates about curriculum
content raged in the columns of national newspapers, and the
recently established system of comprehensive state education
attempted, once again, to ensure the 1944 principle of equality
of education for all, popular cinema consistently undercut such
attempts in its routine representations of female experience. Education for girls, insofar as it was valued at all, seemed still to be
more concerned with preparation for wife and motherhood than
in developing the potential resources of the individual woman:
Newsom's reactionary demand that women should 'relearn the
graces which so many have forgotten in the last thirty years' seems,
in respect of popular film at least, to have been a superfluous one.
Women's magazines of the period, though they did not concern
themselves much with pedagogic matters except to answer reader's
queries about (largely vocational) post-school provision for their
readers' daughters, did occasionally carry a feature about school
life such as that in *Woman's Own* (9 May 1964): 'It's living dolls
for the under-15 class – 14 year olds get classes in mothercraft
and their charges are real babies'. Here again is the assumption
that whatever else a woman might want to be, she will surely
be a mother. The fact that, following the introduction of the first
British-made contraceptive pill in June 1963 women, for the first
time ever, had a choice about whether or not to become mothers,
is, almost wilfully, it seems with hindsight, quite ignored.

The Women's Movement

But perhaps it was precisely the possibility of women taking control
of their fertility, combined with the other factors cited above concerning female claims for moral and economic independence from

established patriarchal conventions, which underlies the emphasis on women as sexual spectacle (in *Goldfinger* and *Tom Jones*), or as incompetent childlike dependents (in *Mary Poppins, Summer Holiday* and *Marnie*) or as, for a variety of reasons, dangerously perverse (*Summer Holiday, Marnie, Tom Jones* and *Goldfinger*). Maybe the typically misogynist representation of women in the films that attracted the biggest audiences at the British box office is evidence of widely held fears about the consequences for society of the practical equality of women. Though the women's movement doesn't figure as such in any of these films, yet it is present by implication very near the surface of several of them, producing ambiguities within the text that can sometimes hardly be contained by the textual structure. In this the sixties films have more in common with those of the forties than those of the fifties in which, as we have seen, typical themes concerned masculinity and national unity. But whereas in the forties the problems for society pursuant on female independence occupy a central place in the text, in the sixties the issue is, as it were, pushed to the sidelines. Thus the apparent focus on youth, pleasure and authenticity masks a deep uneasiness about the consequences of the claim to pleasure and authenticity as they might be understood by women. Liberation for youth, for the individual, is all very well – but for women? There's an altogether different matter. This new version of the double standard is at its clearest in *Marnie* but, as we have seen, it is also evident in *Tom Jones, Mary Poppins* and *Goldfinger*.

Lady Belleston in *Tom Jones* and Winifred Banks in *Mary Poppins*, exemplify the range of objections to the women's movement's proposition that the democratic concept of equal rights for all citizens includes women in the general term 'citizen'. Lady Belleston is constructed as a quasi-comic figure, thus one not to be taken too seriously. Yet her understanding of 'independence' and the lengths to which she is prepared to go to impede the romance of the hero and heroine, besides placing her in the class of 'pantomime villain' also reveal a deep distrust of the group of confident, mature women for whom, within the diegesis, she stands. Her appallingly cynical remark about rape, for example, hardly stays within the bounds of villainous comedy – certainly for the female reader to whom this subject can never be a comic one. At the other extreme Winifred Banks is portrayed as a sweet-natured incompetent: reviewers referred to her as a 'silly suffragette',[18] a 'twittering idiot of a suffragette',[19] and as 'the sentimental little mother with her comical attachment to the suffragette movement'.[20] Her high spirited involvement with the woman's suffrage movement of the Edwardian period in which the film is set has the consequence, within the diegesis, of demeaning the movement itself. Suffragism, in this film, is reduced to a frivolous diversion for well intentioned women who apparently lack the firm (male) guidance which should remind them where their true interest and loyalty lies; that is with the family.

In line with the other films popular at the sixties box office there are relatively few women to be seen on the screen in *Goldfinger*, (after the initial pan around the borders of the Miami swimming pool). Even fewer have any significant narrative function: there are only the Masterson sisters Tilly and Jill, Pussy Galore and her flying circus. Tilly, Jill and Pussy follow each other as 'partners' to the central male character, James Bond. But what is interesting for our purposes is the other narrative traits which these three women have in common. The actions of all three are motivated by a very limited view of self interest and are highly susceptible to male influence, and they are all suggested to be incompetent in at least one narratively crucial skill. Jill is working for Goldfinger because, as she tells Bond, 'he pays me' but is easily persuaded by Bond to change sides. Tilly is trying to avenge her sister's death but her incompetence with a gun leads to Bond's capture and her own death. Pussy is supposed to be a competent pilot and a trustworthy accomplice to Goldfinger, yet it is Bond who takes over at the end of the film when she panics as the punctured plane loses altitude, and it is Bond's kiss which persuades her to betray Goldfinger. None of Goldfinger's male accomplices – Oddjob, for example – are so susceptible to the forces of good (Bond). Thus the diegetic implication is that women don't act on principle or out of belief but are always subject to the twin forces of short-term self-interest and male influence. In the case of Pussy Galore and the flying circus, the implication of lesbianism is thrown in for good measure. It is curious that at the time when legal attitudes to male homosexuality were finally being liberalised there should be this (admittedly minor) 'backlash' against female homosexuality. But just as, in the forties, female independence could, it seems, only be understood through examination of the prospects of uncontained female sexuality, so perhaps the apparent female solidarity of the sixties was most easily conceived of as women's sexual rejection of men – hence its characterisation as female homosexuality, or lesbianism.

In the struggle between Mark and Marnie for power and the control of meaning in *Marnie*, Tipi Hedren articulates many feminist objections to patriarchal dominance. She points out the legal inequities of the marriage contract, the man's right to 'take possession' of his wife. She refers to the infuriating male habit of failing to understand or respect female utterances:

> *Mark*: Are you sure you haven't misplaced an odd husband or two, somewhere in your travels?
> *Marnie*: I told you, I've never been married.
> *Mark*: Near misses?
> *Marnie*: No. No lovers, no beaux, no steadies, no gentlemen callers, nothing.
> *Mark*: You know I find it hard to believe you, Marnie. There must have been a great many men interested in you.
> *Marnie*: I didn't say men weren't interested in me. I said I wasn't interested in them.

And

> *Marnie*: But I don't need your help.
> *Mark*: I don't think you're capable of judging what you need, or from whom you need it. What you do need, I suspect, is a psychiatrist.
> *Marnie*: Oh Men! You say 'no thanks' to one of them and Bingo, you're a candidate for the funny farm.

She asserts the woman's right to lead a life independent of men:

> Oh we don't need men Mama, we can do very well for ourselves.

And she queries Mark's claim to 'love' and 'know' her – hence his understanding of both love and knowledge:

> *Mark*: It's horrible, I know, but I do love you.
> *Marnie*: You don't love *me*.
> I'm just something you've – caught.
> You think I'm some kind of animal you've trapped.

And

> *Marnie*: Why can't you just leave me alone?
> *Mark*: Because I think you're sick, old dear.

> *Marnie*: *I'm* sick! Well take a look at yourself, Old Dear.
> If you're so hot to play mental health week, what about you?
> You've got a pathological fix on a woman who is not only an
> admitted criminal but who screams if you come near her.
> So what about your dreams, Daddy dear?

Yet though the diegesis permits these assertions their context
is structured in such a way that, slowly and deliberately as the
narrative unfolds, the audience is forced to collude with Mark's
meanings, rather than with Marnie's. Both the thriller construction
and what Doane has called the 'medical discourse' are drawn
together to privilege the narrative authority of the male protagonist
who is also, at the same time, the 'investigator' (from the thriller)
and the 'doctor' (from the medical discourse). The woman must
concede that her 'way of looking' is in itself 'ill': 'woman' here
includes both the protagonists Marnie and Bernice *and* those female
audience members inclined to subscribe to Marnie's meanings. The
assertions of the women's movement are articulated, argued and
refuted.

REPRESENTATIONS OF WOMEN AND FEMALE READERS

We have examined in some detail the interface between female
audience members – female readers – and the representations of
women offered in our sample of top box office hits. Since the films
we have been discussing are those which achieved the maximum
exposure at their initial release we can assume that the images of
women – both the 'heroines' and the minor characters motivating
the narrative and peopling the screen – were seen, considered and
discussed by large numbers of cinema-goers: men and women, boys
and girls. The questions which provoked this study concern, at
base, the relation between popular cultural representations of the
'real' world and actual developments in attitudes, expectations,
behaviour and so on on the part of the inhabitants of this world,
from which, we must remember, cinema audiences are drawn. This
is clearly an extremely complex relation: there is no question here
of simple cause and effect. But the fact remains that attitudes,
behaviour and so on do change, and did change markedly in the
period 1945–1965. The difference between, for example, Margaret

Lockwood in *The Wicked Lady* and Julie Andrews in *Mary Poppins*, cannot be entirely accounted for on the basis of plot and genre – they are also qualitatitively different as types of heroine. In order to acount for the significance of the difference we must consider the historical context of the representation.

We have looked to the films themselves, asking what specifically female experience they attempted to represent and what were the terms of such representations – considering both the available discursive materials and some theoretical propositions intended to elucidate the spectatorial process. Taking the question the other way about, as it were, we have also considered some of the more important social developments of the period which specifically concerned women, asking whether, and in what terms, these developments and the debates preceding them found a place in the fictional worlds presented on the cinema screen.

Screen Women

Love and marriage are the most frequently represented of all the experiences which, we might expect, would generate different meanings on the basis of the reader's gender, yet there is very little discussion of these meanings within the films. Love, and its validation, marriage, are not conceived as problematic terms – though it is of course true that many narratives are constructed around obstacles in the course of love, or disruptions to marriage. It is precisely because the progress of romance to love, and love to marriage is so universally assumed in these films that obstacles or disruptions, when they occur, are able to function as primary constituents of narrative enigmas. They disrupt the assumed path, thus engaging the audience by stimulating their desire to know, not *whether* but *how* the disruption will be resolved, the obstacle overcome.

The question of motherhood, however, is dealt with quite differently despite the equally ubiquitous conventional link between marriage and motherhood. There are many fictional mothers either actually represented or implied in the diegesis, but when the nature of 'mothering' is explored, mothers are invariably shown to be a disruptive, destructive and altogether negative group responsible for all manner of individual and social distress. It is the incompetence or malevolence of mothers that, by and large, is emphasised.

Friendships between women receive, on the whole, a similarly

negative treatment. Very few are of any significance in plot development, therefore audience attention is not focused on them, and
those that do figure are generally defined through their adversarial
features rather than their supportive ones. Female friendships are
thus construed as the source of problems, not pleasures.

Women are rarely shown to have either knowledge or power
relevant to the narrative, and in cases where they do possess the
one they invariably lack the other: hence knowledgeable women
are disempowered and powerful women are ignorant – within the
terms of the diegesis.

Finally, and in contrast to the representations of friendships or
of female wisdom, there are rather a lot of representations of rape
or other forms of the assault of women by men. Indeed in the
sixties such representations are particularly noticeable both for their
excessive brutality and for the frequency with which they occur on
screen.

Real Women

Turning to the issues which a glance at the social history of the
period suggests to be of particular relevance to female audience
members, we find that in these most popular films such issues
are conspicuous by their absence. Despite the important debates
about equal pay and the fact that women continued, in increasing
numbers, to seek paid employment in addition to their domestic
responsibilities, fictional female characters throughout the twenty
year period were defined principally through attention to their
emotional state rather than to their practical activities. Though it
is true that women are seen 'working' on screen their work is rarely
the focus for audience attention, and if it is the representation is
invariably offered as a problematic aspect of the character – such
as in the cases of Kate in *East of Eden*, or Marnie. In addition
the peripheral representations of working women, those minor
characters and mere figures peopling the screen, bear little relation
to the actual contours of the female workforce in the period. As we
have seen the largest group of working women on screen was that
of maids and domestic servants of one kind and another, whereas
this form of work was of minimal importance, compared with other
forms, in the 'real' world inhabited by audiences.

Similarly, whereas the divorce rate rose more or less steadily
(allowing for the slight fall in the early fifties) and divorce reform

was a subject of major social importance throughout the period, there are almost no references to divorce in the films which attained the status of box office hit. Where the subject did arise the preferred reading always implied support for those who opposed reforms to the divorce laws.

Despite the intentions of the 1944 Act, education for boys and girls continued to be substantially different in both the content of the curriculum and the importance generally accorded to it. Indeed the avowed aim of equality of opportunity which characterised discussion of education in the forties seems, by the sixties, to have been abandoned by some influential educationalists in theory, as well as by many classroom teachers in practice. This regression is mirrored in both the films' overall lack of attention to the subject of education and in the differences in 'life' goals apparently considered to be appropriate for men and women.

These social reforms – to do with work and pay, with the regulation of divorce and with education – were instrumental in the precipitation of the women's movement in the sixties, arguably the most significant issue of the decade for women (if not also for men). As we have seen, such implicit references to female 'emancipation' as do occur in the films of the mid-sxties all collude in demeaning the movement, in diminishing its importance and exaggerating, through ridicule, violence or both, its negative significance for the maintenance of patriarchal order. Treatments of this subject were so reactionary that it is hard to escape the conclusion that they must have been fuelled by deep seated fears (probably on the part of women as well as men) about the long term social consequences of true gender equality. The exchange between Hugh Griffiths and Edith Evans at the Vauxhall gardens masked ball in *Tom Jones* summarises, albeit in the guise of comedy, one aspect of these fears:

> *Aunt Western*: Do you imagine that a woman of stature can be arrested, in a civilised country?
> *Squire Western*: Humph. Civilised country. Where women are above the law.

The question is, to which law are they referring? The law of democracy, or the law of patriarchy? The confusion of the two may serve the interests of the patriarch, but it is a mischievous device as far as women are concerned.

Conclusion

Narrative cinema from the classic period (which includes most of the films we have been discussing) itself specifies the spectator: it must do so in order to attract, through the mechanisms of marketing, a sufficiently large audience to ensure the survival of the industry. Such a spectator, as John Ellis argues,[1] must be 'curious' and 'expectant' about the resolution of an enigma about to be proposed through the film, but at the same time must not be so clearly defined as to exclude too many potential audience members by allowing them to reject any connection between themselves and the 'proposed' spectator. Hence the tendency, in films produced in order to attract a mass audience (this applies to all the films in our sample, by definition), to remain within the consensual ideological trends in society. As Ellis suggests, the ordering of the cinematic institution through the operations of genre and the star system begins the necessary process of specifying the proposed spectators, but neither genre nor stars, on their own, can secure economically viable audiences. Themes and issues with which any particular film concerns itself must be of interest to the putative spectator, but since the largest possible number of spectators must be interested in the product (the film and its propositions) it follows that the propositions of the film must be more or less in line with contemporary received wisdom (or, dominant discourses) about the particular issues concerned. The putative spectator can then sufficiently identify with the specified spectator to willingly, indeed 'expectantly', purchase a ticket and enter the darkened auditorium.

But in the case of the routine representations of women there is more going on, it seems, than this relatively straightforward operation of the 'lowest common factor' or 'highest common denominator' (which it is depends on our point of view) identified in Ellis' discussion. Our exploration of popular film shows that screen representations, in the period 1945–1965, performed a consistently repressive function in respect of women. There are, simply, no depictions of autonomous, independent women either inside or outside the structure of the family, who survive unscathed at the narrative's close. How is it then, that such apparently negative representations could continue to be so popular with audiences

210

of which at least fifty percent (we are entitled to assume, because of the size of cinema audiences during most of the period) were women? To illuminate this question we must turn once again to our discussion of audience activity and, in particular, spectatorial strategies; a discussion in which the status of the text is put into question and attention focused on the ways in which readers and audiences *make use* of the text.

The psychoanalytical model accords primary significance to the psychic activities of the individual (gendered) subject, attempting in particular to account for the operations of desire and pleasure, of identification and disavowal and the ways in which these terms can account for the complexities of the interface between the reader and the screen. In drawing on the insights afforded by this model, however, we should bear in mind recent feminist theoretical discussion of limitations in both Freud's and Lacan's accounts of the formation of feminine subjectivity, since these limitations may put into question accounts of the production of pleasure and the operation of desire – particularly those based in Freudian or Lacanian propositions.

The semiotic model acknowledges the arbitrariness of the relation between the sign and its referent, revealing, in the process, the underlying structure of myths. Thus biological determinism (arguably present in both the psychoanalytic and the sociological accounts of spectatorial activity) is put into question by means of a demonstration of cultural determinism. The 'artificial' or 'man-made' (the term is used advisedly here) relation between biological and cultural determinisms is made apparent.

The sociological model comes closest, if only implicitly, to acknowledging the existence of audience groupings separable from the 'ideal reader' imagined in the textual construction. This model both enables and requires comparisons between the diegetic and the real: such comparisons are just as likely to generate speculation about the constraints of the real world as to ensure compliance with them. It depends, in the end, not on the text but on the reader: however, as we have seen, the sociological model of spectatorial activity accords small importance to the actual members of the audience, substituting the claims of the dominant discourse to interpret or name 'the real'.

Thus though we share de Lauretis' assertion that cinema is indeed a 'technology of gender', one which, in relation to female self determination within patriarchal order, has certainly acted as a brake, slowing down the processes involved, we must also recognize that such a technology is a two-edged sword. Popular cinematic representations of women may attempt (and in this period certainly have attempted) to enforce patriarchal order's requirements of its female subjects, but in so doing have also revealed these requirements for what they are. Bearing in mind our discussion of the variety of processes in which the female reader may engage when confronted with what are, invariably, repressive representations of women, we can acknowledge that these representations may be used by some women in the audience to enable their recognition of the inequities of patriarchal order and thence to strengthen their resolve to resist. This is an admittedly optimistic conclusion, but it is still a possible one.

Appendix:
Synopses of Films

The format of this Appendix is as follows:

Film Title
Director, Production Company, Country, Year
Actors
Synopsis

All About Eve
Joseph Mankiewicz, 20th Century Fox, US 1950.
Bette Davis; Celeste Holm; Ann Baxter; George Sanders; Thelma
    Ritter; Gary Merrill; Marilyn Monroe.

Witty story of intrigue and power struggles in the world of the
theatre. Eve (Baxter) inveigles her way into the life of Margot
Channing (Davis), a celebrated star who is pre-occupied with her
advancing age (she is 40), and usurps her position. In the end she
too is threatened by an admiring and manipulative acolyte.

All That Heaven Allows
Douglas Sirk, U I, US 1955.
Rock Hudson; Jane Wyman; Agnes Moorhead.

A widow (Wyman), mother of two young adult children, becomes
involved with a local tree farmer (Hudson). Despite opposition
from both her peer group and her children, and after much heart
searching, she goes to join him in his Thoreauesque life outside the
town.

The Belles of St. Trinians
Frank Launder, London Films, UK 1954.
Alastair Sim, George Cole; Joyce Grenfell; Hermione Baddely; Irene
    Handl.

213

Alastair Sim (in drag) is the headmistress of a wickedly anarchic girls' boarding school regarded with terror by both the Ministry of Education and the local constabulary. This highly successful farce was based on Ronald Searle's cartoons, and initiated a series, the last of which was made in 1966.

The Bells of St. Mary's
Leo McCarey, RKO, US 1945.
Bing Crosby; Ingrid Bergman.

A Catholic school in a run down Irish neighbourhood of New York is threatened with demolition to make way for the car park of a new office block. Against this background the newly-arrived pastor (Crosby) and the headteacher (Bergman) negotiate their differing methods of education.

Black Narcissus
Powell and Pressburger, Archers, UK 1946.
Deborah Kerr; David Farrar; Sabu; Jean Simmons; Kathleen Byron; Flora Robson.

A nun in an Anglo-Catholic convent in the Himalayas is 'unhinged' by the combination of the location, the climate and the charismatic presence of a local expatriate (Farrar). In a struggle with the mother superior (Kerr) she falls to her death and the convent subsequently disbands.

Brief Encounter
David Lean, Cineguild, UK 1945.
Celia Johnson; Trevor Howard; Stanley Holloway; Joyce Carey; Cyril Raymond.

Laura (Johnson) tells in flashback the story of her love affair with Alec (Howard) whom she met by chance while on a routine shopping trip. Both are happily married and decide to end the affair almost before it has begun.

Caesar and Cleopatra
Gabriel Pascal, Rank, UK 1945.
Claude Rains; Vivien Leigh; Cecil Parker; Stewart Granger; Flora Robson; Stanley Holloway; Jean Simmons; Michael Rennie.

'An elaborate screen treatment of Bernard Shaw's comedy about Caesar's years in Alexandria. Britain's most expensive film is an absurd extravaganza for which the producer actually took sand to Egypt in order to get the right colour. It has compensations however in the sets, the colour, the performances and the witty lines, though all its virtues are theatrical rather than cinematic and the play is certainly not a major work.' Halliwell 1987.

Calamity Jane
David Butler, Warner, US 1953
Doris Day; Howard Keel; Allyn McClerie.

Musical set in the nineteenth-century American west. Calamity Jane (Day), dressed in her habitually scruffy buckskins, visits Chicago to bring a star attraction to the Deadwood saloon. She and Katie Brown (McLerie) become friends, then rivals and, after Calamity has learned the vital skills of 'femininity', they are re-united in a double wedding with their respective sweethearts.

The Captive Heart
Basil Dearden, Ealing, UK 1946.
Michael Redgrave; Jack Warner; Basil Radford; Mervyn Johns; Jimmy Hanley; Gordon Jackson; Gladys Henson; Rachel Kempson; Karel Stepanek.

The stories of several British prisoners of war before, during and following their long imprisonment in a German camp, and in particular of a Czech who impersonates a British officer in correspondence with the latter's wife in UK with whom he is eventually united.

Caravan
Arthur Crabtree, Gainsborough, UK 1946.
Stewart Granger; Anne Crawford; Jean Kent; Dennis Price.

Period melodrama set in England and Spain and following the fortunes of the hero (Granger), his 'highborn' sweetheart (Crawford), her villainous husband (Price) and the Spanish gipsy (Kent) who nurses Granger after he is left for dead by Price's agents.

Carry On Spying
Gerald Thomas, Anglo Amalgamated, UK 1964.
Hattie Jacques; Kenneth Williams; Joan Sims; Sid James.

Ninth in the long-running Carry On series: here the successful formula of crude stereotyping and slapstick comedy is deployed in a spy thriller format in which the British team faces the evil STENCH network. The varied European settings and the relatively lavish displays of technology constitute a direct reference to the contemporary James Bond films.

Conflict
Curtis Bernhardt, Warner, US 1945.
Humphrey Bogart; Sydney Greenstreet; Alexis Smith; Rose Hobart.

'A man murders his wife and is apparently haunted by her; but the odd happenings have been arranged by a suspicious psychiatrist'. Halliwell 1987. Though released in 1945 the film was completed in August 1943.

The Corn is Green
Irving Rapper, Warner, US 1945.
Bette Davis; Nigel Bruce; Rhys Williams; John Dall; Joan Lorring.

'In 1895 Miss Moffat starts a village school for Welsh miners, and after some tribulations sees one of them off to Oxford'. Halliwell 1987.

The Curse of Frankenstein
Terence Fisher, Hammer, UK 1957.
Peter Cushing; Christopher Lee; Hazel Court; Robert Urquhart.

'A lurid revamping of the 1931 Frankenstein, this time with severed eyeballs and a peculiarly unpleasant and uncharacterised creature, all in gory colour. It set the trend in nasty horrors from which we have all suffered since, and launched Hammer Studios on a long and profitable career of charnelry'. Halliwell 1987.

The Dam Busters
Michael Anderson, ABPC, UK 1954.
Michael Redgrave; Richard Todd; Ursula Jeans.

Scientist Barnes Wallis (Redgrave) and RAF Squadron Leader Gibson (Todd) successfully collaborate in bombing the Ruhr dams in 1943 using a specially invented bouncing bomb. This celebrated incident from British war history is described with a loving and apparently documentary attention to detail though the film's meritocrtic ideals have a distinctly 50s air.

Doctor At Sea
Ralph Thomas, Rank, UK 1955.
Dirk Bogarde; Brigitte Bardot; Brenda da Banzie; James Robertson Justice; Maurice Denham.

Newly qualified Dr Sparrow (Bogarde) escapes the unwelcome advances of his senior partner's daughter by going to sea as a ship's doctor. Thereafter follows a series of comedy routines purveying familiar stereotypes of British farce – foreigners, unions, women, the class system – against a travelogue background of blue seas and skies.

Doctor in the House
Ralph Thomas, Rank, UK 1954.
Dirk Bogarde; Kenneth More; Kay Kendall; Muriel Pavlow; Donald Sinden; Donald Houston.

First of the popular 'Doctor' series, the film details the medical training of Simon Sparrow (Bogarde), making the most of its medical context and 'student' protagonists to produce comic set pieces in the British music hall tradition.

Dr. No
Terence Young, UA, UK 1962.
Sean Connery; Ursula Andress.

First of the successful series of James Bond films based on Ian Fleming's novels. In this one Bond (Connery) is pitted against a master criminal operating in the West Indies, and the series' format of lavish spectacle, violent action and female characters' susceptibility to Bond's charismatic sexuality, is established.

East of Eden
Elia Kazan, Warner, US 1955.
James Dean; Raymond Massey; Julie Harris; Jo Van Fleet; Richard Davalos; Burl Ives; Albert Dekker.

Based on a Steinbeck novel, the film is set in California during the First World War. Adam (Massey) has brought up his twin sons Aron (Davalos) and Cal (Dean) alone since their mother (Van Fleet) deserted the family soon after the children's birth. Aron is obedient and 'good', Cal is difficult and 'bad'. The film follows Cal's various attempts to 'find' himself and to win his father's love, which he eventually does with the help of Abra (Harris), initially his brother's girl but who discovers she loves Cal.

From Here To Eternity
Fred Zinneman, Columbia, US 1953.
Frank Sinatra; Burt Lancaster; Montgomery Clift; Deborah Kerr; Ernest Borgnine; Donna Reed.

'Life in a Honolulu barracks at the time of Pearl Harbour. Cleaned up and streamlined version of a best seller in which the sexual frustrations of a number of unattractive characters are laid bare. As a production, it is Hollywood in good form, and certainly took the public fancy as well as establishing Sinatra as an acting force.' Halliwell 1987.

From Russia With Love
Terence Young, UA, UK 1963.
Sean Connery; Robert Shaw; Lotte Lenya; Eunice Gayson; Lois Maxwell.

A Russian spy joins an international crime ring in order to kill the British agent Bond/007 (Connery) and steal a vital new piece of intelligence equipment from 'the West'. This second James Bond film develops the successful formula of the first, this time with Venice and Istanbul amongst the spectacular locations.

The Glenn Miller Story
Anthony Mann, U-I, US 1954.
James Stewart; June Allyson; Frances Langford; Louis Armstrong; Gene Krupa.

Musical biopic telling moments from the life of the celebrated band leader, emphasising his rise from obscurity to stardom, his marriage and his patriotic death while entertaining US troops stationed in Europe during the Second World War.

Goldfinger
Guy Hamilton, UA, UK 1964.
Sean Connery; Honor Blackman; Gert Frobe; Harold Sakata; Lois
  Maxwell; Shirley Eaton; Bernard Lee.

James Bond (Connery) versus Auric Goldfinger (Frobe): after a
series of lavish and spectacular adventures in Miami, Switzerland
and Kentucky, Bond discovers and foils Goldfinger's plan to plant
a Chinese nuclear device in the US gold reserves at Fort Knox in
order to disable Western economies and increase the value of his
own holdings. This was the third of the Bond films.

Gone With The Wind
Victor Fleming (George Cukor, Sam Wood), MGM, US 1939.
Vivien Leigh; Clark Gable; Olivia de Havilland; Leslie Howard;
  Barbara O'Neill; Hattie McDaniel; Butterfly McQueen; Thomas
  Mitchell.

The biggest box office hit ever: this celebrated and lavish film tells
the story of a southern belle, Scarlett O'Hara (Leigh), her stirring life
during the period of the civil war, and her stormy relationship with
Rhett Butler (Gable).

The Great Escape
John Sturges, UA, US 1963.
James Garner; Steve McQueen; Richard Attenborough; James
  Donald; Charles Bronson; Donald Pleasence; James Coburn;
  David McCallum; Gordon Jackson.

'Allied prisoners plan to escape from a German prison camp. Pretty
good but overlong POW film with a tragic ending'. Halliwell 1987.

Guys and Dolls
Joseph Mankiewicz, Samuel Goldwyn, US 1955.
Marlon Brando; Jean Simmons; Frank Sinatra; Vivian Blaine; Stubby
  Kaye.

A young hoodlum (Brando) takes a bet that he can charm a Salvation
Army officer (Simmons), on a mission to save souls in a run-down
area of the city. Musical romance with a series of song and dance
set pieces in a studio bound 'New York'.

The Happiest Days of Your Life
Frank Launder, British Lion, UK 1950.
Margaret Rutherford; Alastair Sim; Joyce Grenfell.

A girls' school, headmistress Rutherford, is billeted on a boys' school, headmaster Sim, with farcical consequences prefiguring the later St. Trinians cycle.

A Hard Day's Night
Dick Lester, (UA) Proscenium, UK 1964.
The Beatles; Wilfrid Brambell; Norman Rossington; Victor Spinetti.

The film combines documentary detail with fantasy and farce in an action-packed account of a twenty-four hour trip from Liverpool to London by the British pop music group, the Beatles, who were approaching the height of their popularity at the time.

Help
Dick Lester, (UA) Walter Shenson, UK 1965.
The Beatles; Leo McKern; Eleanor Bron; Victor Spinetti.

'An oriental high priest chases the Beatles around the world because one of them has a sacred ring. Exhausting attempt to outdo *A Hard Day's Night* in lunatic frenzy, which goes to prove that some talents work better on low budgets.' Halliwell 1987.

Henry V
Laurence Olivier, Rank/Two Cities, UK 1944.
Laurence Olivier; Robert Newton; Leslie Banks; Esmond Knight; Renee Asherson; George Robey; Leo Genn; Felix Aylmer.

'Shakespeare's historical play is seen in performance at the Globe theatre in 1603; as it develops the scenery becomes more realistic. Immensely stirring, experimental and almost wholly successful production of Shakespeare on film, sturdy both in its stylization and its command of more conventional cinematic resources for the battle.' Halliwell 1987.

Here Come the Waves
Mark Sandrich, Paramount, US 1944.
Bing Crosby; Betty Hutton; Sonny Tufts; Ann Doran.

'A sailor falls in love with identical twin Waves. Empty headed, professionally executed musical recruiting poster.' Halliwell 1987.

High Society
Charles Walters, MGM, US 1956.
Grace Kelly, Bing Crosby; Frank Sinatra; Celeste Holm; Louis Armstrong; Louis Calhern.

Musical remake of *The Philadelphia Story* (1940). A rich heiress (Kelly) about to enter into her second marriage returns, at the last minute, to the arms of her first husband (Crosby). Their romance is parallelled by that of the two journalists (Holm and Sinatra) covering the wedding.

Hobson's Choice
David Lean, British Lion/London, UK 1953.
Charles Laughton; John Mills; Brenda da Banzie; Prunella Scales.

Domestic comedy set in nineteenth-century Lancashire. Da Banzie is the eldest of Laughton's three daughters and efficiently runs both his home and his boot and shoe shop. Though at 30 she is considered an 'old maid' she defies her father, marries their skilled employee (Mills) and sets up a rival business.

I Live in Grosvenor Square
Herbert Wilcox, ABP, UK 1945.
Anna Neagle; Rex Harrison; Robert Morley; Jane Darwell; Nancy Price; Dean Jagger.

'A Duke's daughter falls in love with an American air force sergeant.' Halliwell 1987. Topical romance which was successful at the British box office and intiated the Wilcox/Neagle 'London' romances.

It Always Rains on Sunday
Robert Hamer, Ealing, UK 1947
Googie Withers; John McCallum; Jack Warner; Edward Chapman; Sidney Tafler.

An escaped convict (McCallum) claims refuge from his sweetheart of long ago (Withers), now married with a son and adult step-daughters. Her dilemma is played out against the Sunday routines of London's East End, the interactions of the family, and the thriller format of the manhunt.

Jassy
Bernard Knowles, Gainsborough, UK 1947.
Margaret Lockwood; Patricia Roc; Dennis Price; Basil Sydney.

'A gipsy servant girl falls in love with her master but is accused of murder. Period romantic melodrama of the *Man In Grey* school; poor of its kind despite high production values.' Halliwell 1987.

The King and I
Walter Lang, 20th Century Fox, US 1956.
Deborah Kerr; Yul Brynner; Rita Moreno.

'Musical remake of Anna and the King of Siam, from the highly successful stage production. The film is opulent in lush detail but quite lacking in style.' Halliwell 1987.

The Life and Death of Colonel Blimp
Powell and Pressburger, GFD/Archers, UK 1943.
Roger Livesy; Anton Walbrook; Deborah Kerr; Roland Culver; Ursula Jeans.

The film chronicles the experience of Clive Candy (Livesy), a British officer, drawing attention to the differing codes of militarism and masculinity operating in the British and German armies in the First World War, and following their evolution in the 1939–1945 conflict. To those who opposed both its export and its release, the film portrayed the British high command unfavorably, while others claimed it showed an admirable capacity for self criticism which augured well for British victory.

Madonna of the Seven Moons
Arthur Crabtree, Gainsborough, UK 1944.
Phyllis Calvert; Patricia Roc; Stewart Granger; John Stuart; Jean Kent; Nancy Price; Peter Glenville; Peter Murray Hill.

Melodrama set in pre-war Florence and Rome, concerning the fatal consequences of the heroine's (Calvert) 'split personality'. As Maddalena she is the devout, retiring wife of a wealthy Roman and mother of Angela (Roc); as Rosanna she is the mistress of the leader (Granger) of a gang of petty crooks in the picturesque back streets of Florence.

The Man Who Knew Too Much
Alfred Hitchcock, Paramount, US 1956.
James Stewart; Doris Day; Bernard Miles; Brenda da Banzie.

Remake of the 1934 spy thriller involving a kidnapped child and her father's efforts to rescue her.

Marnie
Alfred Hitchcock, Universal, US 1964.
Sean Connery; Tipi Hedren; Martin Gabel; Diane Baker; Louise Latham.

Psychological thriller in which Mark (Connery) pursues and marries Marnie (Hedren), seeking to explain and 'cure' both her criminality and her frigidity. In a flashback sequence at the end of the film a childhood trauma is revealed to be the cause of her 'problems'.

Marty
Delbert Mann, UA, US 1955.
Ernest Borgnine; Betsy Blair.

The story of a couple who, because they each consider themselves to be unattractive, had given up hope of love and marriage. Borgnine is Marty, a 34-year-old Italian butcher from the Bronx who lives with his mother, and Blair is the girl he meets at a dance where she has been abandoned by her blind date.

Mary Poppins
Robert Stevenson, Walt Disney, US 1964.
Julie Andrews; Dick Van Dyke; Glynis Johns; David Tomlinson; Hermione Baddely; Elsa Lanchester; Jane Darwell.

Musical about a magical nanny (Andrews) and her subversive, though ultimately therapeutic, interventions into a middle-class Edwardian household. Animation, live action and studio versions of stereotypical London exteriors are combined in a series of storybook versions of conventional Britishness as imagined by Hollywood.

Mildred Pierce
Michael Curtiz, Warner, US 1945.
Joan Crawford; Eve Arden; Ann Blyth; Jack Carson; Zachary Scott.

The generic codes of film noir and the family melodrama are employed to tell the story of Mildred Pierce (Crawford), the break-up of her marriage, her rise and fall as an entrepreneur, and the fate of her two daughters.

Millions Like Us
Launder and Gilliat, Gainsborough, UK 1943.
Patricia Roc; Gordon Jackson; Moore Marriott; Eric Portman; Anne Crawford; Basil Radford; Naunton Wayne; Joy Shelton; Megs Jenkins.

The film deals with female call-up in the UK during the Second World War, and follows a group of young 'mobile' women as they are drafted to a munitions factory in the countryside far from their homes. They come from a cross-section of classes and regions and the understanding that develops between them is exemplary of the Ministry of Information's ideal of a patriotically united home front.

Mr Skeffington
Vincent Sherman, Warner, US 1944.
Bette Davis; Claude Rains.

'A selfish beauty finally turns to her discarded dull husband; when he is blind he doesn't mind her faded looks.' Halliwell 1987.

Oklahoma
Fred Zinneman, Rodgers and Hammerstein, US 1955.
Gordon Macrae; Shirley Jones; Rod Steiger; Gloria Grahame.

Musical story of the mid-west. 'A cowboy wins his girl despite the intervention of a hired hand.' Halliwell 1987.

Old Acquaintance
Vincent Sherman, Warner, US 1943.
Bette Davis; Miriam Hopkins; Gig Young; John Loder; Dolores Moran.

'Two jealous lady novelists interfere in each other's love lives. A dated but rather splendid battle of the wild cats, with two stars fighting their way through a plush production and a rather overlong script.' Halliwell 1987.

On The Waterfront
Elia Kazan, Columbia, US 1954.
Marlon Brando; Eve Marie Saint; Lee J Cobb; Rod Steiger; Karl Malden.

Set among the dockers of New York, the film chronicles the struggle of Terry Mulloy (Brando), the young brother of a corrupt union official, to recognise his awakening conscience and lead the dockers in defence of the union. He is encouraged by Edie Doyle (Saint) and the local priest (Malden).

Passport to Pimlico
Henry Cornelius, Ealing, UK 1949.
Stanley Holloway; Margaret Rutherford; Basil Radford; Naunton Wayne; Hermione Baddely; Jane Hylton; Betty Warren; Sidney Tafler.

Children playing on a bomb site find an ancient document which shows that Pimlico was owned by the Burgundian crown and is thus a part of France. The consequences are developed in a comic fantasy in which the dual restrictions of British convention and post-war austerity are overturned.

Piccadilly Incident
Herbert Wilcox, ABP, UK 1946.
Anna Neagle; Michael Wilding; Michael Laurence; Frances Mercer; Coral Browne.

Diana (Neagle) and Alan (Wilding) meet and marry during the blitz in wartime London and are then separated by their service duties. When she returns to the UK after three years marooned on a Pacific island Diana finds that Alan, after mourning her loss, has remarried and had a son by his new American wife. The film's ostensible concern is the legitimacy of this child.

A Place of One's Own
Bernard Knowles, Gainsborough, UK 1945.
James Mason; Barbara Mullen; Margaret Lockwood; Dennis Price.

'A couple buy a house they find to be haunted, and their young companion is affected by the place. She is cured by a mysterious doctor whose body had been found several hours before.' BFI filecard.

Private's Progress
John Boulting, British Lion, UK 1956.
Ian Carmichael; Terry Thomas; Richard Attenborough; Dennis Price.

'An extremely innocent young national serviceman is taught a few army dodges and becomes a dupe for jewel thieves. Celebrated army farce with satirical pretensions; when released it had something to make everyone in Britain laugh.' Halliwell 1987.

A Queen is Crowned
Castleton Knight (Producer). Rank, UK 1953.

Documentary record, in technicolor, of the June 1953 coronation of the British Queen Elizabeth II, with a narration by Laurence Olivier.

Reach For The Sky
Lewis Gilbert, Rank, UK 1956.
Kenneth More; Muriel Pavlow; Dorothy Alison; Sidney Tafler.

Biopic about the flier and hero of the Second World War Douglas Bader (More). The details of his RAF training, his recovery from the accident in which he lost both his legs and his celebrated wartime bravery are suggested to be exemplary of the British character and fighting spirit.

Rear Window
Alfred Hitchcock, Hitchcock, US 1954.
James Stewart; Grace Kelly; Raymond Burr; Thelma Ritter.

A news photographer (Stewart), confined to his chair by a broken leg, observes the daily routines of the inhabitants of the neighbouring apartment block. Convinced that a man has murdered his wife, he enlists the help of his girlfriend (Kelly) in investigating his suspicions. The film is thus concerned with scopophilia and with gender-based power relations and is consequently understood by many as a paradigm for the cinema itself.

Rebel Without a Cause
Nicholas Ray, Warner, US 1955.
James Dean; Natalie Wood; Jim Backus; Sal Mineo; Ann Doran;
    Dennis Hopper.

The narrative covers an eventful twenty four hours in the life of
its adolescent hero, Jim (James Dean). At the opening he is drunk,
disorderly and disaffected – by the close he has 'grown up'. The
film was noted for its implicit criticism of the parental generation,
held culpable for the delinquent behaviour of their young, and for
locating the problem in the wealthy classes.

The Road to Utopia
Hal Walker, Paramount, US 1945.
Bob Hope,; Bing Crosby; Dorothy Lamour.

Fourth of the popular musical comedy 'Road' films, this one is set
in the California gold rush.

Saturday Night and Sunday Morning
Karel Reisz, Bryanston/Woodfall, UK 1960.
Albert Finney; Rachel Roberts; Shirley Ann Field; Hylda Baker.

One of the first 'kitchen sink' films heralded as the British 'new
wave'. Arthur Seaton (Finney) is a young factory worker living
with his parents in a northern industrial town. He has an affair
with a married woman (Roberts) and meets a girl he wants to
marry (Fields). The film's explicit reference to private and public
moral codes marked a clear change in British cinema.

The Searchers
John Ford, Warner, US 1956.
John Wayne; Jeffrey Hunter; Natalie Wood; Vera Miles; Ward
    Bond.

Set in the late 1860s the film details the five-year search for Debbie
(Wood) abducted by Comanches when they attacked her home and
murdered her family. Ethan (Wayne) and Marty (Hunter) follow
this western quest through spectacular landscapes and varying
weather conditions, returning periodically to the isolated Texan
settlers' community.

Seven Brides for Seven Brothers
Stanley Donen, MGM, US 1954.
Howard Keel; Jane Powell; Jeff Richards; Russ Tamblyn.

'In the old west, seven hard working brothers decide they need wives, and carry off young women from the villages around. Disappointingly studio bound western musical, distinguished by an excellent score and some brilliant dancing, notably the barn raising sequence.' Halliwell 1987.

The Seventh Veil
Compton Bennett, Theatrecraft, UK 1945.
James Mason; Anne Todd; Herbert Lom; Albert Lieven; Hugh McDermott.

Psychological drama about a concert pianist (Todd) and the reasons for her pathological belief that her hands are irreparably damaged. Lom is her psychiatrist and Mason the misogynist cousin who, as her guardian, has brought her up and overseen her professional training.

The Slipper and the Rose
Bryan Forbes, Paradine, UK 1976.
Margaret Lockwood; Richard Chamberlain; Gemma Craven; Kenneth More; Michael Hordern; Edith Evans.

Lavish musical production of the Cinderella story.

A Song to Remember
Charles Vidor, Columbia, US 1944.
Cornel Wilde; Merle Oberon; Paul Muni; george Coulouris; George Macready.

Unexpectedly popular Hollywood musical biopic about the life of Chopin and his relationship with George Sand.

South Pacific
Joshua Logan, Magna, US 1958.
Rossano Brazzi; Mitzi Gaynor; Ray Walston; John Kerr; Frances Nuyen; Juanita Hall.

Musical set against the background of the US/Japanese conflict in the Second World War. In 1943 a young US Navy nurse (Gaynor) falls in love with a locally resident middle-aged Frenchman (Brazzi) who becomes a war hero.

Spellbound
Alfred Hitchcock, David O Selznick, US 1945.
Ingrid Bergman; Gregory Peck; Leo G Carroll; Michael Checkov.

Bergman is a psychiatrist; she falls in love with her amnesiac patient who believes himself to be a murderer.

A Stitch in Time
Robert Asner, Rank, UK 1963.
Norman Wisdom; Edward Chapman; Jerry Desmonde; Jeanette Storke.

Vehicle for the popular British slapstick comedian, Norman Wisdom, who plays a butcher's boy falling for a nurse during a stay in hospital.

Summer Holiday
Peter Yates, ABP, UK 1962.
Cliff Richard; Lauri Peters; Melvyn Hayes; Una Stubbs; Teddy Green; Ron Moody; Lionel Murton; David Kossoff.

Musical travelogue in which four young London Transport mechanics led by Cliff Richard take a specially fitted, red, double-decker London bus across Europe to Athens, encountering various light-hearted adventures on the way.

They Were Sisters
Arthur Crabtree, Gainsborough, UK 1945.
James Mason; Phyllis Calvert; Dulcie Gray; Hugh Sinclair; Anne Crawford; Peter Murray Hill.

'One of three sisters tries to rescue another, ill treated by her sadistic husband, but the sister kills herself. At the inquest the former is given custody of the children.' BFI filecard.

Tom Jones
Tony Richardson, Woodfall, UK 1963.
Albert Finney; Susannah York; Hugh Griffith; Edith Evans; Joan
    Greenwood; Diane Cilento; David Warner; Freda Jackson; Wilfrid
    Lawson; George Devine; Joyce Redman; Rachel Kempson.

Based on Fielding's classic eighteenth-century novel, the film
chronicles the adventures of Tom (Finney), the illegitimate ward
of a worthy west country squire, in his home, on the road after
his banishment, and in London as he seeks reunion with his true
love Sophie (York), daughter of the bucolic neighbouring squire.

A Town Like Alice
Jack Lee, Rank, UK 1956.
Virginia McKenna; Peter Finch.

'Life among the prisoners of the Japanese in Malaya, especially
one who is finally reunited with her Australian lover. Genteelly
harrowing war film, formlessly adapted from the first part of a
popular novel; a big commercial success in its day.' Halliwell 1987.

Von Ryan's Express
Mark Robson, 20th Century Fox, US 1965.
Frank Sinatra; Trevor Howard; Sergio Fantoni.

'In an Italian POW camp during World War II, an unpopular American Captain leads English prisoners in a train escape. Exhilarating
action thriller with slow spots atoned for by a nail biting finale,
though the downbeat curtain mars the general effect'. Halliwell
1987.

The Way to the Stars
Anthony Asquith, Two Cities, UK 1945.
John Mills; Rosamund John; Michael Redgrave; Stanley Holloway;
    Joyce Carey; Felix Aylmer; Trevor Howard; Jean Simmons.

Set during the latter part of the Second World War as American
fliers join the RAF station near the small country hotel in which
much of the action takes place. The romance, marriage, motherhood
and bereavement of the hotel manageress is central among other
individual dramas played out against the wartime background.

The Wicked Lady
Leslie Arliss, Gainsborough, UK 1945.
Margaret Lockwood; Patricia Roc; James Mason; Michael Rennie; Griffith Jones; Enid Stamp-Taylor; Martita Hunt; Felix Aylmer.

Costume drama set in Restoration England. Barbara (Lockwood) steals Caroline's (Roc) fiancé Ralph (Griffith Jones) but, quickly bored with marriage, starts to lead a secret nocturnal life as a highwayman. She meets and partners Capt. Jerry Jackson (Mason) but betrays and kills him, adding to the murders she has committed. Caroline becomes engaged to Kit (Rennie), the only man Barbara has ever loved. During Barbara's attempt to kill Ralph so that she might marry Kit, he shoots her and she dies alone as the other three discover her double life.

Woman in a Dressing Gown
J Lee Thompson, Godwin/Willis, UK 1957.
Anthony Quayle; Yvonne Mitchell; Sylvia Sym; Andrew Ray; Carole Lesley.

Marital drama told mainly from the point of view of the wife (Mitchell) as her marriage is threatened by her husband's (Quayle) affair with a younger woman (Sym). The film stands out for its careful attention to the domestic details of the lower middle-class urban setting and for its sympathetic attention to the different desires of its protagonists.

Yield to the Night
J Lee Thompson, ABP, UK 1956.
Diana Dors; Yvonne Mitchell; Michael Craig.

Anti-capital punishment drama based on the Ruth Ellis case. Dors plays the lead and her accomplished performance surprised many, particularly since she spends most of the film in her prison cell accompanied only by her warder (Mitchell) and dressed in a voluminous nightdress, without make-up, as she awaits execution.

The Young Ones
Sidney J Furie, ABP, UK 1961.
Cliff Richard; Robert Morley; Carole Grey; Melvyn Hayes.

Musical comedy set in London in which a youth club is threatened with demolition by a property tycoon (Morley) whose son (Richard), a member of the club, organises resistance. To raise the necessary funds the teenagers put on a musical in an abandoned theatre and its success unites the generations.

Zulu
Cy Endfield, Paramount/Diamond, UK 1964.
Stanley Baker; Jack Hawkins; Michael Caine.

'In 1879 British soldiers stand fast against the Zulus at Rorke's drift. Standard period heroics, well presented and acted.' Halliwell 1987.

Notes

INTRODUCTION: WHAT DOES 'POPULAR CINEMA' MEAN TO WOMEN?

1. Angus Calder, *The People's War* (Cape, 1969).
2. Ian Christie, *Powell, Pressburger and Others* (BFI, 1978).
3. Helen Taylor, *Scarlett's Women: Gone With The Wind and its Female Fans* (Virago, 1989).
4. Annette Kuhn's book *Cinema, Censorship and Sexuality* (Routledge 1988), offers a detailed study of the early formation of censorship regulations in Britain c. 1909–1925 in which the various moral, political and economic constraints to which these regulations have been subject, are explored.
5. Teresa de Lauretis, *Technologies of Gender* (Macmillan, 1987).
6. Diegesis: The fictional world proposed by the narrative.
7. E. H. Carr, *What Is History* (Macmillan, 1961).

CHAPTER 1: POPULAR FORMS AND POPULARITY

1. *Tribune*, 23/11/45.
2. *To-Day's Cinema*, 16/1/45, p. 9.
3. *Kinematograph Weekly*, 22/11/45, p. 24.
4. Carr, 1961, op. cit.
5. *Kinematograph weekly*, 19/12/47 p. 47.
6. Curran and Porter, *British Cinema History* (Weidenfeld & Nicolson 1983 p. 372).
7. The films selected for detailed analysis in this book are chosen from amongst those whose 'popularity' is corroborated by means of a correlation of seven categories listed in three sources.
8. *Kinematograph Weekly*, 13/12/56 p. 8–9.
9. *Kinematograph Weekly*, 17/12/53 p. 10.
10. Curran and Porter op. cit., p. 372.
11. Dickinson and Street, *Cinema and State: the Film Industry and the British Government 1927–1984* (BFI, 1985, p. 228).
12. For details of the American industry c. 1930–1949, see Douglas Gomery, *The Hollywood Studio System* (BFI/Macmillan, 1986).
13. Dickinson and Street op. cit., p. 233.
14. Ibid., pp. 235–6.
15. Later to become ACTT, The Association of Cinematograph and Television Technicians.
16. Public Record Office, Board of Trade 64 2188 quoted in Dickinson and Street, op. cit., p. 170.

17. Monopoly, the future of British films. ACT London 1946, quoted in Dickinson and Street, op. cit., p. 172.

18. Public Records Office, Board of Trade 64 4519 quoted in Dickinson and Street, op. cit., p. 216.

19. Hansard, 5th series, vol. 452, column 775, 17/6/48. Quoted in Barr, *All Our Yesterdays* (BFI, 1986, p. 14).

20. *Parliamentary Debates* (Lords) vol. 272, col 372. 2/2/66. Quoted in Dickinson and Street, op. cit., p. 239.

21. *Cambridge Historical Encyclopaedia of Great Britain and Ireland* (Guild/Cambridge University Press, 1985, p. 325).

22. Newsom, *The Education of Girls* (Faber & Faber, 1948, p. 109).

23. Ibid., p. 103.

24. Elizabeth Wilson, *Only Halfway to Paradise: Women in Postwar Britain 1945–1968* (Tavistock, 1980, pp. 35–36).

25. William Beveridge, *Voluntary Action* (Allen & Unwin, 1948, p. 264).

26. *Sexual Behaviour in the Human Male 1948; Sexual Behaviour in the Human Female, 1953.*

27. Elizabeth Wilson, op. cit., p. 110.

28. For example, Melinda Mash, 1989, doctoral research at Middlesex Polytechnic.

29. Richards and Sheridan, *Mass Observation at the Movies* (Routledge, Kegan & Paul, 1987).

CHAPTER 2:   POPULAR CINEMA IN BRITAIN, 1945–1965

1. The correlative method employed here of ascertaining which films were in fact most successful at the box office yields a list of around thirty titles for each year, of which we can recognise between five and ten as being markedly more popular since they are cited in three or more different sources. From this smaller group a further selection of titles is necessary in order to engage in the detailed study of the textual construction of female characters required by our questions about the representations in and readings of popular cinema. The analyses presented in Chapters 4, 5 and 7 will be in respect of six titles from each of three moments in our period, and the narrative characteristics of these three groups will be considered more fully in Chapter 3.

2. Though, by the sixties, films set during the Second World War were 'historical' pictures as well as 'war' films we should note the difference between such films and *Zulu*, which dealt with the more remote conflict of the Boer war. The fact remains that all three are war films first, history films second.

3. John Cawelti, 'Chinatown and generic transformation in recent films, in Mast and Cohen', *Film Theory and Criticism, Introductory Readings*, 3rd edn (Oxford University Press, 1985, p. 519).

4. Pam Cook, *The Cinema Book* (BFI, 1986).

5. Steve Neale, *Genre* (BFI, 1980, appendix B). Neale has addressed

some of the problems implicit in generic classification more recently by means of a useful survey of genre studies during the 80s in *Screen*, vol. 31, no. 1 (Spring 1990).

6. Ibid., p. 54.
7. *Picturegoer*, 30/3/46.
8. *Sight and Sound*, Autumn 1956.
9. *Tribune*, 3/8/56.
10. *Daily Sketch*, 27/7/56.
11. Richard Dyer, *Stars* (BFI, 1982); *Heavenly Bodies: Film Stars and Society* (BFI/Macmillan, 1987). Janet Thumim, 'The Star Persona of Katharine Hepburn', in *Feminist Review*, vol. 24 (1986).
12. *Films Illustrated*, vol. 5, no. 52 (December 1975).
13. *New Statesman*, 16/12/50.
14. *Time*, December 1946.
15. *Pictureshow*, 19/5/45.
16. *Picturegoer*, 2/2/46.
17. *Picturegoer*, 18/8/45.
18. Ibid.
19. *Picturegoer*, 28/4/45.
20. Ibid.
21. *Today's Cinema*, 25/5/55.
22. *Sunday Times*, 10/7/55.
23. *Daily Herald*, 4/8/56.
24. *Hollywood Reporter*, 16/2/55.
25. *Woman*, 2/6/56.
26. *Evening Standard*, 17/12/64.
27. *Daily Express*, 15/12/64.
28. *Daily Worker*, 19/12/64.
29. *Daily Express*, 19/4/61.
30. *Evening Standard*, 13/3/56.
31. *Evening Standard*, 25/3/63.
32. John Ellis draws attention to the function of the star text in modifying possible readings of the film text: 'the film is one text, the star is another text passing through it. The result is a system in which any film is guaranteed to signify over and above its connotations as a textual system' in 'Made in Ealing', *Screen*, vol. 16, no. 1, 1975.

CHAPTER 3:   THE FILMS: NARRATIVE THEMES

1. Hermeneutics: 'the art or science of interpretation' – OED. In this context the successive cruxes of action by which the reader is led into and through the plot, thereby discovering the narrative.
2. Visual Pleasure and Narrative Cinema, first published in *Screen*, 1975.
3. The hallucinogen Lysurgic Acid.

CHAPTER 4: THE CONSTRUCTION AND DEFINITION OF FEMALE CHARACTERS

1. *Manchester Guardian*, 1944.
2. *Picturegoer*, 20/1/45.
3. *Pictureshow*, 3/6/44 p. 4.
4. *Woman's Own*, May 1963, p. 44.
5. *Woman's Own*, September 1963.
6. Though there are no such characters in the sample group of six films under discussion here some popular box office hits did dwell on older female characters, chiefly in order to reveal the 'tragedy' of aging, for a woman. An example is *Picnic* (Logan, Columbia, US 56).
7. John Coleman in the *New Statsman*, 5/7/63.
8. The figures cited here refer to mentions in *Woman, Woman's Illustrated, Woman and Home, Woman and Beauty, Woman's Own, Woman's Journal*, in 1945–1946, 1955–1956, 1963–1965.
9. Maids in films: mid-forties = 6; mid-fifties = 3; mid-sixties = 9.
10. Performers in films: mid-forties = 4; mid-fifties = 3; mid-sixties = 7.
11. Nurses in films: mid-forties = 4; mid-fifties = 10.
12. Waitresses in films: mid-forties = 2; mid-fifties = 4; mid-sixties = 7.
13. Teachers in films: mid-forties = 5; mid-fifties = 1.
14. Nurses in magazines: mid-forties = 7; mid-fifties = 7; mid-sixties = 5.
15. Shops/small businesses in magazines: mid-forties = 5; mid-fifties = 7.
16. Only five of these mentions refer specifically to catering itself, including waitressing, the rest being related jobs.
17. Catering and domestic work in films: maids = 18; waitresses = 11; housekeepers = 5.
18. Radiography in magazines: mid-forties = 2; mid-fifties = 1; mid-sixties = 1.
19. Physiotherapy in magazines: mid-fifties = 1.
20. Bacteriology in magazines: mid-sixties = 1.
21. Health visiting in magazines: mid-forties = 1; mid-fifties = 1; mid-sixties = 1.
22. Performers in cinema: mid-forties = 4; mid-fifties = 3; mid-sixties = 7.
23. Performers in magazines: 14, of which acting = 5; musician = 2.

CHAPTER 5: THE NARRATIVE RESOLUTIONS OF FEMALE CHARACTERS

1. MFB 22.
2. *Motion Picture Herald*, 15/12/45.
3. *Kinematograph Weekly*, 15/12/45.
4. *Woman*, 9/2/46.

5. *Picturegoer*, 2/2/46.
6. *Pictureshow*, 28/1/46.
7. 'A chilling – if over fancy – performance from Louise Latham as the misguidedly penitent mother', *Daily Cinema*, 1/7/64.
8. The politics of this reading are rather more complex than is suggested here: the 'multi-racial' future is one based on unequivocally 'white' values. The dominant group, in the film's mid-fifties context of the emergent Civil Rights movement in the USA, is seen to be able to 'contain' its opposition.
9. These respondents are from Melinda Mash's research data at Middlesex Polytechnic.
10. *Films and Filming*, August 1964.
11. *Sight and Sound*, Autumn 1964.
12. *Sight and Sound*, August 1955.
13. *Films in Review*, March 1955.
14. Ibid.
15. *Woman*, 8/10/55.
16. *Sight and Sound*, August 1955.
17. *Daily Mail*, 22/3/46.
18. *Daily Express*, 23/3/46.
19. *Daily Mirror*, 22/3/46.
20. *Kinematograph Weekly*, 28/3/46.
21. Source obscured, 24/3/46, BFI Microfiche.
22. Lévi-Strauss, *Structural Anthropology*, 1968. According to Levi-Strauss it is in the relation between the characters and events of myth that meaning resides, and this film clearly offers a variant of the many tales which deal with man's negotiation of the material and the spiritual in the context of his temporal existence.
23. *Amateur Cine World*, January 1965.
24. *Evening Standard*, 17/12/64.
25. *Financial Times*, 18/12/64.
26. *Daily Worker*, 19/12/64.
27. *News of the World*, 20/12/64.
28. *Motion Picture Herald*, 7/9/46.
29. I am indebted to the 1989–90 BFI Diploma students for their attention to this point.
30. *Kinematograph weekly*, 14/12/44.
31. *Motion Picture Herald*, 27/1/45.
32. MFB 11, 1944.
33. *New Statesman*, 16/12/44.
34. *Motion Picture Herald*, 27/1/45.
35. *Sunday Times*, 17/12/44.
36. *Time and Tide*, 23/12/44.
37. Source and date obscured, BFI microfiche.
38. *Daily Sketch*, 16/11/45.
39. *Tribune*, 23/11/45.
40. *Kinematograph weekly*, 22/11/45.
41. *Today's Cinema*, 16/11/45.
42. *Motion Picture Herald*, 15/12/45.

43. The word first appeared in the name of the committee of cardinals charged with the foreign missions of the eighteenth-century Roman Catholic church, the Congregatio de Propanda Fide, notorious for their activities which have been popularly remembered as the Inquisition.

CHAPTER 6: THE FILM AUDIENCE AND THE FEMALE READER

1. The editors of *Cahiers du Cinema* analysis of Ford's Young Mr Lincoln, published in translation in *Screen*, vol. 13, no. 3.
2. Laura Mulvey, *Visual and Other Pleasures* (Macmillan, 1989, Introduction, p. vii).
3. Ibid., p. 159.
4. Mary Ann Doane, *The Desire to Desire* (Indiana University Press, 1987, p. 67).
5. Laplanche and Pontalis, *The Language of Psychoanalysis* (Hogarth Press, 1985, p. 208).
6. Doane, 1987, op. cit., pp. 38–70.
7. Jacqueline Rose, *Sexuality in the Field of Vision* (Verso, 1986, p. 217).
8. de Lauretis 1987, op. cit., p. 13.
9. Ibid p. 37.
10. Doane, 1987 op. cit.
11. Ibid p. 182.
12. Ibid p. 181.
13. For example Morley 80, 86; Hobson 82; Radway 84; Modleski 84; Ang 85; Buckingham 87; Taylor 89.
14. David Morley, *The Nationwide Audience: structure and decoding* (BFI, 1980); *Family Television: cultural power and domestic leisure* (Comedia, 1986).
15. Janice Radway, *Reading The Romance: women, patriarchy and popular literature* (University of North Carolina Press, 1984).
16. Morley, 1980, op. cit., p. 153.
17. Radway, 1984, op. cit., p. 187.
18. Ibid., p. 100.
19. Ann Oakley, *The Sociology of Housework* (1974).
20. Ibid., p. 179.
21. Melinda Mash research, Middlesex Polytechnic.

CHAPTER 7: FEMALE READERS AND THE FILM TEXT

1. *Woman in a Dressing Gown* (J. Lee-Thompson, UK 57), for example.
2. Melinda Mash research, Middlesex Polytechnic.
3. *Daily Express*, 26/5/56.
4. *Daily Cinema*, 1/7/64.
5. *News of the World*, 12/7/64.
6. *Daily Worker*, 11/7/64.

7.   *Sunday Telegraph*, 12/7/64.
8.   *Films and Filming*, August 1964.
9.   *Films in Review*, August 1964.
10. Oakley, 1974, op. cit.
11. Doane, 1987, op. cit., pp. 67, 69.
12. *Movie*, Spring 1965.
13. *Spectator*, 14/8/64.
14. Wilson, 1980, op. cit., for example.
15. Auxiliary Territorial Service.
16. 1/2/51; *Longman's 20th Century Chronicle* (1988).
17. *The Belles of St. Trinians*, 1964; *Blue Murder at St. Trinians*, 1957; *The Pure Hell of St. Trinians*, 1960; *The Great St. Trinians Train Robbery*, 1966.
18. *Daily Telegraph*, 18/2/64.
19. *Spectator*, 25/12/64.
20. MFB 373.

CONCLUSION

1.   John Ellis, *Visible Fictions* (Routledge, Kegan & Paul, 1982, chapter 5).

Bibliography

Allen, R., *Speaking of Soap Operas* (University of North Carolina Press 1985).

Ang, I., *Watching Dallas: Soap Opera and the Melodramatic Imagination* (Methuen, 1985).

Barr, C. (ed.), *All Our Yesterdays: 80 Years of British Cinema* (BFI, 1986).

Barr, C. *Ealing Studios* (Cameron & Tayleur and David & Charles, 1977).

Beauvoir, S. de, *The Second Sex* (Jonathan Cape, 1953).

Beauvoir, S. de, *Memoirs of a Dutiful Daughter* (Andre Deutsch and Weidenfeld & Nicolson, 1959).

Bennett, T. and J. Woolacott, *Bond and Beyond: The Political Career of a Popular Hero* (Macmillan 1987).

Broad, R. and S. Fleming, *Nella Last's War* (Sphere, 1983).

Buckingham, D., *Public Secrets: Eastenders and its Audience* (BFI, 1987).

Calder, A., *The People's War: Britain 1939–1945* (Jonathan Cape, 1969).

Calder, A., and D. Sheridan (eds), *Speak For Yourself: A Mass Observation Anthology 1937–1949* (Cape, 1984).

Carr, E. H., *What is History?* (Macmillan, 1961).

Cawelti, J. G., 'Chinatown and Generic Transformation in Recent American Films', in Mast and Cohen (eds), *Film Theory and Criticism* 3rd edn (Oxford University Press, 1985).

Code, L., *Epistemic Responsibility* (University Press of New England, 1987).

Cook, P., *The Cinema Book* (BFI, 1985).

Curran, J., and V. Porter (eds), *British Cinema History* (Weidenfeld & Nicolson, 1983).

Dickinson, M., and S. Street, *Cinema and State: The Film Industry and the British Government 1927–1984* (BFI, 1985).

Doane, M., *The Desire to Desire: The Woman's Film of the 1940s* (Indiana University Press, 1987).

Durgnat, R., *A Mirror for England* (Faber, 1970).

Ellis, J., *Visible Fictions* (Routledge, Kegan & Paul, 1982).

Ellis, J., 'Made in Ealing', in *Screen* vol. 16, no. 1 (1975).

Ellis, J., 'Art, Culture, Quality: Terms for a cinema in the 40s and 70s', in *Screen* vol. 19, no. 3 (1978).

Foucault, M., *The History of Sexuality* vol. 1 (Allen Lane, 1978).

Foucault, M., *The Order of Things* (Tavistock, 1970).

Friedan, B., *The Feminine Mystique* (Victor Gollancz, 1963).

Gledhill, C., (ed.), *Home is Where the Heart Is: Studies in Melodrama and the Woman's Film* (BFI, 1987).

Gomery, D., *The American Studio System* (BFI/Macmillan, 1986).

Halliwell, L., *Seats In All Parts* (Grafton, 1986).

Halliwell, L., *Film Guide* 6th edn (Grafton, 1987).

Hill, J., *Sex, Class and Realism: British Cinema 1956–1963* (BFI, 1986).

Hobson, D., *Crossroads: The Drama of a Soap Opera* (Methuen, 1982).

Hoggart, R., *The Uses of Literacy* (Penguin, 1958).

Kuhn, A., *Cinema, Censorship and Sexuality* (Routledge, 1988).

Kuhn, A., *The Power of the Image: Essays on Representation and Sexuality* (Routledge, Kegan & Paul, 1985).

Kuhn, A., *Women's Pictures: Feminism and Cinema* (Routledge, Kegan & Paul, 1982).

Laing, R. D., *The Divided Self* (Penguin, 1965).

Laing, R. D., *The Bird of Paradise and the Politics of Experience* (Penguin, 1967).

Laing, R. D., and A. Esterson *Sanity, Madness and the Family* (Tavistock, 1964).

Laplanche, J., and J-B. Pontalis *The Language of Psychoanalysis* (Hogarth Press, 1985).

Lauretis, T. de, *Alice Doesn't: Feminism, Semiotics, Cinema* (1984).

Lauretis, T, de, *Technologies of Gender: Essays on Theory, Film and Fiction* (Macmillan, 1987).

Modleski, T. *Loving With a Vengeance: Mass Produced Fantasies for Women* (Methuen, 1984).

Modleski, T. *The Women Who Knew Too Much: Hitchcock and Feminist Theory* (Methuen, 1988).

Morley, D., *The 'Nationwide' Audience: Structure and Decoding (BFI, 1980).*

Morley, D., *Family Television: Cultural Power and Domestic Leisure* (Comedia, 1986).

Mulvey, L., *Visual and Other Pleasures* (Macmillan, 1989).

Neale, S., *Genre* (BFI, 1980).

Neale, S., 'Questions of Genre and Problems with Quality', in *Screen*, vol. 31, no.1 (1990).

Oakley, A., *The Sociology of Housework* (1974).

Pirie, D., *Hammer: A Cinema Case Study* (BFI, 1980).

Radway, J., *Reading the Romance: Women, Patriarchy, and Popular Literature* (University of North Carolina Press, 1984).

Richards, J., and D. Sheridan (eds), *Mass Observation at the Movies* (Routledge, Kegan & Paul, 1987).

Rose, J., *Sexuality in the Field of Vision* (Verso 1986).

Taylor, H., *Scarlett's Women: Gone With The Wind and its Female Fans* (Virago, 1989).

Thompson, E. P., *The Making of the English Working Class* (Penguin, 1968).

Williams, R., *Keywords: A Vocabulary of Culture and Society* (Fontana, 1976).

Williams, R., *Culture and Society* (Penguin, 1961).

Wilson, E., *Only Halfway To Paradise: Women in Postwar Britain 1945–1968* (Tavistock, 1980).

Winship, J., *Inside Women's Magazines* (Pandora, 1987).

General Index

Index of Film Titles

246